The WAR
of the
LAMB

The WAR
of the
LAMB

THE ETHICS OF NONVIOLENCE
AND PEACEMAKING

JOHN HOWARD
YODER

Glen Harold Stassen,
Mark Thiessen Nation,
and Matt Hamsher, *editors*

BrazosPress

a division of Baker Publishing Group
Grand Rapids, Michigan

© 2009 by Martha Yoder Maust

Published by Brazos Press
a division of Baker Publishing Group
P.O. Box 6287, Grand Rapids, MI 49516-6287
www.brazospress.com

Printed in the United States of America

"A Theological Critique of Violence" is reprinted with permission of the United Church of Christ from *New Conversations*, 16 (1994): 2–15.

"Politics: Liberating Images of Christ" was previously published under the auspices of the Theology Institute at Villanova University in *Imaging Christ: Politics, Arts, Spirituality*, ed. Francis A. Eigo (Villanova, PA: Villanova University Press, 1991), 149–69.

Library of Congress Cataloging-in-Publication Data
Yoder, John Howard.
   The war of the lamb: the ethics of nonviolence and peacemaking / John Howard Yoder; Glen Harold Stassen, Mark Thiessen Nation.
       p.   cm.
   Includes bibliographical references and index.
   ISBN 978-1-58743-260-6 (pbk.)
       1. Nonviolence—Religious aspects—Christianity. 2. Peace—Religious aspects—Christianity. 3. Just war doctrine. I. Stassen, Glen Harold, 1936– II. Nation, Mark. III. Hamsher, Matt. IV. Title.
   BT736.6.Y6158 2009
   261.8′73—dc22   2009030021

09   10   11   12   13   14   15   7   6   5   4   3   2   1

In keeping with biblical principles of creation stewardship, Baker Publishing Group advocates the responsible use of our natural resources. As a member of the Green Press Initiative, our company uses recycled paper when possible. The text paper of this book is comprised of 30% post-consumer waste.

Contents

Introduction: Jesus Is No Sectarian

John H. Yoder's Christological Peacemaking Ethic

GLEN HAROLD STASSEN

*T*he *War of the Lamb* presents surprises for readers whose perception of John Howard Yoder is based on stereotypes of Mennonites or of Yoder. He planned this book himself, before his sudden death in 1997. So *The War of the Lamb*—its plan as a whole as well as most of the individual essays—represents Yoder's own intention and is a true development of his own thought. Of course, indications pointing toward these developments can be found in his earlier publications, since Yoder was incisively logical and logically coherent. But in several ways, these ideas develop beyond what many people associate with the thought of John Howard Yoder.

Arguing on the Basis of Effectiveness

Yoder is well known for arguing on behalf of an ethics of faithfulness rather than effectiveness.[1] In *The War of the Lamb*, however, he describes how Tolstoy, Gandhi, and King had a "cosmological conversion," in which they each saw God as the ruler of the universe. Therefore, they believed that action faithfully in tune with God's rule is likely to be more effective. Yoder agreed. He himself had a cosmological and eschatological faith in the lordship of Christ. It was grounded in his own Christ-centered Mennonite faith and strengthened by his doctoral study with Karl Barth and Oscar Cullmann. Yoder noticed the theme of God as ruler of the universe and highlighted it in Tolstoy and King because it was a central theme in his own faith; he also saw something analogous in Gandhi. In *The War of the Lamb*, he writes:

> To say "the means are the ends in process of becoming" is a cosmological or an eschatological statement. It presupposes a *cosmos*—a world with some kind of discernible moral cause-effect coherence. Unlike Kant, for whom the hereafter was needed to make the moral accounting come out even, this view claims coherence within history. But for this claim to work, one must believe that in some sense suffering is redemptive, or (as King will say it) "there is something in the universe that unfolds for justice." For Gandhi, that cosmic validator was the great chain of being, represented literally or at least symbolically by the notion of reincarnation. For King it was the black Baptist vision of another Moses leading his people from Egypt, another Joshua fighting at Jericho, a promised land we can see from the mountain top, a cross on Golgotha from which one can see the heavens opening. King also said it in terms of the American dream, the humanism of the fathers of the republic, and even in terms of the federal politics of the Kennedy brothers.[2]

> To say with King that "love is the most durable power in the world," or that "there is something in the universe that unfolds for justice," is not to claim a sure insight into the way martyrdom works as a social power, although martyrdom often does that. It is a confessional or kerygmatic statement made by those whose loyalty to Christ (or to universal love, or to *satyagraha*) they understand to be validated by its cosmic ground. Suffering love is not right because it "works" in any calculable short-run way (although it often does). It is right because it goes with the grain of the universe, and that is why *in the long run* nothing else will work.[3]

> If your rejection of violence is cosmically based, as for Tolstoy, Gandhi, and King—i.e., if its validation is not pragmatic—the impact of that kind of commitment will in fact be greater effectiveness. Perseverance in the face of sacrifice and creativity in the face of dismay are heightened for those who believe that the grain of the universe is with them.[4]

Yoder here makes several arguments that nonviolent action is usually more effective than violent action. In addition, he argues insightfully for accurate, balanced ways of assessing that comparative effectiveness. He is not giving up effectiveness; he is restoring it to its proper, but limited, place within sound theological and eschatological ethics.

Yoder writes that the last chapter of *The Politics of Jesus*, which argued for faithfulness over effectiveness, unsettled some readers because they erroneously thought it was a call for withdrawal from social involvement. It was "offensive to contemporaries because it seemed to some to constitute an *argument* to the effect that even in other times and settings, such as our own, withdrawal from social involvement" was mandated. "It was not that, as my other writings make clear," Yoder writes, "but it is fascinating that readers thought so."[5]

Refuting Reinhold Niebuhr's Marginalizing of Pacifism

Reinhold Niebuhr marginalizes nonviolence. He says nonviolence is idealism without responsibility for effectiveness. He writes of "the failure of liberal Protestantism to recognize the coercive character of political and economic life. To refuse the use of any coercive methods means that we do not recognize that everyone is using them all the time, that we all live in and benefit or suffer from a political and economic order that maintains its cohesion partially by the use of various forms of political and economic coercion."[6] Niebuhr argues from the need for coercion to the need for force, and then violence, and then war (often eliding these different categories into one). He argues that "responsible" Christian ethics must recognize this need in national policy. For national policy, we need to be pragmatic, and to have a strong sense of sin, the tragic, and the ambiguous. Thus, as Yoder has pointed out, the test that Niebuhr applies to Christian ethics is its adequacy for national policy, not for Christian witness in churches. By contrast, Yoder shows ways that nonviolent witness can claim "responsible" political involvement, over against Niebuhr as well as over against sectarian ethics of withdrawal.

Niebuhr sees Christian pacifism as based on a legalistic absolute—love as pure unselfishness, nonresistance, or nonviolence, absolutistically understood.[7] "Religious absolutism in its pure form is either apocalyptic or ascetic. In either case, it is not compatible with political responsibility. When apocalyptic, as in the thought of Jesus, it sets the absolute principles of the coming Kingdom of God, principles of uncompromising love and nonresistance, in sharp juxtaposition to the relativities of the economic and political order and assumes no responsibilities for the latter."[8] "It knew that [the effort to achieve a standard of perfect love] could only be done by disavowing the political task and by freeing the individual of all responsibility for social justice."[9] But moral absolutes have no place in the necessary pragmatism of public policy, Niebuhr says. "We can find no stable absolute in the shifting situation of the social struggle where everything must be finally decided in pragmatic terms."[10]

Yoder breaks this stereotype at four key points:[11]

1) Christian ethics is for the witness made by churches. The test of its adequacy is not whether national policy will adopt it, but whether it is faithful to the gospel of Jesus Christ. We cannot make the interests of the president of the United States, with all his or her mixed motives and pragmatic or nationalistic calculations, into the judge of the adequacy of Christian witness. To do so is to fall into the error of Constantinianism, making Christian ethics into a chaplain for Christendom. In our post-Christendom context, Christian

ethics is for witness by churches as alternative communities. Jesus Christ is Lord, and the president is not Lord.

As Mark Thiessen Nation documents in the fifth chapter of his *John Howard Yoder: Mennonite Patience, Evangelical Witness, Catholic Convictions*,[12] Yoder goes to great lengths to redefine *responsibility* so it does not mean playing by Constantinian rules of acquiescence to the power structure. And as Yoder has shown throughout his writings and certainly demonstrates in *The War of the Lamb*, he strongly believes Christians are called to speak to the world on questions of effective practices for peace and justice.

2) Yoder has a realistic view of national policies and sinful churches. He argues in *The War of the Lamb* that churches and nations have usually acted neither on the basis of nonviolence nor even of just war theory, but on the basis of nationalism, right of state, or crusade.

3) The norm for Christian pacifism is not an absolute rule, or an absolute principle—not even nonviolence—but the Lord, Jesus Christ. Jesus Christ does not proclaim an absolute rule, but kingdom breakthroughs, hope in the Holy Spirit, and hope that churches can sometimes respond to the gospel. Ernst Troeltsch and most ethicists influenced by him, including Niebuhr, claim that churches of the sect type depend on norms that take the form of absolute legalism. By "the sect type," they mean to include Christian pacifists and other Christian congregations that see themselves as alternative communities— alternatives to the secular society—and they see sectarians as basing their ethics on absolute rules. Therefore, since the society will not accept absolute norms, these witness groups must either withdraw from responsible engagement in society or try to force their norms on society by authoritarian takeover. So Niebuhr writes of "religious absolutism as expressed in the Sermon on the Mount." This is a nineteenth-century idealist interpretation of the Sermon on the Mount that I have worked to correct, showing the Sermon on the Mount gives us norms that are not legalistic prohibitions but grace-based practices, kingdom breakthroughs, transforming initiatives.[13] For Yoder, the norm is not a legalistic absolute, but Jesus Christ as Lord.[14] This then requires thick exegesis of the way of Jesus Christ, as Yoder famously has done in *The Politics of Jesus*. And it requires a hermeneutic for what witness to Jesus as Lord means in societies such as ours. Jesus was no apolitical idealist. The Jesus of the gospel story "is not simply different from the Jesus of the liberal optimism that Niebuhr attacked," writes Yoder. "He is also different from Niebuhr's ethic of responsibility, by being a much more consciously political figure, in his statements, public action, and formal teaching, than Niebuhr was willing to admit. Therefore the Jesus of this story represents an option Niebuhr did not have on his scale."[15]

4) Yoder consistently calls for a Christian witness to the state, as his book by that title indicates. There he writes, "Our purpose is to analyze whether it is truly the case that a Christian pacifist position rooted not in pragmatic . . .

but in christological considerations is thereby irrelevant to the social order."[16] We do not expect the state to follow a legalistic or perfectionistic absolute, or to understand and submit to the gospel of Jesus Christ.

He names political leaders who have been faithful, including my own father—for which I am grateful.[17] He rejects the label *sectarian* for his own method,[18] and instead intentionally advocates a method in which a Christian pacifist does not seek to control history, but does advocate peacemaking practices that are effective in reducing the society's and the government's violence. Thus, here in *The War of the Lamb*, he offers one section on pacifism, a second section on just war, and a final section on peacemaking practices that are proving effective. This means churches are not faced with the absolute either/ or that either the government will become nonviolent or we have nothing to say to them. We can develop an ethic that prods politicians to be less violent and to engage in justice-making and peacemaking initiatives that are effective in decreasing war and violence. This is what Yoder does in the third section of this book. He is not susceptible to Niebuhr's claim that pacifists are perfectionistic absolutists who have nothing to say to the "real" world.

For a strikingly fair and accurate description of Niebuhr's arguments and contributions, and for more extensive refutation, I recommend Yoder's newly published book, *Christian Attitudes to War, Peace, and Revolution*.[19] It also includes a fuller history of nonviolence in many church traditions and of the theory of "justifiable war," as well as assessments of ecumenical discussions of these questions. It outlines as well liberation theology and arguments about effectiveness of nonviolence versus war and revolution.

Arguing for a Public Ethic—At Home in Churches, and Abroad in Society

In his plans for this book, Yoder wrote that the title intentionally points to the Quaker understanding, symbolized by William Penn as governor of Pennsylvania and Roger Williams as governor of Rhode Island, that nonviolence does not require us to withdraw from having and carrying out an effective public ethic in pluralistic society. Nor is it based on weakness. It is based on the triumph of the Crucified. "Thus the stereotypical vision, that a Christian commitment governed by such more critical and more promising visions drawn from the experience and the witness of the Christian community can properly be categorized as 'apolitical' or 'unrealistic' (as was done in the heritage of Ernst Troeltsch by the brothers Niebuhr) misreads the facts."[20] Gandhi's concern for effectiveness and Gene Sharp's massive study of the effectiveness of nonviolent action "break apart Niebuhr's dichotomy. They argue for the effectiveness of nonviolence."[21] Here Yoder's emphases on the dynamic providence of God, the resurrection triumph of the crucified Jesus, and the effectiveness of nonviolence guide us in making a public witness.

"The Science of Conflict" (chapter 10 below) argues that we need to incorporate research by political scientists like Robert Johansen on new theories in international relations and on a nonviolent world police force, and research in anthropology, sociology, and psychology on aggression and conflict resolution. Christians should not withdraw from or ignore such research, but trust there is truth here and incorporate it into our thinking, our theories, and our theological ethics.

When John Howard Yoder and I were planning our book, *Authentic Transformation: A New Vision of Christ and Culture*, I wanted to conclude by offering our own revised typology of relations between Christ and culture. I wanted to enable readers to visualize how we would correct H. R. Niebuhr's typology with a better typology. But John was so genuinely troubled by how Niebuhr's typology was being used to convince Mennonite students to desert their own tradition and its pacifism that he refused to include even an alternative typology.[22] When I then began to urge, "Let's not cop out, ..." John immediately flushed bright red. I had never seen the always logical John Howard Yoder show such intense emotion. I knew immediately what he was thinking of—the Niebuhrian stereotype of Mennonites as "copping out" from responsible engagement in the social struggle. I rushed to explain that I meant we should at least provide a typology of ways churches *evade* the way of Jesus. We should not cop out from identifying the temptations to unfaithfulness. John immediately accepted this—and the red subsided. The result is the concluding chapter of *Authentic Transformation*, with its typology of ways of evasion. When the book was finished, John said to me and coauthor Dianne Yeager, "I am so glad we set Glen free to write the concluding chapter."

As this incident shows, Yoder deeply opposed being understood as advocating an ethic of withdrawal. He was deeply committed to developing an ethic loyal to the lordship of Christ over all of life, and not only over private life or only over churches. His themes of the lordship of Christ, the normativity of the way of Jesus for all Christians and not only Christians in peace churches, and his books *The Christian Witness to the State*, *The Politics of Jesus*, *Priestly Kingdom*, *Body Politics*, *For the Nations*, and now *The War of the Lamb*, all point to a witness in pluralistic society that includes a public ethic expressed in thin, secular language as well as in thick, Christian discipleship language. It resembles Michael Walzer's argument that our ethic is grounded in thick, particular communities and that it is also expressed in thin understandings that are widely shared in pluralistic societies.[23]

Yoder mentions this public ethic in at least these six different books; it is no minor theme, despite its being overlooked by some interpreters. We need to be able to speak the languages of the pluralistic society in order to become articulate about which languages are useful for communicating our witness, which first need to be transformed, and which must be flatly rejected. We need to understand and assess society's languages in order to develop antibodies against being manipulated into supporting unjust ideologies of the powers and authorities.[24] Yoder hated to be seen as offering a particular Anabaptist witness that mainstream church traditions could pat on the head—and therefore marginalize—because it was misinterpreted as lacking a public ethic. He wrote about the lordship of Christ for all Christians in all of life, and for all persons and powers and authorities in all of life. In this he resembled Dietrich Bonhoeffer.

In his first two books, written in German and now translated as *Anabaptism and Reformation in Switzerland*, Yoder argues that the Anabaptists did not withdraw. They engaged in some thirty public debates and discussions with the Zwinglian and Calvinist reformers, and they wanted to continue the dialogue.[25] It was the magisterial reformers who withdrew from the debates. It was the magisterial reformers who resorted to the power of the state to force the Anabaptists out of the discussion and out of participation in society. Yoder's whole life was a resumption of that discussion, a participation in scholarly debates, and a defense of young Mennonites and others from being pushed out of participation by the dominant, Ivy League, mainstream discussants. *The War of the Lamb* now develops his public ethic on peace and war beyond what is generally known.

Churches can witness publicly by modeling innovation, by their own faithful practices inside church communities. Churches have taken action in founding orphanages, hospitals, universities, and in practicing agricultural missions and other forms of service. The states have noticed this. Church practices have stimulated innovations in state policies. This is one form of public witness.

As Mark Thiessen Nation has written of Yoder's "messianic community":[26]

> Moreover, our life together is comprised of "a covenanting group of men and women who instruct one another, forgive one another, bear one another's burdens, and reinforce one another's witness."[27] This community provides mutual support. But more than that, "the existence of a human community dedicated in common to a new and publicly scandalous enemy-loving way of life is itself a new social datum."[28] In fact, claims Yoder, this "alternative community discharges a modeling mission. The church is called to be now what the world is called to be ultimately."[29] Thus, it is important to realize that the church exists as a witness to the gospel of Jesus Christ. But it is also important to note that this community exists to give its "life for a society."[30] And as this community gives its life for the world around us, we still must attend to the identity of this community because "only a continuing community dedicated to a deviant value system can change the world."[31]

Churches also witness publicly by *translating multilingually*: that is, making selective and tactical use of normative language in the society. This is what Michael Walzer calls "thin shared understandings," including those parts of the government's claims that point partway toward gospel norms. "The Christian can speak to the statesmen," Yoder claims, "without failing to take account of their differing presuppositions, using pagan or secular terminology to clothe social critique without ascribing to those secular concepts any metaphysical value outside of Christ."[32] We should learn to speak the language of the society in which we live, adopting a multilingual method.[33] "Every secular hope is true and necessary as a criticism of ingrown and complacent 'religion,'" Yoder writes. "Secular hopes are necessary because secular language is the only language there is. If we do not say 'Jesus Christ is Lord' in language that men can understand, then we are not saying it at all." In other words, the problem is not translation; it is whether the translation "is big enough and true enough to say everything that the name Jesus Christ must mean."[34] We must assess translation languages by the norm of the way of Jesus, affirming what is helpful and correcting or criticizing what is not.[35]

Churches can advocate the societal implications of Christian normative practices, such as racial inclusion, conflict resolution, feeding the hungry, and democratic decision making.[36] We may make tactical alliances with secular assumptions such as relativism, liberation, Gandhi, or the Enlightenment.

> We may be tactical allies of the pluralist/relativist deconstruction of deceptive orthodox claims to logically coercive certainty, without making of relativism itself a new monism. We will share tactical use of liberation language to dismantle the alliance of church with privilege, without letting the promises made by some in the name of revolution become a new opiate. . . . We shall not grant, with Tolstoy and Reinhold Niebuhr, that to renounce violence is to renounce power. We may then find tactical alliances with the Enlightenment, as did Quakers and Baptists in the century after their expulsion from the Puritan colonies, or with the Gandhian vision, as did Martin Luther King, Jr.[37]

In *For the Nations*, Yoder criticizes communitarians for focusing exclusively on the strategy of modeling internally, and he criticizes liberals for focusing exclusively on secular political witness. The communitarians among us "will not risk the challenge of telling the world that servanthood, enemy love, and forgiveness would be a better way to run a university, a town, or a factory. They pull back on the grounds that only they have already experienced the power and novelty of that threefold evangelical cord in the worship and ministry of the church. They affirm integrity but at the cost of witness." On the other hand, what Yoder calls the "public Catholics" and liberals among us "are concerned not to look foolish to their sophisticated neighbors by making any claims or promises linked to the particularity of the Jew Jesus (or of their own denominational past). By dropping the particular baggage of normative servanthood, enemy love, and forgiveness, they think they might make it easy . . . to talk their neighbors' language, but they do so at the cost of having nothing to say that the neighbors do not already know."[38]

We need a third way. It can be found in a free church community that witnesses to the lordship of Christ over all of life—in the community and in the world. "Only a believing community with a 'thick' particular identity has something to say to whatever 'public' is 'out there' to address," Yoder writes. "And . . . only the community that welcomes the challenge of public witness can justify . . . its distinctive witness."[39]

Yoder further articulates this third way in the following quotations: "Over against the sanctification of the existing structures of society and the glorification of Christian individualism . . . we affirm with the New Testament and with the free church tradition through the ages that the church as a new kind of social structure, a new kind of human community, is a third option."[40] "The entire Christian community is sent into the world to 'communicate a message and gather its hearers into communities.'. . . What we do about social justice or about education should then be no less 'missionary' than what we do about crossing linguistic or political borders and communicating our convictions to unbelievers."[41]

Experiencing Overpowering Grace

In chapter 7 of this volume, Yoder writes:

> Hugh Barbour's exposition of the subjective religious experience of radical Puritanism in England, under the heading "The Terror and Power of the Light," interprets profoundly the rootage of the renunciation of violence in the inner experience of overpowering grace. What the Anabaptists of the sixteenth century called *Gelassenheit*, or what the early Dunkards called *perfect love*, or what frontier farmer preachers of the nineteenth century called *humility*, or what their Wesleyan contemporaries called *sanctification*, represent closely related but distinguishable labels for the view of human dignity that frees the believer from temptations to feel called to set the world right by force. Probably this commonality is more important subjectively for the peace churches' peace witness than any of the more standard ethical issues I was reviewing before.

Here we see Yoder's own personal resonance with the inner experience of overpowering grace. This comes from a lecture at Swarthmore College in 1995, near the climax of his life, before a highly academic audience. He had been reviewing and analyzing the ethical argument of the U.S. Catholic bishops' *Challenge of Peace*. But he was dissatisfied with a purely ethical analysis because it overlooked a deeper faith dimension that was important for him and for the religious experience of the historical peace churches—the experience of God's grace that underlies the peace churches' peace witness. The experiential dimension and spiritual commitment crucial for peace church traditions cannot be reduced to ethical argument.

Yoder was so gifted in analyzing ethical arguments, and so firm in criticizing dualists who reduce spirituality to inner life without public mission, that
some have missed his witness to a piety of suffering love, following Jesus
Christ as Lord, as revealer of God's way out of vicious cycles of retaliation,
and as promise of eschatological hope. I want to offer my own testimony that
while editing chapter 3 on hope, re-reading it carefully, I was hit by a deeper
unifying vision of John's own spiritual insight that even I, engrossed in his
theological-ethical vision as I am, had not quite fully seen—even though I
knew all the parts. Different dimensions of his unifying vision came together
in one illuminating flash, beginning in how he shows Tolstoy's conversion
and climaxing in King's cosmic hope. I urge you to ponder that chapter very
sensitively. Much of the heart of Yoder's own faith and vision are here.

Twice in *The War of the Lamb* Yoder emphasizes that Tolstoy, Gandhi,
and Martin Luther King's stances were deeply grounded in their faith in God
who rules the cosmos, God who is much bigger than a particular ethical law.
He is saying that Tolstoy, Gandhi, King, and the Puritans, Anabaptists, and
Pentecostals, as well as ordinary farmers, have an experiential faith in God
as Lord of the universe. For Yoder, it is faith in God, and in who God is, as
revealed in Jesus Christ. It is Christological, eschatological, and ecclesiologi-
cal. It is holistic.

But I was thinking too generally of the cosmic vision as faith in God's
sovereignty. Now I see it is the specific revelation in Christ that retaliation
and domination are vicious cycles throughout history. And that participation
in God's redemptive suffering and nonviolent confrontations and actions of
deliverance, as revealed in Christ, is how God's sovereignty works in history.
Tolstoy saw this in the Sermon on the Mount, and King saw it in God's love
revealed in Jesus. Gandhi caught Tolstoy's vision to a large extent, and translated much of it into his Hindu context, though without faith in Christ and
with a different understanding of God. King experienced a brilliant flash when
his African American Baptist loyalty to Jesus' love combined with Gandhi's
practice of nonviolent direct action and then connected experientially during
the Montgomery Bus Boycott. Jesus' way is not passive suffering; it is the way
of deliverance, the way of overcoming, when we are down.

In his book *Nevertheless* and elsewhere, Yoder says that nonviolence is not
adequately understood as an absolute ethical rule; it is loyalty not to a law
but to Jesus.[42]

The pacifism of the messianic community depends "on the confession that
Jesus is the Christ and Christ is *Lord*. It is therefore in the person and work
of Jesus, in His teachings and His passion, that this kind of pacifism finds
its rootage, and in His resurrection that it finds its enablement. . . . It follows
that the character of such a position can be known only in relation to Jesus
Christ. . . . Just what it means to believe in Jesus as Christ, just what it means

to follow Jesus Christ as revealer of the nature and will of God, cannot possibly be figured out on our own resources."

It is not moralism, the stuffy fear of ever making a mistake, nor is it reducible to living by rules; it is participation "in that human experience, that peculiar way of living for God in the world and being used as instruments of the living of God in the world, which the Bible calls *agape* or *cross*."

> When we speak of the pacifism of the messianic *community*, we move the focus of ethical concern from the individual asking himself about right and wrong in his concern for his own integrity, to the human community experiencing in its life a foretaste of God's kingdom. The pacifistic experience is communal in that it is not a life alone for heroic personalities but for a society. It is communal in that it is lived by a [community] of men and women who instruct one another, forgive one another, bear one another's burdens, reinforce one another's witness. . . .
>
> The existence of a human community dedicated in common to a new and publicly scandalous enemy-loving way of life is itself a new social datum. A heroic individual can crystallize a widespread awareness of need or widespread admiration: only a continuing community dedicated to a deviant value system can change the world. . . .
>
> Those who uphold it would affirm that the discipleship of which they speak is a necessary reflection of the true meaning of Jesus and that the call to follow Jesus is a call addressed to all. . . . But the standards by which such a life is guided are not cut to the measure of [people] in general. They can be clearly perceived—to say nothing of being even modestly and partially lived—only through that reorientation of the personality which Jesus and His first followers called repentance. Repentance initiates that true human existence to which all are called. But as long as a given [individual] or a given society has not undergone that change of direction, it is not meaningful to describe how. . . they would live as pacifists. It is thus not possible to extrapolate from this stance of faith a strategy for resolving the urban crisis tomorrow. It is not a position which can be institutionalized to work just as well among those who do not quite understand it or are not sure how much they believe in it. . . .
>
> Another disadvantage of this position is that it does not promise to work. The resurrection is not the end product of a mechanism which runs through its paces wherever there is a crucifixion. There is about the Christian hope in the kingdom that peculiar kind of assurance which is called faith. . . .

"Nevertheless," Yoder concludes, "this position is closer than the others to the idiom of the Bible and to the core affirmations of the Christian faith." Here is a core statement, in *Nevertheless*, of Yoder's own faith.

Yoder's faith in the lordship of Christ was probably strengthened by his engagement in many PhD seminars with Karl Barth and Oscar Cullmann at the University of Basel, since these two theologians emphasized the lordship of Christ over all. Barth drafted the Barmen Confession of those pastors who resisted Adolf Hitler and resisted relegating Christ's lordship to a private or only inner-churchly realm. Yoder has influenced Anabaptists and many others to move from a two-kingdom dualism in which Christ is Lord only over an inner realm to emphasizing the lordship of Christ over all of life.

Hence Yoder argues in *Preface to Theology* that the main point of the doctrine of the Trinity is to make clear that the revelation in Christ is the revelation of who God really is. To claim an ethic based on God as Creator that contradicts the revelation in Christ is to deny the unity of the Trinity. Like his teacher, Karl Barth, and like Claude Welch, he emphasizes God's unity and guards against those interpretations of the Trinity that he sees moving toward tritheism.[43] The central point throughout *Preface to Theology* is that God revealed in Christ, and in the Spirit, is really who God is; God is not instead a distant ruler whose ethics differs from Jesus Christ's ethics.[44]

This helps us understand Yoder's appreciation of Lisa Cahill's argument that just war theorists, who are used to reasoning with rules like "never intentionally attack noncombatants," often interpret pacifism as also a rules-based ethic. Pacifists like Yoder are saying something much deeper. They are committed to the way of Jesus—as revelation of the way and character of God—who is Lord of the universe.

John Yoder himself had a deep experience of the sovereignty of God as revealed in Jesus Christ. This is why he flushed bright red with shock to think I was saying pacifism "cops out" from responsible action in the public sphere. If I had meant that, it would have denied his cosmic faith in the sovereignty of God in the whole universe, grounded in God's revelation of Christ. It would have denied his commitment to serving God faithfully in all of life. It would have accepted a raft of unfriendly stereotypes of Anabaptists as "irresponsible" in a major part of life. It would have attacked their faith in God.

Many in the Anabaptist tradition are affirming a need for greater attention to the experience of the Holy Spirit in our lives.[45] Such an articulation is implied by and needed for what Yoder here speaks of as the deeply subjective "inner experience of overpowering grace." He identifies this experience of God's presence as important for radical Puritans, Anabaptists of the sixteenth century, the early Dunkards, frontier farmer preachers, their Wesleyan contemporaries, and Pentecostals around the world whose experience of God's presence in the Holy Spirit is also an experience of Jesus Christ as Lord, powerfully present and sovereign. In chapter 10 of *For the Nations*, he concludes: "The closest the Jesus of the Gospel accounts came to projecting the shape of the church was the description in Matthew (18:15–20) and in John (14–16; 20:19–23) of the Paraclete [Holy Spirit] to empower forgiveness and discernment. That is the warrant for continuing prophetic clarity."[46] In chapter 11, "The Spirit of God and the Politics of Men," he refers to the work of the Holy Spirit seventeen times. He focuses on the Holy Spirit's work for grace-based justice and forgiveness. "The Spirit of God on the other hand enables a justice of grace. We pray

to be forgiven as we forgive others."[47] Throughout his writings, he emphasizes
that congregations need to be organized to practice discernment of the guiding
of the Spirit, listening carefully to all members who have a word to share, and
seeking clarity together. Additionally, the experience of Jesus Christ as Lord,
powerfully present and sovereign, is here in *The War of the Lamb*. This is an
ongoing tradition; our mission is to continue and deepen its development,
with special attention to the experience of the Holy Spirit, as witness to what
Jesus has taught (John 14:16; 15:16; 16:14; and 1 John 4:1–3).

Honoring Jesus's Roots in Judaism

In his essay for scholars of Asian religions and elsewhere, Yoder emphasizes
Jesus's roots in Judaism.[48] "Since the Middle Ages Christians are accustomed
unquestioningly to considering Christianity as having arisen over against Judaism. We therefore fail to discern the great extent to which the early Christian
attitude toward the Roman Empire was simply that of faithful Jews." The
nonviolence of Jewry since Jeremiah depends upon a worldview uniquely
tuned to befit the Jewish sociology of dispersion and the synagogue:

> The life of every human being is sacred. Blood is the presence of life given by
> God alone, which only God has the right to take back. Any bloodshed is sacrifice.
> Long before the rise of Christianity, Jewish saints and sages had gone about the
> process of mitigating the judicial power to kill, through more careful rules of
> evidence and warnings against the dangers of bias and self-interest; by rabbinic
> times the actual execution of capital punishment was practically excluded by
> their understanding of Torah.
>
> God is sovereign over the cosmos in general, and therefore also over our op-
> pressors no less than over us.

Yoder spells out several corollaries that follow. He bases some arguments
on God the Creator, not only God the Son. He emphasizes "the risen Jesus as
cosmic Lord, whose ultimate control of events can be trusted, when we cannot govern the world."[49] "The early Christians were Jews, and . . . Jews since
Jeremiah believed that God had abandoned kingship and war as instruments
of His concern for justice within history. . . . Jesus' pacifism was not an innovation; it was an intensification of the nonviolence of Jeremiah, Ezekiel,
and the singer of the Servant passages of the book of Isaiah."[50]
He suggests six reasons why early Christians not only insisted on their
own nonviolence, but also developed an ethic critical of Caesar's policies and
demands. Theirs was not a sectarian, dualistic, two-kingdom ethic in which
the lordship of Christ was normative only for their own actions among fellow
Christians. Their ethic gave them norms for critically assessing what Caesar

did.[51] It gave them norms for criticizing, transforming, and making use of terms employed in the surrounding society.[52]

Constantinianism actually began two centuries before Constantine, with Justin Martyr's Neoplatonic split that marginalized Jesus and Jesus's way. Justin wrote that we must obey Jesus in how we worship, but "*in all else we obey you, O Emperor.*" Constantinianism was not first of all about there being a Christian emperor, but about Christians weakening, thinning, or giving up any ethic that was critical of the emperor's policies and demands for loyalty.

"In view of the gospel bases cited above [the five christological bases for radical reformation criticism of Constantinianism cited in chapter two, below, on "Gospel Renewal"], the simplest way to cut to the core of reform is to claim that the teachings of Jesus are to be taken as normative moral guidance. One finds the reasoning as simple as a syllogism: is Jesus authorized to speak for God in matters of morality? If so, then when he teaches, 'you have heard that it was said . . . , but I say to you,' must not his teachings have at least the same authority as earlier Mosaic and prophetic moral commands? Therefore, the six so-called "minor precepts" of Jesus in Matthew 5 must be no less binding than the Ten Commandments or the two great commandments. Of the six minor precepts, three deal with killing and with love of the enemy. If that is the law of the Lord, then we are called to obey it."[53]

Letting Just War Theory and Pacifism Be Friends

Yoder argues that just war theory and pacifism should not be seen as enemies but as complementary. They both battle side by side against the usual war ethic, which is either crusade or justification of whatever wars the state decides to wage. Yoder also performs immanent criticism of just war theory, within its own terms, showing how it could be improved.

He comments that "Childress is right." By this he means that James Childress is right that just war theory, rightly understood, is based on the presumption against violence. Yoder argues this in an essay that he labels "A Think Piece on How Just War Thinking and Pacifism Coinhere."[54] And he comments: "Take note of other parallel efforts by Duane Friesen in [the] Whitmore Book and by Richard Miller in [his] book; possible paper on the theme of bridging over. Bounce it off Paul Ramsey on 'come clean.'"[55] Yoder's main point is that "the just war people who invest all their energy in discussing their relationship to the few pacifists on their left are in political reality tacit allies to the unjust warriors on their right. My purpose here is not to make debating points, but to clarify the substance of a perennial debate by looking at the diverse ways in which language is used to attempt to make sense of the debate but at the same time also (often unintentionally) tends to obfuscate."[56] And then he prods just war theorists critically, incisively, to take their own principles seriously and to build the church practices needed to reject war when it is unjust. Anything less is not honest.

Nor does pacifism refuse responsible involvement in political action while just war affirms it. Yoder writes:

> Nonviolent action is in any case involvement and not withdrawal. It is a form of involvement to maintain, as all serious nonviolent activist strategies have done, a broad range of forms of pressure within the existing order, at the same time that one seeks to replace it. The work of Martin Luther King Jr. included a very strong affirmation of the use of the American courts and appeal to the American constitution against specific injustices within the American system. Likewise, King's activity presupposed strong investment in obtaining and using the vote, and in calling the courts to implement the Constitution.
>
> Gandhi had his reasons for trusting less to litigation than King was later to do, but he created his own political party, which ultimately became the governing party, and before that he brought into being (first of all in South Africa) the powerful educational instruments of the Ashram and popular journalism.[57]

Advocating Active Strategies of Peacemaking

Yoder planned the three sections of *The War of the Lamb* in memos dated "4 September 97" and "November 1997."[58] In his plan for "Section I. Nonviolence: The Case for Life and Love," he specifically named the two chapters we have included as chapters 1 and 2. At the bottom of his memo, he wrote: "now the question is whether in addition any of the following should belong. . . . Maybe redo the Sermon on the Mount from *The Original Revolution*?" Shortly before he died, he sent me an extensive rethinking of the structure of the teachings in the Sermon on the Mount in response to what I was writing on that subject. I would love to have seen what sort of "redoing" he would have done. I am impressed with his highly insightful and exegetically accurate interpretation of the Sermon on the Mount in *The Original Revolution*. We wanted to include it even though he did not have a chance to rewrite it, but Herald Press now republishes *The Original Revolution* with a new introduction by Mark Thiessen Nation. Nevertheless, we are struck by his interpretation's call for personal experience of conversion and *metanoia* in response to the presence of the kingdom:

> "Repent! For the kingdom of God is at hand!" Under "repentance," we think of remorse, regret, sorrow for sin. But what [John the Baptist and Jesus] were calling for was a transformation of the understanding (*metanoia*), a redirected will ready to live in a new kind of world.
>
> The teachings which follow refuse to measure by the standards of "common sense" or "realism" or "reason": they testify to the novelty of the kingdom that is at hand. Jesus will therefore be describing for us a morality of repentance or

of conversion, not a prescription of what Every Man can and should do to be happy; not a meditation on how best to guide a society, but a description of how a person behaves whose life has been transformed by meeting Jesus.[59]

Yoder also considered including "the Abraham chapter in *Original Revolution*." I believe this essay is brilliant and incisive, as well as biblically faithful. It answers the question so many ask: "If Jesus taught all this peacemaking in the Sermon on the Mount, what about the Old Testament's wars and God's role in them?" But it too is now readily accessible in *The Original Revolution*, and we want our readers to be enticed to read that book. In fact, we encourage people to read *The Original Revolution* and this book as a pair. Yoder's essay on Abraham argues convincingly that we should not read passages in the Hebrew Scriptures for their contrast with the New Testament, but in their own context. Then we see how they differ from what cultures of that day were assuming—not whether wars are right or wrong, but whether our security depends on our military might or on God. The consistent message of the Hebrew Scriptures, over against the surrounding culture, is that our security depends on God's providence not our might, and on our doing justice and being faithful to God. Again and again, God rescues the people—not because of their expertise in battle but because of God's faithfulness. The answer is, "God will provide." The answer is based on faith in and experience of God's providence.

We also recommend reading the chapter "The Original Revolution" from that book because it answers the question of eschatology, of living in the new era of the kingdom versus living in the old era. Crucial for Yoder's understanding of peacemaking is God's bringing the kingdom. He speculated in his plan for this book whether to include "Maybe a section on OT and Eschatology," but in his last memo, he wrote that the book should be kept significantly shorter than *Royal Priesthood* so it would sell better. We recommend reading chapters 5–7 of his *For the Nations*, and "Peace Without Eschatology?" in his *Royal Priesthood*.[60]

His plan for the second section was exactly as we have it, except that he intended to include his lecture at the American Academy of Religion in January 1997, "The 'Power' of 'Nonviolence.'" It repeats arguments for the effectiveness of nonviolent action, and against Reinhold Niebuhr's either/or dichotomy between pure, powerless nonviolence and pragmatic, effective violence, arguments that Yoder already makes in other essays in the book. Its style is detached and academic, spending almost the first half defining terms. For the sake of readability of this book, and in the interest of avoiding repetition, we have decided not to include it.

His plan for the third section was to include chapters 12, 13, and 15 in the present book. In addition, he considered including, in his words, "Something more from South Africa. . . . Something from Warsaw Series 1983 (currently lost), Something from the Heck lectures? Look for." We have found these, and are including chapters 10 and 11, both of which are from the Heck lectures, but were repeated in his South Africa lectures and/or Warsaw lectures. We also included "Politics: Liberating Images of Christ" as chapter 14. Yoder's theological ethics is thoroughly Christ-centered, and we wanted to make clear that he bases his advocacy of peacemaking practices on God's revelation in Christ. We also included this chapter because of its incisive clarity about liberation theology, economic justice, and unjust ideologies.

His third section on "Nonviolent Action and Conflict Management" develops a positive theology of peacemaking, or what we have come to call "just peacemaking." It includes the just peacemaking practices of nonviolent direct action, conflict resolution, democracy and justice, support for the United Nations, international cooperation, and participation in alternative communities. Just peacemaking works to fill out what Yoder argues for in chapter 6 below under last resort, just intention, truthfully informed populace (which is required for supporting voluntary associations), diplomacy, and nonviolent action), and what he argues for in his third section, especially in shifting from interpretations of nonviolence and the Sermon on the Mount as passivity to transforming initiatives:

1) Yoder argues that we should speak not simply of nonresistance or nonviolence, but of *nonviolent direct action*. "Nonviolence means active strategies: So what is normally meant as an alternative is specific undertakings, initiatives, strategies, procedures, nonviolent action and not simply nonviolence as a negative, abstract term. . . . Think of all the trouble we would have in developing a Christian understanding of marriage if the only word we had for it were non-adultery and we had to make our affirmations in the form of negations." Therefore, Yoder defines nonviolent action as "involvement and not withdrawal. It is a form of involvement to maintain, as all serious nonviolent activist strategies have done, a broad range of forms of pressure within the existing order, at the same time that one seeks to replace it." He defines nonviolence not simply as a deontological obligation of faithfulness, but as a teleological action designed for the purpose of allowing peacemaking initiatives to work: "I propose to use [nonviolence] here . . . as designating modes of activism that renounce violence, in order that other kinds of power (*truth*, *consent*, *conscience*) may work."[61]

2) Similarly, he writes extensively on *conflict resolution*. Both nonviolent direct action and conflict resolution go beyond the debate between just war theory and pacifism to develop a proactive peacemaking ethic. Both are practices not only for Christians, but are normative for public ethics. Both call for peacemaking practices and initiatives by non-Christians as well as Christians in the secular world.

3) His positive peacemaking ethic also emphasizes *practices of justice*. He praises the development of religious liberty, egalitarian democracy, anti-

authoritarian education, the humanizing of corrections, and raising the status of women, slaves, and original Americans. "These specimens of critical social impact may be thought of as second-order nonviolence. . . . They reflect patterns of loving community in the wider society, which are first meaningful within the faith community." They are expressions of normative New Testament practices in public ethics—as expressions of the normativeness of Jesus's lordship in society.[62]

4) He advocates United Nations peace brigades, and commends Robert Johansen's work in international peacemaking.

All these are practices of the new paradigm of just peacemaking. John and I were dialoguing in my home about just peacemaking theory as it was developing. He urged that the new paradigm of just peacemaking clearly state that it does not replace the paradigms of pacifism and just war theory, but that it adds a crucial dimension: peacemaking action. I was clear on that, and John expressed his support for the project. It enables pacifists as well as just war theorists to advocate a much-needed public ethic, with practice norms rather than legalistic absolutes, and therefore not to be marginalized as in Niebuhr's stereotype without a relevant word to say to the state. That is what John was working to develop in his third section of *The War of the Lamb*.

This third section shows nonviolence is not passive but active, not withdrawn or sectarian but engaged in the world and communicating with social science studies. Indeed, the theme of the whole book as Yoder planned it is engagement, interaction, dialogue. John Howard Yoder was no monolinguist: he spoke English, French (every day with his wife, Annie), German (he wrote his first two books in German, now translated by my son), Spanish (in order to lecture in Argentina), and he learned to read Dutch in order to translate Berkhof's *Christ and the Powers*, thereby influencing us to make "the powers" a significant category in our ethics. He also advocated a multilingual method in Christian ethics.[63] That included learning from and dialoguing with social science, anthropology, just war ethics, Catholics, Protestants, experts in diverse religions, and humanists. This theme of multilingual dialogue runs throughout *The War of the Lamb*—by intention.

Nonviolence

The Case for Life and Love

1

A Theological Critique of Violence

The dominant view of the moral challenge of violence, in terms of the amount of literature it generates and the shape it gives to debates, is *casuistic*.[1] It assumes that by the term *violence* we can clearly designate some kinds of cases, clearly differentiated from other behaviors that are not violent. Then it considers the reasons why in this or that case such violent activities may or may not be morally justified. Much depends upon defining terms and comparing competing modes of moral argument. Since that is the dominant mode of our world, I shall need to converse with it, but I shall do that only after setting the scene more broadly.

First I propose to begin where the Bible does, by telling and interpreting a very ancient story. I shall not lay a prior theoretical groundwork by explaining why telling stories is a respectable theological thing to do, though that discussion is much in vogue in the guild. I shall not justify the authority of the book where we find these stories, although in some circles that would need to be done. I shall not throw any etymological light on the word *violence* or its Hebrew counterparts, as if definitions could settle moral matters.

As soon as the human story is situated outside the original innocence of the garden of Eden, one man kills his brother (Gen. 4). The first epistle of John tells us one reason for the murder,[2] but Genesis does not. Cain represents the culture of the farmer, tied to the land from which he drew the vegetables that he offered in sacrifice but that Yahweh did not accept. Abel represents the flock-herding nomad. Genesis does not tell us why either of them brought sacrifices. There had been no account thus far of the origins of sacrifice. Nor

27

are we told why the shepherd's sacrifice was more acceptable to Yahweh, although an anthropologist could offer some hunches.

It is not for us to make Genesis consistent by explaining what Abel was doing with flocks when Genesis 2 had foreseen a vegetarian culture. Ritually sacrificing and eating animals does not come until chapter 9. What we can say *is* in the intention of the text is that this first homicide drags Yahweh back into the fallen history which he had thought he had banished from his presence. We might think that divine intervention becomes necessary to protect the rest of humanity against the danger of this murderer in their midst. But the opposite is the case. Yahweh acts to protect Cain against the primeval vengeance he has every reason to fear. But why does Cain have reason to fear it?

A century ago, amid the debates around Darwinism, the mocking question was "where did Cain get his wife?" In Genesis, the rest of humanity is first alluded to not as a resource for affection or procreation or community, but as a threat. The very first reference to the rest of humanity is "whoever finds me will slay me."[3]

That is the primeval definition of *violence* for our present purposes: that there are people out there whose response to Cain's deed is *mimetic*. They will quasi-automatically, as by reflex, want to do to him what he had done to Abel.[4] It will not occur to them not to do so. It will seem self-evident to them that that is what he has asked for by what he did.

Later cultures have developed theories—many of them—to explain why this primitive retaliatory reflex is morally justified, politically functional, or even divinely demanded as a sort of cosmic redress. All of those theories are worthy of respectful attention, since they bespeak the claims of our fellow humans to some kind of moral dignity. They testify to the trust that, if things happen in patterns, those patterns must somehow be valid. Yet my task here cannot be to catalogue those constructs, even less to measure the parcels of truth which each of them might contain. None of them was around way back then to explain why Cain knew he was in danger.

Yahweh himself has no interest in vengeance. He does warn Cain that the earth that he has soiled with his brother's blood will no longer nourish him. That is more a statement of fact than a judicial pronouncement. In anthropological terms, Cain will move from agriculture to the cultural stage of crafts and city-building. But the divine initiative that matters is that *Yahweh intervenes to protect Cain's life from the universally threatening vengeance.* The sign of the protection is a mark placed on Cain; its verbal formula is a threat of vengeance: "If any one slays Cain, vengeance shall be taken on him sevenfold."[5] The threat is so massive that it will not need to be carried out. No one will attack Cain, even though he has it coming, for fear of the sevenfold backlash. This was an extreme measure, but it worked. Cain did survive, to become the ancestor of urban culture, of metalworking, and of music.

This strand of the story soon reaches its dead end, however, with the boast of Cain's distant descendant Lamech. Whereas in Cain's case Yahweh's threat of sevenfold retaliation does not need to be carried out, Lamech boasts that he himself retaliates seventy-sevenfold (Gen. 4:23–24). That suffices to characterize the way in which the retaliatory reflex, by its very nature, runs amok. It breaks loose from the preventive, protective function that it was supposed to discharge and becomes itself the engine of destruction.

René Girard, literary critic turned anthropologist, has been attracting increasing attention to his general theory of the origins of primitive culture in a foundational transaction prior to history but reflected in myth and legend. By that foundational covenant, the escalating spiral of retaliation is broken off before it explodes. At that point a transaction, redirecting the communal vengeance against an innocent victim, replaces the spiral as the guarantee of society's peace.

Girard's theory is too complex for the ordinary nonspecialist like me to know whereby it might be validated or falsified,[6] but in any case the threads he pulls together impress one with a kind of genial verisimilitude. His reconstruction seems to fit with stories like that of Lamech. The only way to keep Lamech's pride in his incommensurate retaliation from putting an end to history was to find some way to soak it up, to buffer it, to keep it from running free, yet without ignoring its provocation. The civil order arises to replace private violent vengeance: regulating it, mitigating it, yet also thereby legitimizing it.

I doubt that Girard's etiology explains *all* the modes of bloodshed. Other forms of killing would seem to have their evolutionary origins less in retributive mechanisms than in the hunt or in battle. Those cultures in which a "brave" is accredited as a true man by killing do not argue the legitimacy of the massacre by some claim that the victims had provoked it. In such settings it would seem rather that people of that other tribe are not fellow humans; they are of another, less worthy species. They are not part of the community whose peace is our concern. Their God is not our God. Their being human bears no divine image. Likewise, it is unclear how Girard's explanations of how violence is covert, at the roots of a culture, would illuminate systems where persistent overt violence maintains dominance over whole classes of others: other races, inferior classes, or the society's own women and children.[7]

But my concern here cannot be to pose as an amateur anthropologist. Whether or not the Girardian etiology represents ancient prehistory with total accuracy, the metaphor is very helpful. I propose to make do with the kind of argument that Girard represents: namely, that the bloodiness of ancient human cultures is not best understood as compatible with later rationalizations, either functionally as part of maintaining social order, or theologically as maintaining a cosmic balance. Those interpretations are modern. They are rationalizations in the technical sense; i.e., they are efforts to impose by a mental exercise a sense-giving framework upon realities that do not have that kind of meaning. That is why our struggles in the name of enlightenment against xenophobia, militarism, patriarchy, or the death penalty are so far from the mark.

But then if the phenomenon of violence is not rational in its causes, its functions, and its objectives, neither will its cure be rational. The cure will have to be something as primitive, as elemental, as the evil. It will have to act upon the deep levels of meaning and motivation, deeper than mental self-definition and self-control. It will have to be *sacrifice*. There will have to be innocent suffering.

That is not only a statement about ancient cultures; the bloodiness of our modern culture cannot be explained rationally either. The most widely credited accounts of what was going on in the Pentagon and the White House, as well as in Baghdad, from July 1990 to March 1991,[8] give more attention to the needs of the several actors to appear manly than to other moral criteria. Some accounts locate this need inside the psyche of George H. W. Bush or of Saddam Hussein; others locate it in the minds of their respective publics, or their media. The several accounts agree that only a small part of the decision process was the rationally quantified weighing of competing risks and values, or of legal obligations and prohibitions. That is true of Saddam Hussein, who is crazy; it is no less true of George Bush or of Norman Schwarzkopf, who are shrewd and sane. It is probably as true regarding power abuse in the school or in the family as it is regarding war.

More than ethics is involved, then, in our coming to grips with what violence means. Whether that *more* needs to be sought deeper in the order of the impersonal cosmos that surrounds us, or deeper in the psyche inside us, or deeper in the decree of a person-like God, who responds to misbehavior in ways that can be compared to an angry person, is a choice we need not resolve. Why could it not be all of the above? For our purposes it suffices to recognize that *there is a destructive reflex at work, which will not go away and whereby violence propagates itself.*

One thing that can be done with this reflex is to channel it by the application of a justification that is at the same time a restraint; we call that the *state*, or *law and order*.[9] Or we can attempt to manage it by appealing to the world of magic and metaphor; we call that *sacrament*. We can attempt to come to grips with it in the framework of a set of mental constructs; we may label it *mimesis* as does René Girard or compare it to the eye-for-eye balancing of the ancient Hebrews. We may call it *retribution* or *compensation*, as does legal theory. We may call it *expiation*, or the restoring the balance of a tilted cosmos. In another context, another discipline, the word will be *deterrence* or *self-affirmation*. C. S. Lewis argues that the imperative of equivalent retribution is part of the human dignity of the offender.[10]

To Overcome the Retributive Impulse, We Need the Sacrifice of the Cross

Not long ago the television news hounds, with their usual nose for blood, were interviewing the father of one of the victims of the first man in years whom California was going to execute for murder.[11] The father was rejoicing in the prospect of attending the execution, but he said he would like even more to be able to replicate formally, as a means of execution, the chase and the stabbing as they took place in the original murder. His reason? "An eye for an eye, ya' know."

It is a fascinating fluke of culture transmission that this phrase, "an eye for an eye," whose primary place in the Christian canon is that Jesus set it aside, should lead its own life down through Western history as validation for the reflex of mimetic destruction. That phrase appears only three times in the Mosaic corpus, never in a literarily important place. In none of the three places does the text call for the death penalty for murder.[12] The phrase is used once when death is prescribed for accidentally killing a woman in the course of fighting a man, once for blasphemy, and once for perjury in a capital case. In short: the notion of cosmic symmetry is there in the ancient rhymed phrases but not in the actual Hebrew jurisprudence, and not in the nature of God.

Nevertheless, that ancient rhyme rolls on down through Western civilization as if it were the law of gravity. René Girard would say that it *is* the law of gravity.

By putting the facts about the violence reflex in an explanatory and (some hope) regulatory framework, these efforts to channel it or manage it have several things in common:

(1) They are undertaken after the fact. None of them can or does claim to describe the *origin* of the phenomenon of reflexive vengeance.
(2) They grant, concede, or posit that the reality of the destructive reflex cannot be managed or removed by describing, defining, or explaining it.

The response that is needed then is not a new way to *think* about it—what we might properly call a *theological critique*—but something to be *done* about it. The response is divine judgment; not an explanation, not an evaluation, but an intervention.

The name of that intervention is "Jesus." How best to interpret the meaning of Jesus, and especially of his becoming victim, will depend on which of the descriptions of the problem we choose to draw on. I mention only a few of these descriptions. If you can make sense of a sacrificial worldview, Jesus is the last high priest and the last victim. If your worldview is juridical, then Jesus is the vicarious offender who bears the penalty humanity had earned. If your worldview is political realism, Jesus is the advocate of the people whose leadership called down on him the death penalty of the Romans. Psychody-namic analysis, or Girard's deep anthropological vision, or feminism can say it yet other ways. Tolstoy, the doctrinaire poetic oversimplifier, could speak of "breaking the chain" of evil. Gandhi, and Gandhi's pupil Martin Luther King Jr., replicated it as a model for social change in our time.

What all of these (in detail deeply different) modes of connection have in common is that the thing to do with violence is not to understand it *but to undergo it*. In no case is the solution that we should escalate our power to coerce. We cannot beat the destructive reflex at its own game. Whichever idiom we use to articulate its claim on us, for our own setting and for the mental agenda of our particular interlocutors, the answer is the cross.

Sometime in August of 1525, in the pastor's residence of the parish of St. Martin's in Basel, Johannes Hausschyn, who as a humanist preferred to use the Hellenized name Oecolampadius, was confronted by some men called Anabaptists. They were responding to his having attacked them from the pulpit. While they were talking, a man from Zurich joined the group. He exclaimed that, "what is needed is divine wisdom, in order to discern honor in the cross, and life in death. We must deny ourselves and become fools."

I have been working away at the problem of violence, beginning with the bad news rather than the good, because that was our assigned theme. The good news, however, is that out of death life has come and does come. The salvation of the world comes not from shrewder management or better luck but from the divine condescension of the cross.

This is not a rare insight, present only at one place, one high point, within the apostolic writings. Every major strand of the New Testament, each in its own way, interprets the acceptance by Jesus of the violence of the cross as the means, necessary and sufficient, of God's victory over the rebellious powers. Violence is not merely a problem to solve, a temptation to resist, a mystery to penetrate, or a challenge to resolve with a theodicy. It is all of that, but that is not yet the good news. The good news is that the violence with which we heirs of Cain respond to our brothers' differentness is the occasion of our salvation. *Were it not for that primeval destructive reflex, there would have been no suffering servant, and no wisdom and power of God in the cross.*

That this is the case does not make it any less necessary to review and update the arguments about the legitimacy of violence in the defense of vic-tims or against oppression. That is the theme of the rest of this essay. Yet this observation about the place of the destructive reflex in the divine economy may encourage us to direct our energies less toward explaining and evaluating, and more toward participation in the reconciliation story.

Paul wrote to the church at Corinth: "The weapons of our combat are not fleshly."[13] We would expect the sentence to go on to say something like, "not fleshly *but spiritual*." That would fit with Paul's acceptance of his weakness, expressed elsewhere in the same letter, as his own privileged mode of ministry.

But that is not what he says. He says, "The weapons of our combat are not fleshly but mighty." They can "destroy strongholds." The opposite of "flesh" is *strength*. If we can face the great tacit assumption of Genesis 4—that the destructive reflex characterizes the fallen world—we may be empowered to see clearly that the cross of Jesus Christ is not only cultic but also *cosmic*. Innocent suffering is the victory over the vengeful urge, and over the institutions that exploit it, on an anthropologically far more fundamental level than our usual theories of the state or of social hygiene.

To illustrate: In our society, unlike in the rest of the industrialized world, the forces of enlightenment have been losing ground for twenty years in the effort to abolish the death penalty. Some of the reasons for the setbacks were tactical. It may have been a mistake in the long run to trust the courts to set aside as "cruel and unusual," or otherwise as unconstitutional, penalties that legislatures could reinstate. It may have been a tactical mistake to base so much of the case against judicial killing upon the racial and economic inequities of its application in some states. But I have come to the impression that there was a deeper mistake.

We have projected the tacit claim that there is something uncouth about the destructive reflex itself, rather than granting it a deep anthropological legitimacy. Instead of posing the foundations for a nonretributive society upon ways of processing the deep demand of blood for blood, such as Jewish reverence for the sacredness of life, or the Christian interpretation of the cross of Christ in word and sacrament (and in discipleship), or on Enlightenment visions of restraining governmental absolutism, or even on psychodynamic therapeutic analogues of all the above, we have tried to make our culture ashamed of its vengefulness. That shame has backfired in a new wave of executions.

We have not been able to transfer to capital punishment the insight Gandhi and King taught us about racial oppression, namely that *the victim of violence most to be pitied is its perpetrator*. The perpetrator is not as free, or as in control, or as effective, or as satisfied with himself or herself as he or she thinks. This was the case for the imperial bureaucrats Gandhi faced, as well as for the white police officers King faced. This is hardly less true when the power being abused is that of office, or that of gender. Only when we retrieve an awareness of the foundational place of retribution in our social psyche can we hope to discover the role of redemption in a newly pertinent form.

Inventory of the Definition Games

Few important themes have been as subject as ours to the damage done to dialogue by a particular style of foundationalism. This form of foundationalism hopes to resolve matters of substance by seizing the microphone—that is, by controlling the definition of terms. Yet I here define *fundamentalism* as that form of theological culture that assumes there are no hermeneutical problems, since what I take a text to mean is what it has to mean. *Foundationalism*, its name linguistically parallel, makes a similar but opposite mistake. It assumes that since there are hermeneutical problems, we should and can resolve them before entering into the substance of the debate by making a ruling on how terms must be used.

In the case of the subject at hand, the most basic and most widely accepted ruling usually proposed is to distinguish between *legitimate* and *illegitimate* violence. Sometimes it is called the distinction between *force*, which is legitimate, and *violence*, which is not. What makes the difference between these two, for one set of thinkers, is not a difference between different kinds of deeds. What matters is governmental authorization. The same act can be *force* if government authorizes it and *violence* if not. We may call this view *legitimist*.

For another set of advocates of resolution by definition, the primary criterion is *justice*. Some of these call themselves *liberationist*, though that designation opens a new set of questions. *Force* for them is legitimate when it is directed against an unjust regime; the *violence* that supports or imposes an unjust social system is what should be rejected morally.

For both parties, although they take opposite sides in the political conflict, the moral logic is the same. There is—for both—no point in defining violence as such; what matters is the *goal* toward which an activity is directed.[14] The capacity to coerce, they argue, is like the pressure in a firefighter's hose. Aimed at a burning building it is good; aimed at people marching in the street it is bad.

The classical form of that claim to be able to discriminate morally between acceptable and unacceptable force is the so-called just war tradition, which has been slowly developing for millennia in the hands of political philosophers, Christian theologians, and diplomats. That tradition asks a variety of commonsensical questions in order to evaluate the claim that in a particular case (that meets the criteria of the tradition), an action that inflicts harm in a responsibly structured way is morally preferable to letting some adversary inflict some other harm, which one can argue would be greater.[15] The just war argument works for both legitimist and liberationist applications. All that needs to be changed is the content of terms like *legitimate authority*, *proportion*, and *necessary means*.

There is another, more ambitious set of definitional proposals. They reach much further than regulating overt harm. They propose to include under the term *violence* every kind of limitation imposed on the potential of people for self-fulfillment.[16] The injustice built into the institutions of any society can be called violence whenever we can identify who its victims are. Sometimes the phrase is *structural violence*. If the children in an urban slum die because the healthcare delivery system available to middle-class children a few kilometers away does not reach them, those children are just as dead as if guns had killed

them. Others have used the phrase *latent violence* to allude to the fact that
in authoritarian societies, even though the streets are quiet, the iron hand of
enforcement is always just under the surface.[17]

In some cases, these efforts to redefine are the expression of a desire to
achieve greater objectivity and analytical refinement, without partisan political
payoff. This is the case for the analyses of peace studies academics like Johann
Galtung. More often the intention of the definitional argument is ideological
in the strong sense of that word. Then the argument about defining violence
already constitutes part of the combat for control of the conflictual system.
One seeks to stipulate the terms of analysis so that the other posture is wrong
not by virtue of successful dialogue but by definition.

An escalated form of the ideologized definition is the therapeutic vision of
Frantz Fanon, a psychotherapist who interpreted the Algerian independence
movement of the early 1960s. The specific context of oppression there was
that a tenth of the country's population, those of European origin, were administering the country as a part of France, while the Arab majority claimed
the right to national independence. Fanon's claim, sharpened by Jean-Paul
Sartre (who wrote the preface to Fanon's book, thereby guaranteeing its sale
in France), was that violence exercised by the colonized against the settlers,
the persons called oppressors, was necessary for the underdogs to become
psychically independent. The necessity was not merely practical and political,
but therapeutic:

> I need to kill you not because you have wronged me, the Algerian rebel should
> say to the adult European colonist, or even to a child, but because your kind of
> people have wronged my kind, and my rising up to destroy you is a necessary
> component of restoring my [collective] self-esteem. Whether you are *personally*
> guilty of oppressing me or not is not decisive. Whether the particular tactics of
> the uprising in which I participate will be successful is not decisive either. My
> psychic enfranchisement is an autonomous moral value. You are part of the
> slaveholder class; previously my class had no rights; now it is your turn, and
> my shedding your blood proves to me my own manhood.[18]

In a completely different setting, but structurally not as different as one
may want to think, there is the redemptive role of violence in the films of
Sylvester Stallone.[19] Rambo does not use finite and proportionate means for
a just cause in a situation of last resort. Neither he nor any objective arbiter
weighs costs, benefits, or the probability of success. That violence is the first
resort and that it is disproportionate is necessary to the story. (Rambo himself
in the story has suffered some early trauma which he has the right to take out
on whoever gets in his way.) Other Stallone fighters may be differently driven,
but the correlation between disproportionate harm and restored self-esteem
is parallel.[20]

Straightening Out the Conceptual Tangle

There is no simple or self-evidently right way, in our present setting or in moral discourse in general, to clear this all up by once more reshuffling the words. A wide survey of dozens of usages over thirty years might be possible, but it would document the complexity rather than clarify anything. Certainly, from the point of view of pastoral care and mental hygiene, there is value in the point already made by Jesus (Matt. 5:21–22): that to despise a fellow human is "as bad as" or is "potentially equivalent to" killing. Yet that is not a statement about political ethics. Most of the time I would rather that you despise me than kill me. The same is true of the realms of latent or structural violence. If their effect is to heighten sensitivities, they are helpful; when, however, they are used backhandedly to imply that killing is not so bad, because nonlethal injustices are "violent" too, they lose the original point. What I can do, instead of reviewing the entire foundational/definitional game, is to begin again with a nonfoundational, ordinary language review of the theme, disavowing the claim that this is the *only* right way to use the words.

Violence is a verbal noun. *To violate* is a transitive verb; it can only be used with an object. One cannot simply violate or do violence; one can only violate someone or something; one can only do violence to some value. The object can be a law, a border, a person's integrity, or a promise. To evaluate violence morally, then, is to evaluate the worth of the value violated. An unjust law or a promise to do evil perhaps should be violated; the rights or integrity of a person or a community should not. If exceptions to that prohibition need to be made, they must be justified by some kind of argument that takes into account the values at stake and how they collide.

The most responsible way to think carefully about what is being claimed in that case is to say that violence is unavoidable, and that what needs to be determined, by some kind of weighing of evils,[21] is which kind of violence is less objectionable. Then the lesser violence can be held to be justifiable; but it is still violence. Calling it *force* or *redemption* is obfuscation. Liberation or some other form of justice may be its goal, *but the activity being discussed is still killing people on purpose.*

What Needs to Be Evaluated, and What Is Assumed

What needs to be evaluated is the moral weight of arguments for the necessity of this kind of violence to prevent some other evil or achieve some greater good. I am not saying that this is the *only* way to define the words, or the shape of the moral choice: I am saying that if we define it thus simply we can meaningfully dialogue about it, whereas some of the other definitions make moral discourse less accountable. For our purposes, it will be more useful to begin with the worst-case phenomenon of killing,[22] and then derive from it our understanding of milder forms, than to broaden the term at the outset to cover all forms of less-than-loving behavior.[23]

If then the simplest issue is the case for justifiable violence, on the grounds of the claim that the values thereby violated weigh less than other undesirable outcomes, we have a question simple enough to think about critically, and so classical that we can review how it has been thought about before.

Before stipulating that that is the simplest argument and going on to converse with it, let me take note that there are other subquestions, also debatable, that hide beneath that stipulation:

(1) *There is the assumption that we possess a very high level of accuracy in information about the facts of the case.* This is presupposed in order to be sure that the values being weighed against each other are in fact as the tradeoff image defines them. All utility calculation, of which this is a subtype, makes that assumption of reliable predictability, if not omniscience.[24] Yet in complicated institutional settings, where many different actors interrelate conflictually, with some of them able to manage the availability of information to some of the others, such a high level of accuracy is hard to guarantee.

(2) *There is the assumption that one can ascertain the legitimacy of the bearer of the legitimate violence.* In the ideal setting of an orderly domestic society this argument is not impossible to deliver; the local police officer is legitimate. But that ideal setting is exceptional rather than typical. In conflictual situations part of what is in doubt is usually legitimacy; often legitimacy is claimed for both sides. That is the very meaning of *revolution*. But by the nature of the case there is often no criterion of legitimacy above the fray, or as in half of Europe today, any credible authority,[25] and there is no criterion of legitimacy that does not beg the question.[26] Fanon and Rambo claim that the unacceptability of the way things are justifies using violence.

(3) *There is the assumption that some way exists to quantify the different values violated over against each other.* The life we destroy in battle is worth less than some other life we defend; the institutions we destroy are worth less than the ones we promise to create. The language of *proportion* is classically used here, as if that weighing were somehow possible; yet the values violated are incommensurable.[27]

I do not propose to review these assumptions or the others like them critically from the inside; together they compose the texture of the consequential reasoning of the just war tradition. They are the standard components of that tradition, of which the case for justified violence on behalf of the poor is one application. For the purpose of the present discussion, I grant that although the components of that argument are severally subject to logical question, it remains *prima facie* convincing to many who think about it and self-evident to many who do not. It therefore merits being tested head-on, by virtue of my ecumenical respect for those who hold to it, despite the disrespect earned by its less-than-irresistible logic.

If we assume that there is a *prima facie* case for lethal violence, in some restricted case, and that it can touch all the bases of cause, authority, proportion, last resort, necessary and legitimate means, etc., then where does the "theological critique" begin? If only an *ethical* critique were intended, that would be plenty, since ethics is also theology. But it is more fitting to begin at the other end, with the language of doxology.

Celebrating the Faith in the Face of Violence

"I believe," the creed says, "in one God, the Father Almighty, Maker of heaven and earth, and of all things visible and invisible." That God is almighty will have something to do with why we assume we need to impose our choice of the lesser evil on world history. But for now I note that if "all things visible and invisible" are of God's making, if (as Locke said much later about human creativity) God has "mixed his labor" with things, then they are God's. That is why we should not violate them. What is wrong with violence is that what is violated is a creature of the sovereign God. Of human life in particular, Genesis further says (although the creed does not) that the creature is characterized by the "image and likeness" of God. I do not propose to review the various meanings given to that Hebrew phrase; *any* possible meaning must be part of what makes it wrong to violate the life or dignity of a human being.

The theological critique of violence begins, then, by recognizing that *the majesty of the creator God is what is under attack*. To reduce a life-threatening situation to a clash of quantifiable group interests without recognizing the uniqueness of the human life one proposes to destroy is not merely misdirected politics or cost-benefit pragmatism with the coefficients wrong; it is first of all *blasphemy*.

There are many ways to sin against God and neighbor, but it is a mistake to level them all out as if the values at stake were all of the same size or shape. Some argue that in order to be consistent we must treat all sins the same and not make one sin worse than another.[28] Yet to shed human blood is, according to Genesis 9, an offense against the divine image; that is not said of lying or stealing, coveting, bearing false witness, or disrespect to parents. *Violence* is qualitatively on a different level from other offenses. Many other offenses would be less drastic if not escalated by the admixture of coercion. After other offenses one can make amends to the victim; not after killing. Fratricide, as demonstrated in Genesis 4 and in 1 John 3, is the chief of sins, because God's making my fellow human to be my partner in the care of the cosmos is the crown of creation.

The creed goes on: "I believe in one Lord Jesus Christ" and then uses seven words to describe the action of Christ: begotten, crucified, buried, risen, ascended, seated, coming. For our purposes we can concentrate on the verbs. First there is the triptych-like, threefold downward movement: three passive verbs, *kenosis*, and all past tense. Then the threefold victory: three active verbs, also past. Then comes the dangling seventh verb, in timeless present: "coming."

The theological critique of violence implicit in the first triptych addresses the pride and self-justification presupposed by the just war argument. The just war argument presupposes the possession of power. That is why Christians did not think that way during the first three centuries. The early Christians were not pacifist in the sense that, when called by the draft, they did not serve. There was no draft. They were not pacifist in the sense of asking Nero to call off the superpower struggle against the Parthians. Neither they nor Nero, not having read Locke or Rousseau, thought of Nero as being accountable to "the people" in general or to Christians in particular. But they *were* nonviolent. They saw in the passion and death of their Lord the model of divine-human virtue to place over against other visions of human prospering. Doing without dominion was not for them a second-best alternative to glory; *it was the way to participate in the victory of redemption.*

The theological critique of violence implicit in the active panel of the triptych addresses the element of despair in the just war argument. Violence is the only way, the last resort, the just war common sense says, *because there is no other actor for good on the scene.* We must tough-mindedly take on the dirty work and the moral ambivalence of dealing death to our fellow creatures, because otherwise history would get out of hand. But confessing Jesus Christ risen, ascended, and seated at the right hand of the Father meant, in the first century, that history *cannot* get out of hand.[29] The medieval and high Protestant word for "seated at the right hand" was *providence*. There is a potential for saving outcomes in the human drama, and there is a potential for redemptive outcomes out of suffering, if Jesus Christ is viceroy over the cosmos. We short-circuit that providential potential when we decide to be providence ourselves, at the expense of the fellow humans on whom we inflict the violence that we claim is lesser.

The critique of violence implied in the final verb, "coming [to judge]," restates as vindication what the three active participles [risen, ascended, seated at the right hand of God] described as authority. The redemption that is now going on in history under providence will be ratified as the last word. The evil that is now being condoned by the patience of God will come to an end. That the way of the suffering servant is after all the way of the Lord of hosts, which today we have to believe against appearances, will then be manifest so that every knee will bow.

That should be enough, but the creed goes on: "I believe in the Holy Spirit, the Church Universal, Forgiveness, Resurrection, and Eternal Life, Amen."[30] That the human communion in which our trust centers is not a nation-state or a regime, that sins are forgiven, that the sanction of death is revoked: these are not major new theological affirmations, yet they round out the holism of our vision of the world where violence is out of order. This third article is not just an addendum. All of this concrete reconciliation and community is the work of the Spirit, who is no less Godself than are the Father and the Son.

My point in putting doxology before ethics was that too often our cultural ethics, especially social ethics, is reduced to a form of engineering: how to do what you have to with the least pain. We calculate costs and benefits on the basis of a deterministic understanding of how history goes. Then the place of piety is to help us live with the inevitable pain.[31] If you are more Wesleyan, your warmed heart will make you try harder. If you are more Calvinist, your confidence in predestination will make you try harder. If you are Lutheran, your trust in God's forgiving you will make you stop trying so hard, but by the paradox of grace that will make you do just as well. For all of the above, dogma and spirituality contribute to the setting or the mood of ethics, but not to its substance.

For our apostolic predecessors, the form of the life of faith in society was not in that sense derivative. They did not have in one corner of their casuistry a place to discuss the pros and cons of killing in extreme circumstances. They were living in and into a new world, one in which that corner had no place.

Jesus and the Politics of Violence

One more exposition: I said nothing until now about the human career of the Jesus of the Gospels, because the creed does not. The creed skips from Bethlehem to Golgotha, from Mary to Pilate. But of course the Gospels do not make that leap, nor did the real story. If there had not been the story in between, there would have been no creed. Because of the metaphysical invasion of our world bespoken by the verb "begotten," there had to be the story in between, for which my name is *The Politics of Jesus*.[32] Named by angelic imperative for the liberator Joshua, greeted by the magi as liberator-designate, and targeted for massacre by Herod for the same reason, Jesus faced the temptation of violence as no other. Our sources give no information concerning his inclinations to covet, steal, bear false witness, or commit adultery. But from the first testing in the desert to the last one in the garden, his unceasing temptation was the plea of the crowds and even of some of his disciples that he should strike out on the path of righteous kingship.

The Gospel Is Not about Delegitimizing Violence So Much as about Overcoming It

Violence, we saw already at the other end of the story, is not a sin like any other. For Jesus it was not a temptation like any other. Jesus did not refrain from violence because he was scrupulous about bloodguilt. He did not, like a cartoon figure incarnating unconditional love so absolutely as to be historically impossible, step off the scale of political pertinence in order to be true to the hyperbolic logic of the Sermon on the Mount (as Reinhold Niebuhr would interpret it in the 1930s). Jesus chose the cross as an alternative social strategy of strength, not weakness. As Paul would write a generation later, it was God's wisdom and power, what God ultimately does about violence.

In thus repeating the classical critical agenda evoked by the case for violence, I do not want to be thought unaware of the misuse that can be made of the gospel themes I have touched upon. What I referred to above as "doing without dominion" can, in the wrong hands, be twisted into an acceptance of evil systems on the grounds of the claim that God is in control. Suffering servanthood can, when involuntary, become pathological. Trusting providence can be twisted into passivity. Discerning in violence a destructive quality *sui generis* can keep us from discerning all of the latent ways we hurt each other without drawing blood. All of these distortions of the cross[33] are connected to the effort to do ethics without piety, social ethics without ecclesiology, law without gospel.

The review of the justification for violence ends where the interpretation of its anthropological origins ended. Violence has been made a problem and has called forth our critique because some advocate its use on various kinds of grounds. But the gospel is not about delegitimizing violence so much as about overcoming it. We overcome it partly by demythologizing its moral pretensions, partly by refusing to meet it on its own terms, partly by replacing it with other more humane strategies and tactics of moral struggle, partly by innocent suffering, and partly by virtue of the special restorative resources of forgiveness and community. Yet all of those coping resources are derivative. At bottom violence is judged—*critiqued* in the deep sense of the verb—because of the passion events.

We participate in that judgment by participating in the cross, the resurrection, the ascension, and the pouring out of the Spirit. That we thus participate in the gathered life of believers goes without saying. What matters for our present study is to appropriate it as grace so that we can participate in the same process no less within the struggles of our wounded world.[34]

2

Gospel Renewal and the Roots of Nonviolence[1]

Most interreligious encounters occur between majority-culture religions. Participants in such conversations, especially within the Western cultural world, can thus be presumed to share common knowledge about the mainstream religious forms of Christendom. That predisposes people to misunderstand what radical Protestantism is. As a result, I need first to clarify what is meant by the label *radical reformation* to describe a specific phenomenon within Western Christianity.[2]

Radical reformation is a repeatable phenomenon, even a syndrome. It recurs in different times and places without the actors thinking that what they are doing derives from predecessors. George Fox knew little of Peter Waldo. Tolstoy was surprised when he learned late in life about the Czech Brethren. Seldom does a radical reformer think he or she is replicating some earlier reformation. Nonetheless, there are common features that authorize the following summary.[3]

The common feature linking all such movements is the notion of re-formation. This includes two essential components. First, there is the conviction that forms matter. Religious reality is not dealt with more authentically by avoiding, ignoring, dispensing with, or abstracting from the concrete historical and institutional shape of things. These may be verbal forms like confessions of faith, institutional forms like episcopacy, or ritual forms like breaking bread together. The platonic or gnostic attempt to heighten religious authenticity by

43

downgrading the formal or cognitive may lead to reformulation, revitalization, or reaffirmation. It may do some good; yet it will not lead to reformation.[4]

Second, there must be the conviction that something has gone wrong and that forms need to be changed. The reason for change will be stated in various ways. There must also be a criterion—whether faithfulness to the past or adequacy for the present, whether formally located in a Scripture, clergy, or market measurement—whereby pressure toward change and criteria for acceptable change can be defined without being arbitrary or vague. Without some such criterion, there will not be reformation.

For reformation to be radical, another pair of complementary requisites is self-evident. First, present agencies are not qualified to reform themselves. A structure that should not exist cannot be counted on to correct itself. If what was wrong with the medieval church was the papacy, the pope could not be the instrument of radical reformation. The change needed is thus not organic evolution to a new and more adequate phase, nor refurbishing and remodeling a basically adequate structure.[5] It must somehow be a new beginning.[6]

Second, that more radical new beginning will therefore demand a more radical criterion. No ephemeral reading of the marketplace of ideas, or contemporaneity, or adequacy will suffice to judge the present with sufficient clarity to enable a new beginning. Only a return to an original charter, which unfaithful development has abandoned, will provide sufficient leverage for new beginnings.[7] Recourse to an ancient charter need not be antiquarian, nor need it deny continuing historical change; however, it does affirm that the movement called upon to undergo reformation has a normative foundation within history, which it is possible to deny and therefore also possible to reaffirm.

The distinction between reformation and radical reformation can be exemplified by two specimens: (1) the difference between the Franciscan and Waldensian movements, and (2) the perceived role of civil government within the sixteenth-century reformations.

There was certainly a beautiful New Testament radicalness about the vision of St. Francis of Assisi. He broke with the cultural patterns of family and economy. He let his life and that of his brothers be totally "made over" by the model of the Jesus of the Gospels. He did not claim, however, that his way was *the* way to be Christian, in any mode that demanded repentance on the part of all his neighbors. By the practice of mendicancy, he made it possible for those with material goods to maintain a good conscience. By creating the tertiary disciplines, he clarified that celibacy was not for everyone. By soliciting and receiving—and then respecting—authorization from Rome, he committed to not rocking the boat of the established church more than it could tolerate. In this, he differed from Peter Waldo who, although he also requested and to his deathbed apparently believed he had received the blessing of the pope, refused to oblige his circles of preachers to submit to the discipline of local bishops. Thus Franciscanism, with all its simplicity, could be co-opted.

Waldo's message and method, preaching the Gospels in the vernacular, was practically the same. The cultural setting was the same. Yet by centering poverty on working with one's hands and living from the gifts of others, rather than on begging as a spiritual discipline, the Waldensians avoided becoming hostages to the wealthy. By refusing to respect the bull promulgated against them in 1184, on the grounds that the pope must have been misinformed, they placed the original gospel call to preach above the contemporary unfaithful institution, even though they went as far as they could to avoid offense.

In the sixteenth century, the *magisterial*[8] reformers clearly and courageously attacked those elements of the late medieval Catholic synthesis they considered to be in error—the theology of the sacraments, the theology of salvation, and the jurisdiction of bishops. However, they did not call into question most of the rest of the changes that had taken place between the first century and their own. They not only affirmed but also heightened the power of civil government in the life of the church and the commitment of church leaders to serve provincial civil governmental interests. They not only affirmed the just war tradition; they declared pacifism heretical.[9] The alternative in the sixteenth century, as in the fifteenth and seventeenth centuries, was what polemicists of the time called *Anabaptist*: namely, movements that first challenged the authority of civil government to set the pace of reform and then proceeded to dispute other elements of the *consensus cinquesaecularis* that Luther, Zwingli, Calvin, and the Anglican divines had not intended to question.

Our concern is with the retrieval of nonviolence in the radical reformation, although it is essential to place it within the setting of the wider reformation. In order to know what the radical reformers had to attack, I must identify what it needed to criticize. Why, centuries earlier, had war become acceptable to Christians?

The progressive decay of the primitive Christian rejection of Caesar's wars[10] had many causes that built up gradually, although the Constantinian transition was the weightiest.[11] Instead of being a small band of believers, each of whom had counted the cost before making the commitment of discipleship, everyone who counted was now a Christian; it was now costly to be a pagan or a Jew. Since everyone was a Christian, Christian morality had to be tailored to the capacities and motivation level of "Everyman." Instead of looking to their risen Lord to bring history to a triumphant conclusion in his own time and way, Christians now knew that the Roman emperor and their God were allies and that the forward movement of history was enforced by the legions. Sometimes this meant that the wars of Christians were crusades, holy causes, like those of Moses. Sometimes they were plain Machiavellian rapacity, though in the interest of Christian people. Sometimes, ideally, notions of just war restraint and episcopally mediated peacemaking mitigated war's destruction, but in principle that was the most one could expect.

The synthesis of Christendom was not simple, so the fitting critique was not simple either. It had at least three theologically distinguishable forms.

Good News

The radical reformers did not sit down like sociologists and project different critiques for each component of the Constantinian slide. Yet the simple Gospel resources on which they drew provided the fulcrum for questioning the system. The continuing critical impact of recourse to the New Testament can be distilled schematically into the following themes, which any reader of the Gospels cannot avoid:

(1) Jesus the Franciscan, the poor peripatetic who calls people to leave valuable things behind and follow him in a new way of life;

(2) Jesus the eschatological Rabbi, who teaches a *fulfilled* understanding of the human situation under God. For example: (a) the law is fulfilled, so not killing is radicalized into not hating, loving one's neighbor is radicalized to mean loving one's enemy, and limiting vengeance is radicalized into renouncing vengeance,[12] all of which is validated on the grounds that it corresponds to the nature of God "your Father";[13] (b) the chain of evil causing evil is broken by the presence of a new alternative behavior issuing from this alternative understanding; and (c) trust in God for one's defense is possible as trust in God for other material needs is possible (Matt. 6:25–34);

(3) Jesus the nonviolent Liberator;[14]

(4) Jesus the Lamb who was sacrificed, the Suffering Servant whom his disciples are called to imitate; and

(5) Jesus the risen, cosmic Lord, whose ultimate control of the world can be trusted when we cannot govern the world.

The Jewish Legacy

Since the Middle Ages, Christians are so accustomed to considering their origins in contrast to Judaism that we often ignore the great extent to which the early Christian attitude toward the Roman Empire was simply the attitude of faithful Jews,[15] as illustrated by the following five points. Each focal theme about Jesus cited above was utterly Jewish. When we turn to interpret the nonviolence of Jewry since Jeremiah in a wider sociohistorical frame, it depends on a Jewish worldview uniquely tuned to befit the Jewish sociology of diaspora and synagogue.[16]

(1) The life of every human being is sacred; blood is the presence of life given by God alone and only God is entitled to take it back. Any bloodshed

is sacrifice. Long before the rise of Christianity, Jewish saints and sages had mitigated judicial power through more careful rules of evidence and by warning against the dangers of bias and self-interest; by rabbinic times the execution of capital punishment was practically excluded by their understanding of Torah.

(2) God is sovereign over the cosmos and therefore also over our oppressors as well as over us. As a result: (a) God can defend justice without our help; therefore, pragmatic calculations of how to keep bad things from happening and how to ensure that good things will happen do not decrease the Torah's claims upon us; (b) We cannot know God's ways when God functions as cosmic sovereign; we therefore cannot claim to be instruments of God's wrath; (c) God may want to chastise us; if we defend ourselves that might be rebellion against God's designs, which are ultimately gracious even if they lead us through times of chastisement; and (d) It is possible for persons under the guidance and blessing of God, faithful to the Torah, to be useful within a pagan society and even to prosper.

The four dominant symbols from the Hebrew story are Joseph, Esther, Daniel, and Daniel's three friends. In each case, there was first pagan pressure that tested the readiness of the faithful one to pay the cost of faithfulness. Each had to be ready to refuse what was asked by the pagan authorities, and to commit civil disobedience for the sake of simple fidelity to the Torah. In each case, that readiness to sacrifice was protected and ratified by the power of God. First of all, the worst outcome was avoided. Then it became possible to find one's position validated, vindicated, and positively rewarded, not only by God but also by the pagan authorities, assigning to the previously disobedient minority figure not merely a tolerated status but the authority to do good in dramatic ways. This usability of pagan power structures for good—not only for the protected people of God but also for the peace of that city—was not explained on the basis of some concept of prudence or nature known to everyone by unaided human reason. It was not yet explained, although that explanation was to make good sense to the rabbis later, that its basis was the covenant made by God with all humanity in the person of Noah. They did not explain it as revealed to everyone by nature and reason, nor as reducible to pragmatic effectiveness in achieving valuable goals.

(3) God may choose to use our faithfulness unto death as a sacrifice to his holiness. What Christians call *testimony* the Jews call *sanctifying the Name*. Testimony—*martyria,* the root of our term *martyrdom*—is what a witness does in the courtroom. One validates with one's own presence and jeopardy, as if before a judge and as if contested, God's claims to be one, holy, and sovereign. The Jewish equivalent is that when a person's faithfulness to the law goes to the point of accepting death as its price, that is a way to give glory to God or to proclaim God's holiness—not despite the cost but because one sacrifices other values to it.[17] Later rabbis did not consider every item of the

law to be worthy of sacrificing one's life. The rejection of bloodshed, incest, and blasphemy are the three points that called for such costly faithfulness. On other matters of the law a Jew might accept an evil that someone asks him to do, for the sake of saving his life or that of another.[18] However, this does not mean that the martyr's death *sanctifies the Name* only when it is inflicted for the sake of one of those three refusals to conform. The suffering of righteous people is thus functional in the divine economy. This applies not only to oneself but also to members of one's people or family who may count, and may be sacrificed, as an extended self.

(4) The Messiah has not yet come. Peace among the nations is a sure promise of God that will be brought about by God in his own time and way. Neither the time nor the way is for us to determine. For us to bless any righteous political enterprise on the grounds that it will make peace is presumption.

(5) Beyond these strands of argument, which belong specifically to the Hebrew understanding that God is active in history, one also finds in the rabbis traces of a general reasonableness. Although not specifically Hebraic, this reasonableness puts in rabbinic terms a kind of wisdom that cultures with a less pronounced view of God could also understand. There was Beruriah, the wife of Rabbi Meier, who said that the way to destroy an enemy is not to kill the person but to destroy the sin that makes him an enemy.[19] There was skepticism about preferring one's life to that of an attacker: "How do you know your blood is redder than his?"[20] There was also the knowledge that a soft answer turns away wrath (Prov. 15:1), whereas human wrath cannot be an instrument of God's judgment (James 1:20).[21]

Disavowing Caesar

Highly critical analysis of ethical language will argue that the early Christians, like the Jews before them, were not pacifist in the sense of being able to project for the Roman Empire a set of nonviolent political policies. Only a modern perspective could find that absence remarkable. They were, however, globally polarized against all that Caesar and his empire meant for the following reasons:

(1) Caesar stood for polytheism and idolatry, which were repugnant to the Hebrew worldview. Many ritual activities involved in soldiering included pagan cultic observance. Sometimes a particular unit of the army would revere a specific divinity as patron.

(2) Caesar himself was sometimes honored in a cultic way, little different from deity. This particular ceremony sometimes functioned as the test for determining whether Christians would be tolerated or aggressively persecuted.

(3) The life of the soldier involved regularly swearing oaths. For Christians the oath was itself idolatrous, being pronounced in the name of a deity. The oath was also an immoral abdication of personal responsibility because it promised unconditional obedience to an unworthy human lord. In addition, the oath was forbidden by the simple teaching of the New Testament (Matt. 5:34–37; James 5:12).

(4) Caesar's agents occasionally persecuted Christians, either directly because they were Christian or indirectly because things they did or refused to do made them appear to be a threat to Caesar's sovereignty.

(5) Caesar's total lifestyle was immoral and blasphemous: pride, vice, immorality, and most of the other deadly sins were dramatically fostered and flaunted in his court.

(6) Although the Roman system was, in its highest self-understanding and by comparison to many alternatives, a relatively decent political order and governed at its best by a high view of law, this legality nonetheless covered patterns of political oppression with regard to subject peoples and economic oppression with regard to slaves and servants. Jewish and Christian understandings of the dignity of the outsider and the enemy had to reject these patterns of oppression.

Later History

We move now from the shared Gospel bases for radical reformation critique to selected specimens implementing that critique in the late Middle Ages.[22] The first exemplar, moving on from where the Waldensians had begun, was the Czech Reformation of the fifteenth century, beginning with Luke of Prague and John Hus, and culminating with the Unitas Fratrum in 1467.[23] The sixteenth century made *law* an issue in a way that predisposes us to be unfair to much that went before. Before Luther, however, law was a powerful critical resource.

In view of the Gospel basis cited above, the simplest way to cut to the core of reform is to claim that the teachings of Jesus are to be taken as normative moral guidance. One finds the reasoning as simple as a syllogism: Is Jesus authorized to speak for God in matters of morality? If so, then when he teaches, "You have heard that it was said . . . but I say to you," must not his teaching have at least the same authority as earlier Mosaic and prophetic moral commands? Therefore the six *minor precepts* of Jesus in Matthew 5:21–48 are no less binding than the Ten Commandments (Exod. 20:1–17; Deut. 5:1–21) or the two great commandments (Matt. 22:34–40; Mark 12:28–34; Luke 10:25–28).[24] Of the six *minor precepts*, three deal with killing and with love of the enemy. If that is the law of the Lord, then we are called to obey it, independent of any calculation about how to bring about good social outcomes.

The rejection of violence by Petr Chelčický was thus firmly founded on the clear moral teaching of Jesus himself,[25] but that does not mean Chelčický was a legalist or only concerned with ethics. His view of history included a precisely worked out interpretation of the wrongness of the Constantinian linkage between church and state. He spelled this out in the image of the church as a net, which ought to hold believers together in a unity distinguishable from the world, as the contents of the net are distinguishable from the sea. Yet two whales, the pope and the emperor, have broken the net; once torn, it no longer serves to gather believers in any way distinguishable from the world at large. Petr was likewise a critic of the feudal class system, serfdom, capital punishment, and the civil oath.

We identify the beginnings of the radical reform movement of the sixteenth century with the breakup of Zwingli's reformation into an established and a radical wing.[26] The first baptisms in Zurich in January 1525 brought into being a movement that spread widely and incorporated people and ideas from other sources. The issue of war did not create the division. Zwingli himself had been a kind of pacifist, as had his teacher Erasmus before him. Because so many other Protestants claim origins in the sixteenth century, the Anabaptist mode of radical reformation has been made prototypical by their enemies, including naming them as heretics in the reformation confessions. While the nonviolence of the Czechs was most like that of Jesus the eschatological Rabbi (I/2 above), that of the Anabaptists was more like that of Jesus the Lamb who was sacrificed, the Suffering Servant (I/4).[27]

That typical or prototypical reading is deceptive, however. It came into recent ethical thought through Reinhold and H. Richard Niebuhr's appropriation of categories drawn from the European experience of Ernst Troeltsch. The British Reformation took a different course, leading to a different repertory of radical shapes in the Baptists, Diggers, Seekers, and Friends. The spiritual roots were nourished by the same recourse to the gospel, within the context of the same Christendom establishment, but the room to grow that the shrub or vine found above the ground was different in the post-Puritan world. That enabled the radicals to make powerfully creative contributions to the development of religious liberty, egalitarian democracy, anti-authoritarian education, humanizing correction facilities, and raising the status of original Americans, women, and slaves.[28] These specimens of critical social impact may be thought of as second-order nonviolence. They apply the commitment to human dignity initially anchored and clarified in the commitment not to kill to other relationships, more broadly.[29]

Tentative Conclusions

After this review, can anything be said by way of summary? Are there important common features amid the variety of these several "radical" phenomena?

These stories tell us that *it is possible to overcome the Constantinian mistake only by a basic renewal of the entire Christian movement*. It is not sufficient to make superficial or formal adjustments in the relationship between church (i.e., episcopal structure) and state (i.e., governmental structure) as long as there is no new definition of what it means to live the faith.

Conversely, *it is possible to renew the entire Christian gospel by overcoming the Constantinian mistake*. It has been done. Whether we center our formulation of the nature of that mistake on the morality of violence or the meaning of church membership, on redefining ritual meanings or inward experience: if renewing the life of faith is to be coherent and thorough, it will necessarily bring with it a renewal of the ethic of nonviolence. Most of the groups described above did not begin their dissident creativity at the point of violence, *but before* their vision of renewal was rounded out and socially viable they had to deal with the question of violence. Waldo, Chelčický, the Zurich radicals in 1523, George Fox in the 1640s, Alexander Campbell, William Booth, and Uchimura Kanzo each had his own focal agenda, local and different each time. Yet within a generation, each had brought into being a community marked by voluntary membership, independence from the state, lay Bible study, shared leadership, economic sharing, and the rejection of war.[30]

On the level of formal analysis, these movements have in common that they replaced a metaphysical dualism by an historical dualism. This becomes clearer in juxtaposition to Asian alternatives, but once that juxtaposition has drawn our attention to the issue,[31] it becomes visible that the same tension separates radical renewers from establishment Christians.

The most concrete social expression of metaphysical dualism is the specifically religious structure of ritual, or sacerdotal office, or esoteric doctrine. The radical renewers rejected or reduced in importance those components of majority religion. They all rejected episcopacy, in the strict sense of an office existing independent of local parish assemblies, and sacerdotalism,[32] in the strict sense of the ascription of unique status to one person per parish. All of them minimized and redefined ritual, although only Mukyokai, the Friends, and the Salvation Army went so far as to declare traditional forms undesirable.[33] All of them rejected ethical role dualism and advocated the same morality for everyone. While quite argumentative and concerned about clarification of ideas, they tended to reject or relativize dogma in the sense of sacrosanct formulation, and to challenge the privileged status of the theological profession. In none of these realms did they reject all forms; that would be the spiritualist option, which has long been recognized as a different kind of claim.[34] But they reconceived those matters functionally and subordinated them to the life of a community.

To say that the dualism of the radical renewers is moral and not metaphysical means that God is understood not primordially as all-encompassing transcendence but as actor within the human story. Monotheism in the Hebraic mode is more appropriately approximated by personalistic than by apophatic or inclusive forms. To speak of God as *spirit* is not to identify a level of being apart from the social and the moral; it is to name *spirit* as a social, moral, and person-like power. This puts in a different light the ordinary debates about religious morality that distinguish between a morality of means and one of ends, or between the Kantian focus on pure obligation and the pragmatic focus on consequences.[35]

To clarify the difference in structure that seems most salient in contrast to Asian models of religion as well as established-church versions[36] of Christianity: probably the most central feature is that for radical Christian communities the dualism that provides orientation is historical and therefore ethical. For the Asian and established-church versions, it is metaphysical and therefore religious. For some, the *religious* is defined by contrast to the *cognitive*, for others by contrast to the body, for others by opposition to the laity. In these various instances, the *religious* is defined by apartness, an apartness rooted in a dualistic picture of ultimate reality. Ordinary people need not do metaphysics to live with rituals, but that is what teachers of contemplation talk about. The purpose of the exercises is to move from the less to the more ultimate. By the nature of the case, this can be done only partially and only by a few.

The Hebraic vision is not one of a division between this world and a more real one, but between the forces of good and evil *in this world*. The teacher's preoccupation is not to encompass everything but to illuminate choice. The Lord God asks not so much that we understand and contemplate as that we serve and love.[37]

3

The Political Meaning of *Hope*

Scholars have been paying renewed attention to the New Testament's own intent in pointing its readers to Jesus.[1] But another kind of change has also been happening. To trace this, we turn to the storyteller turned exegete, Leo Nikolayevich Tolstoy.

Without a doubt, Tolstoy was the most known and read Eastern European in the West during the nineteenth century. He was known first of all for the way he told stories, and in his later years for the letters and periodical articles he wrote critiquing current events. Yet, in his own mind, Tolstoy's most original contribution was his effort to disengage the central meaning of the Christian gospel from the distortions that had been imposed upon it over the centuries and that had made Christianity into the religion of the oppressors.

Tolstoy Was Responding to the Gospel

Tolstoy was a convert. His books *Confession*, *What I Believe*, and *The Kingdom of God Is Within You* are the expositions of the profound change that made of him a different person than he had been before.[2] What led Tolstoy to his change of life direction was the strength he brought to life: his profound narrative perceptiveness. It was his ability to perceive the depths of human being and relating, and to describe that perception dramatically. It was his great gift of narration and the ability to convince the reader that inside the personages in his stories things were really as he recounted them. When Tolstoy applied his skill at analysis and portrayal to a new set of life questions, a multitude of readers all over the Western world were ready to serve as a sounding board. Had he not been the great storyteller, he might have had the same experiences or held the same ideas, but his telling of them would not have been heard.

The trigger for this change came from outside Tolstoy's own mind. It was not a product of simple organic movement, in which what comes later can be explained by what came earlier. Tolstoy responded to the gospel. What *gospel* came to mean to him was illuminated by his literary and critical skills, but it was not the product of those skills. The skills only made more precise and demanding the claims that a message from another world made on him.

The *gospel* does not mean vaguely anything or everything in the Christian message. Within the total Christian tradition, Tolstoy could explain and argue the grounds for choosing to make the Scriptures central. In the Orthodox world, that choice was not self-evident. Tolstoy progressively narrowed the focus by using his skills as an artist and writer, not an ethicist or exegete. In that process of narrowing and centering his vision, within the Scriptures he came to focus on the New Testament, and within the New Testament the Gospels. Tolstoy discerned next that the center of the Gospels' narrative was the proclamation of the kingdom of God; that was less evident a century and a quarter ago than it is now. The center of that proclamation is the Sermon on the Mount. Next, he saw that the six antitheses introduced by "You have heard that it was said . . . but I say to you . . ." are the center of the Sermon on the Mount. The most fundamental of the six antitheses is the replacement of the *lex talionis* by "Do not resist the evil one."

The Cure for Evil Is Suffering, Breaking the Vicious Cycle

Every step of that process of reduction can be debated, yet each can be argued on literary and substantial grounds. The result is what Tolstoy calls the "key" to the Scripture message: the cure for evil is suffering. The link between the work of Christ and human obedience, which had been denied through the centuries, was thus restored.

This centering process represented in Tolstoy is not mere ethical rigor, but a cosmic vision. This one dramatic and scandalous teaching is not only internally shown to be the key to the Scriptures—it is as well the key to what is wrong with the world. Our society is characterized by vengeful violence and the hunger for domination. This explains the rest of the evils in the world. What is wrong with the world cannot be grasped by a mental construct like original sin, nor by a materialistic reduction to a dialectic of structural changes not yet consummated. What is wrong with the world is most fundamentally that people respond to evil with evil. The iron necessity of retaliation intends to preserve human society from chaos, but in reality, it guarantees at best a continuing chain of evil causes that produce evil effects. At worst, it escalates, after the mode of Lamech,[3] or like pouring oil on fire. Nonretaliation is the only way to break the chain of causation.

The good news is that we can be freed from extending the chain of evil causes, evil effects, and reactions in kind. This one key opened the door, in Tolstoy's worldview, to a restructuring of the entire world of Christian life and thought, issuing in a critique of economic exploitation, of military and imperial rule, and of westernization. He had the nerve to construct an entire alternative vision of world history according to which progress results from the faithfulness of the persecuted, the pride of the dominaters goes before a fall, and an empire built on coercion is a house built on sand.

Nonretaliation is probably the best term for this break in the chain of evil for evil, even though for a century and a half the designation *nonresistance* was preferred, thanks to Tolstoy's contemporaries W. L. Garrison and Adin Ballou.[4] Tolstoy himself did not renounce resistance. He worked against the Tsarist regime. In his support of the Doukhobors, he supported acts of civil disobedience and noncooperation with the authorities. In letters and essays read avidly by literate folk all over the West, he troubled the peace of the empire by denouncing governmental stupidity and violence of all kinds.

Nonretaliation is probably also the best term for rendering what was actually meant by the *me antistenai* of Matthew 5:39.[5] Responding in kind is what is rejected. There is no imperative of passivity or of pointless suffering. That passivist meaning has been read into the text by those who have a stake in making its demands seem unreasonable.[6] Jesus did not simply let things happen to himself or to others, or cooperate passively with evil. He was ready to suffer, true; but he chose the time and the shape of his confrontation of the powers.

The stronger proof of what Tolstoy meant for our purposes may, however, be his impact on Mohandas Gandhi. Gandhi wrote:

> Tolstoy's *The Kingdom of God is Within You* overwhelmed me. . . . Before the independent thinking, profound morality, and the truthfulness of this book, all the books given me by Mr. Coates [a Quaker he met in Pretoria] seemed to pale into insignificance. . . . I made an intensive study of Tolstoy's books. *The Gospels in Brief, What To Do?* and other books made a deep impression on me. I began to realize more and more the infinite possibilities of universal love.[7]

What Gandhi respected in Tolstoy was his mental independence and his disrespect for orthodox/catholic tradition, *specifically at the point* where that tradition relativizes the impact of the Sermon on the Mount. It was not the authority of Jesus, nor Tolstoy's romantic attachment to the culture of the peasantry, nor even the notion of loving the enemy that attracted him. It was rather Tolstoy's readiness, on the grounds of intrinsic moral obligation, to reject the dominant Western worldview, with its acceptance of the chain of violent causes and violent effects as self-evidently normative for the Christian. He rejected it on the grounds of a counter-cosmology.

The *conversion* in Tolstoy's story was not what the term has often come to mean in European experience: namely, a change in the convictions or the emotions of an individual or in his or her institutional adherence. The change is rather cosmological. Tolstoy now knows a new truth about the real world, a truth verified by the facts of human experience. The world is that way: it is an arena of domination. It is factually the case that the only hope for history is the law of love. Despite appearances, it is true of the real world that history is borne by those who suffer, not by generals and prelates.

There is of course a certain romanticism in the way Tolstoy identifies evangelical humility and suffering with the particular *mushik* culture within which his folktales were at home. His bad conscience as an aristocrat led him to equate the serfdom of his villagers too simply with the servanthood of Christ. It was articulated too simply, by a romantic in a romantic age, but that does not invalidate his thesis. The way to fulfillment and advancement is not to be a life of slowly clawing one's way upward within the imperial bureaucracy, whether by dint of hard work or through favoritism and fraud, but is the alternative of suffering love.

Gandhi Too Was a Convert

When Gandhi restated what impressed him about Tolstoy, it was not simple moral rigor divorced from concern for effectiveness; it was rather "the infinite possibilities of universal love." We know from the record, and shall see in the texts, that in Gandhi's religious worldview, and in his practice over the next half-century, there was no dichotomy between moral rigor and effectiveness. Gandhi rather synthesized a set of uniquely effective strategies of social pressure for political change, effective in a setting where the ordinary kinds of violence being dreamed and schemed about by ordinary Barabbas-type liberators had no chance of working. It was from Gandhi in turn that Martin Luther King Jr., in another setting where insurrection would not have worked, was to receive a decisive impetus toward formulating uniquely effective strategies for change.

Gandhi too was a convert, but not in the same way. Unlike Tolstoy, who lived near the top of a relatively unified society and as heir to centuries of Christendom's development, Gandhi lived rather at the intersection of two pluralistic worlds. For Tolstoy, to open up a breach in his world required a deep process of internal criticism, provoked both by the subjective deepening of his awareness that his life was meaningless and by the objective conflict between the gospel and the imperial orthodox vision of Christendom. That same wisdom which for Tolstoy demanded that that breach be opened, and that his life be turned around, was offered to Gandhi by his living between cultures, each of them incorporating the same contradictions and injustices as imperial Russia's, but neither in such a blatant manner. Anglo-Saxon society was responsible for the imperial occupation of India and other colonies, but it was also the source of a system of legal principles and institutions that could be applied to undo those injustices. Hindu society seemed stagnant, defeatist, and stratified; yet its fundamental religious vision, far less debilitated by the acids of modernity than is religion in the West, bore the seeds of its own renewal. Living at the frontier between two worlds, learning from both, using each as the fulcrum against which to move the other, Gandhi engaged in a pilgrimage of repeated conversions throughout his life story. His autobiography repeatedly points to events that changed his outlook and his policies. Often those learnings were intellectual and abstract: they came from a mental encounter with a thinker or a book. His story is full of little conversions: once from a book on vegetarianism, once from Tolstoy's *The Kingdom of God Is within You*, once from John Ruskin's *Unto This Last*. Of each he reports that it revolutionized his thought.

At other times the sources of his learnings were more concrete. They came from some failure in his program, from which he learned to be relentlessly self-critical. He could thus describe his entire strategic wisdom as "experimenting with truth."

In taking the power of truth realistically as a force in history, Gandhi moves with Tolstoy but beyond him. Tolstoy affirms that the course of human history was carried by suffering, but cannot explain how. Gandhi sees the cosmos as a unity of spiritual powers, interwoven in an unbroken nexus of causation, making sense of the notion that fasting, prayer, or sexual continence, and above all the active renunciation of violence, can exert spiritual power—"soul force"—upon the adversary one desires not to destroy but to restore to his or her right place in a fuller human community.

Had Gandhi been more at home in the New Testament, he might have spoken of such a power in terms of the *logos* sustaining all of creation, or the risen Lord subjecting the powers of a rebellious creation to his sovereignty. But it was simpler for him to understand the efficacy of renunciation in more Indian terms. Thus a first stage of deepening in the transition from Tolstoy to Gandhi is a more transparent cosmological account of how suffering *works*.

Gandhi Added Organizational Practices

The other side of that same progress is that Gandhi developed social strategies to fit his renewed evangelical/Hindu cosmology. Out of the religious holiday of *hartal* there springs the strategic work stoppage. Out of purity rituals there springs the boycott. Going to jail for refusal to obey an unjust law applies moral pressure to the judge and thereby to the legislator (especially in a democratic society). The illegitimate assembly or procession provokes the oppressor to unveil his illegitimacy by lashing out. It also seizes the attention of the public, including the newspaper readers of London.

To Tolstoy's spiritual diagnosis, then, Gandhi adds both philosophical clarity and organizational genius. The organizational insights arose slowly, and were practiced before they were understood:

(1) The social basis is a communal farm/school/retreat center, the ashram.

(2) Traditional religious forms are appropriated and transformed: the fast, the procession, regular daily prayers.

(3) Gandhi's writing is journalistic: brief, epigrammatic, repetitive, and thoroughly popular.

(4) He appeals to the positive values of Anglo-Saxon law: *habeas corpus*, the right to trial, and the independence of the courts.

(5) The adversary is to be won over, not defeated.

(6) Civil disobedience is not obstruction or coercion, but obedience to a higher power and a refusal to legitimize one's own oppression by co-operating with it.

(7) There is a strong sense of fair play: Gandhi refused to press his advantage to demand more than the original goals of an action. He would not undertake an action when the authorities were under attack from another quarter.

(8) Self-discipline is rigorous: he would terminate a popular action if its nonviolent discipline broke down.

(9) Gandhi called his alternative social vision a "constructive program." He had no interest in simply replacing English oppression (capitalism, urbanization) with Indian oppression.

(10) Gandhi was ready to take positions unpopular with his own people, such as his rejection of untouchability and of Hindu-Muslim enmity.

Martin Luther King Jr. Also Knew Personal Conversion and Practices of Churches

Although fully representative of the black Baptist culture of the American South, Martin Luther King Jr. was also, like Gandhi and like Moses, a beneficiary of the educational resources of the wider society.[8] Following the failure to wrest real freedom for blacks out of the Civil War, the white churches of the North planted a network of quality colleges for black students in the South. Although schools supported by the state were blocked by segregation from providing basic educational opportunities, these colleges represented a strategic corrective, one of the most creative contributions that the white Christians from the North could make. Morehouse College, where King and his father both studied, was such an institution, supported by northern Baptists. It prepared him to continue at Crozer Theological Seminary, the liberal Baptist school in Pennsylvania. It was during his second year at Crozer that King became aware of the achievements of Gandhi. This discovery seems to have been a turning point in his young adult sense of mission. Before this he had heard about nonviolence, but had not been aware either of the theological power of its rootage in the cross of Jesus Christ nor of the social power of organized resistance. This laid the foundation for his later leadership, although he did not set about directly starting a movement.

King chose to return to the congregational pastorate. To this he brought exceptional understanding of white Protestant thought and of the American democratic vision as understood by the cultural leaders of the eastern seaboard. In this he was like Moses and Gandhi: his education equipped him with the cultural information and educational credentials to understand the white world he was seeking to change.

An important component of that power from the wider society was, of course, the official liberal democratic vision of the founding documents of the American republic. Just as Gandhi, a British subject admitted to the London Bar, could appeal to the British sense of due process and the rights of all citizens under the common law, so King could use the egalitarian American vision of the rights of citizens, the independent judiciary, and the fruitful tension between federal and state law.

It is more important that his choice to return to the South and to accept pastoral leadership in the Dexter Avenue Baptist Church of Montgomery, Alabama, was a voluntary act of identification with the cause of black Americans. In this too he was like Moses and Gandhi: he identified with his people. His qualifications would have prepared him to move into teaching or administration in some northern college or divinity school, or to a comfortable middle-class black congregation in the North. He could have escaped from the South. His voluntary turn back toward identification qualified him to speak for victims of discrimination.

While King followed Gandhi in making religion the foundation of his movement, his situation was quite distinct in the ways in which black Baptist religion is different from Hinduism. Hinduism is an ancient majority religious culture, ethically pluralistic and politically conservative. Black Baptist religion is a response to oppression, highly unified in its values, voluntary in its membership, politically critical although dualistic. Whereas Hinduism would form an ashram around the person of its guru and the special disciplines of a spiritual retreat, Baptist polity could form a congregation in every hamlet and on every city block, joining not only in worship but also in extended family solidarity and moral uplift. Throughout the South, where the state, commerce, and the schools were all white-dominated, the churches were the arena where black leadership, self-esteem, and community solidarity could be cultivated without white interference, and where countercultural consciousness and an alternative interpretation of social history could be maintained.

It is important that the church base of the movement was not only black but also Baptist.[9] As contrasted with other forms of Christianity, baptistic piety makes indispensable the personal, mature, and often dramatic religious decision of the individual. There is no cultic ritual around the altar independent from the believer's own participation. There is no self-perpetuating hierarchy keeping the structure of the church going until some special crisis makes an individual want its ministrations. Personal conversion and believers' baptism make one a member of the community. The worship experience commemorates, renews, and projects the drama of conversion into a series of renewed calls to decision and commitment. When the bus boycott movement broke out spontaneously in Montgomery, the rallies held every evening in the churches were a simple transposition of the format of revival preaching.

Gandhi had differed significantly from Tolstoy, even though acknowledging a major debt to him. King, in his turn, differed as well from Gandhi in many ways that would matter for a full account of what each was doing, and why each achieved what he did, and of what the limits of each were.[10] What matters for us at present, however, as we loop back to analyze their reasons, is that both of them specifically accentuated the identity of means and ends, and rejected the ordinary notions of the pragmatic usability of destructive means toward constructive ends.

Cosmological Faith: Right Means Lead toward Good Ends

"The means are the ends in the process of becoming." Any teacher of ethics or of logic can tell you that this phrase is not technically profound. It simplifies what an academic ethicist could subdivide into several different types of ends-oriented and several other types of means-oriented moral reasoning. If this were a technical seminar, we should need to unpack and categorize all of that and to see under what presuppositions the argument would not be logically watertight.

But Gandhi and King were not academics. Though both were the products of white Anglo-Saxon schools, and both of them were intelligent, critical, and synthetic thinkers, each was primarily a communicator to a wide public; one as an editor-publisher and one as a preacher. Each knew how to reach past his immediate readers and listeners to a far wider public for whom his particular fusion of morality and practicality had the ring of truth. That ring of truth was validated not by academic logic but by the resonance between a particular people's entire religious culture and the new empowering response to their oppressive setting, which he was helping them define.

Hope and *incarnation* are not two separate themes. Without forsaking the theme of incarnation, I have begun to report about concretions of hope. To say "the means are the ends in process of becoming" is a cosmological or an eschatological statement. It presupposes a *cosmos*—a world with some kind of discernible moral cause-effect coherence. Unlike Kant, for whom the hereafter was needed to make the moral accounting come out even, this view claims coherence within history. But for this claim to work, one must believe that in some sense suffering is redemptive, or (as King will say it) "there is something in the universe that unfolds for justice." For Gandhi, that cosmic validator was the great chain of being, represented literally or at least symbolically by the notion of reincarnation.[11] For King it was the black Baptist vision of another Moses leading his people from Egypt, another Joshua fighting at Jericho, a promised land we can see from the mountaintop, a cross on Golgotha from which one can see the heavens opening. King also said it in terms of the American dream, the humanism of the fathers of the republic, and even in terms of the federal politics of the Kennedy brothers.

It may have been a tactical error, if taken strictly in terms of argument, for both Gandhi and King to use phrases like "the redemptive power of suffering." By saying it this way, they seemed to be accepting the pragmatists' demand that they meet consequentialism on its own terrain of measurable effectiveness in attaining agreed goals. By speaking of "power," they could be taken by some pragmatists to be attempting to prove the strategic rightness of their methods; by promising a profitable medium-range cost/benefit tradeoff, they could be seen as justifying pragmatically the cost of renouncing violence. The pragmatists' argument in response was then predictable: (1) suffering does not *always* have the promised positive effect, at least not soon enough; and (2) the specific efficacy of the methods of Gandhi were effective against the British, with their traditions of fairness, and those of King against southern local authorities, thanks to the federal government and its constitution, but those methods would not have been as likely to "work" against the Japanese or the Nazis.

It would be a repetition of that tactical error were I here to prolong the argument about relative effectiveness by entering into more precise ends/means arguments. That could be done; the record does not show any more successful violent insurrections against Japanese or Nazi or Soviet tyranny than nonviolent ones. I shall return in a future chapter to the pragmatic claim.[12] But here that would be a red herring.

What Gandhi meant by "the infinite possibilities of universal love" is not that there is a measurable, finite, efficacy potential which can be weighed, in a mechanistic social-science mode, against the also finite and lesser possibilities that can surely be achieved by the use of less loving means. This would have been an arguable position,[13] but it was not his point. Gandhi meant rather to call for a qualitative transformation of the perspective in which one thinks about the possible. To say with King, "love is the most durable power in the world,"[14] or "there is something in the universe that unfolds for justice,"[15] is not to claim a sure insight into the way martyrdom works as a social power, although martyrdom often does that. It is a confessional or kerygmatic statement made by those whose loyalty to Christ (or to universal love, or to *satyagraha*) they understand to be validated by its cosmic ground. Suffering love is not right because it "works" in any calculable short-run way (although it often does). It is right because it goes with the grain of the universe, and that is why *in the long run* nothing else will work.

As we shall see further in another chapter, there should be no surprise about the asymmetry with which different ethical systems talk past each other. Words like *practicality* or *power* have different meanings, depending upon one's system. If your rejection of violence is cosmically based, as it is for Tolstoy, Gandhi, and King—i.e., if its validation is not pragmatic—then the impact of that kind of commitment will in fact be greater effectiveness. Perseverance in the face of sacrifice and creativity in the face of dismay are heightened for those who believe that the grain of the universe is with them. Those who reserve for themselves the "realistic" decision about when to cut their losses by lowering their sights will in fact be less effective. They will be short of wind. Thus it is that a *principled* rejection of violence heightens effectiveness. A renunciation of violence justified only practically, on the other hand (e.g., because one has no arms, or because nonviolence avoids giving the oppressors a pretext for striking back) will in the hard cases not work. There, the pragmatists will sometimes be right, although they will usually be wrong in assuming that some evidently available violent tactic will "work" much better.

Thus we have finished the shift from what I was calling *incarnation* to what I would call *hope*: namely, the real power within history of a vision of the world under God that refuses to be boiled down to progress that can be extrapolated from intrasystemic potentials. When Tolstoy's Christocentric moralism was translated into Gandhi's cosmic vision, it meant that the universe is open toward the future.

Gandhi explained his hope; later, as we saw, in terms of reincarnation, although I doubt that that is where it first began. King was willing to state it in terms of Boston University personalism, or of the American dream—a translation for which he had good tactical reasons, but I doubt that he first found it there. King was a product of the post-Reconstruction black Baptist culture. This community was empowered—by the memories of Moses and David, of Jeremiah and Jesus, and of African ancestors—to create a viable community life and culture against the pressure of white America's rule. Nourished by the biblical narratives as was no other American subcommunity (unless it be the Amish), disciplined by standing up (or bowing uncowed) to legal and illegal oppression, institutionally autarchic because there could be no symbiotic support from the structures of the state, the economy, the country club, or the chamber of commerce, black Baptist America hoped for history only on the grounds of the promise of God,[16] and in its weakness that was its strength.

Martin Luther King Jr.'s most frequent response to the mystery of evil, not an ethicist's answer but a preacher's, was the poem of James Russell Lowell:

> Will the cause of evil prosper?
>   Yet 'tis truth alone is strong
> Though her portion be the scaffold,
>   and upon the throne be wrong,
> Yet that scaffold sways the future;
>   and behind the dim unknown
> Standeth God within the shadow,
>   keeping watch above his own.[17]

I doubt that the reason King found that poetic image convincing was the same as Lowell's. It made sense to King because his people's piety was full of the memories of the first Joshua at Jericho and the second Joshua at Golgotha. The hope of the Christian apocalypse is not utopia, not compensation for suffering, not trust in a Darwinian or a humanistic law of progress, but reasonably founded extrapolation from the cross, the resurrection, and Pentecost.

The Retrieval of *Hope* as an Express Theme in Social Thought

In the early 1950s, in the beginning of the age of Eisenhower, American Protestants were startled to learn that the theme of the second Assembly of the World Council of Churches, to meet in Evanston in 1954, would be "Christ the Hope of the World." Churches of the ecumenical Protestant mainstream had abandoned the language of eschatology to the fundamentalists, preferring to fuse their own liberal version of Christian hope into the promise of America.

There would be little point in our trying to decide whether one factor since then has been more decisive than another in the beginning restoration of the relevance of apocalyptic. One line of causation has obviously been cultural: the breakdown of our mainline hopes and securities.[18] This we need not itemize here.

Another component of the change of mood has been a rising level of honesty in the academic enterprise of reading ancient documents. To this we shall return. It calls for a higher level of imaginative pluralism in handling a variety of styles of discourse. For example, we need imaginative pluralism to rehabilitate the meaningfulness of the apostolic rhetoric about "principalities and powers," whereby the intermingling of creaturely dignity and oppressive rebelliousness is reflected in far more nuanced ways than much modern social science is capable of.[19]

The final chapter of my book *The Politics of Jesus* published a generation ago, and the least documented, sought to make historical sense of the apocalyptic vision of the apostolic generation. That chapter was apparently more offensive to many readers, although (as far as I can see) for less reason, than the rest of my book. I meant simply to exposit, as a matter of historical fact, how the early Christians saw their world as in God's hands under the lordship of Christ. In a setting in which pragmatic ethics—justifying behaviors on the grounds of their projected social effect—could make no sense, trusting Christ's lordship to make sense of history was not withdrawal but responsibility, not self-righteous purity but rationality. Nobody can seriously deny that such trust in Christ's lordship was the reading of the historical prospect by Christian thought in the late first century. Nobody who thinks about it seriously can deny, either, that in most of world history Christians have been in social settings more like that of the early church than like that of the West since Constantine. And in most of the world today Christians are in settings in which calculating actions on the basis of social effectiveness makes little sense.

Yet many readers did not evaluate my report in *The Politics of Jesus* as an effort to read ancient texts empathetically with regard to their original setting. Neither did many critics read it with a view to whether the stance it found in the New Testament would make sense today in continental China or in Afghanistan. It was offensive to contemporaries because it seemed to some to constitute an *argument* to the effect that, even in other times and settings such as our own, withdrawal from social involvement would always be morally right. It was not that, as my other writings make clear, but it is fascinating that readers thought so.

Apocalyptic literature is being read more carefully today than three generations ago, when Albert Schweitzer surprised himself and others with the discovery that there was no separating Jesus's expectation of an imminent kingdom inauguration from the rest of his teaching. Ernst Käsemann is partly the symbol and partly the agent of the growing awareness of this insight in the academic world, although it had been adequately represented, if people had had ears to hear, two generations earlier by less academically respected thinkers like Leonhard Ragaz[20] and Eberhard Arnold.[21] The sociologists of knowledge help us today by articulating the "epistemological privilege of the underdog," making it more evident than before that consequentialist visions of moral reasoning must assume that the agent is in a position of power.

Apocalypse is a genre of communication that we need to learn to read in its own terms, not as an inferior way of "really meaning to say" something else. Neither the Bultmannian reduction of hope to hopefulness, "openness,"[22] or some other dimension of psychic self-understanding, nor the fundamentalist extrapolation of a countdown from the formation of the state of Israel to the battle of Armageddon, is compatible with what these texts meant in the first century.

Whatever else a more thorough unpacking of the apocalyptic mind would tell us, that literature celebrated and proclaimed a vision of history under God, whereby the certainty of the victory of God's cause was correlated with his people's faithfulness but not with their power. The credibility of the dream, whether it be King's famous variations on the theme "from every mountainside let freedom ring!" or something more historic, more Hebraic, is not properly to be measured either by the ability to project a causal sequence under our control from here to where we want history to arrive, nor by our discerning causative forces pointing in the same direction. The credibility of the vision is to be measured by its congruence with what God has already been doing.

> What is of ultimate importance is no longer that I should become good, or that the condition of the world should be made better by my action, but that the reality of God should show itself everywhere to be the ultimate reality.[23]

The fullest substantive definition of that "ultimate reality" is not some formula for ratiocination about ends and means but, thanks to Jesus Christ, God's identification with oppressed humanity, his justifying the godless, and his raising the dead. In the light of that "reality" we shall not stop caring about how "the condition of the world should be made better by my action," but we shall be freed from beginning or ending with that picture of the question. An ethic of incarnation and hope is one that can begin where the creed ends:

> We believe in the Holy Spirit,
> the Holy Church,
> the remission of sins,
> and the resurrection of the flesh.[24]

4

From the Wars of Joshua to Jewish Pacifism

W e have become accustomed to assuming that little is to be gained from the text of the Bible itself for Christian thinking about peace.[1] We assume that what the Scriptures have to say is already well-known but insufficient. This is even more the case for the Hebrew Bible. We have been led to believe that our Old Testament teaches a kind of nationalism which cannot be a model for us, and most Christians believe that the New Testament teaches a kind of pacifism which cannot be a model either.[2] Christian thinking on these matters has therefore been concerned, especially since the fourth century, with finding other sources, in nature or reason or custom, that might give guidance for thinking morally about matters of war and peace. We continue to see the Bible being sifted through as a mine for general slogans about the broad peacemaking purposes of God, which have their place in celebrations and sermons; it is widely taken for granted, however, that specific moral guidance should no longer be sought in the Scriptures.

This assumption is mistaken. In a more extended and more academic treatment, it would be appropriate to converse critically with the traditional developments that have led to that widely accepted consensus. I should then have to identify and critique the contributions especially of Neoplatonism, of Germanic tribalism, and of Roman understandings of civil order. But for our purposes here, it must suffice to restate the simple affirmation that the post-critical reading of the Scriptures has yet more to teach us about national loyalty and the outsider, God and our enemies.

Legalistic Dualism Uproots Us and Jesus from the Historical Narrative

The shape of the question put to us by the phenomenon of the wars of Yahweh has been determined for many of us by the dualism of Petr Chelčický and Leo Tolstoy.[3] As they saw it, from the age of Moses and Joshua to that of David, war was morally obligatory: now Jesus says "but I say to you . . ." and tells us that war is wrong. From that simple shift, in the light it throws on the New Testament, our thoughts can move in several directions.[4]

One way is to say that we stand simply with Jesus, and that in rejecting the warlike dimensions of the Old Testament we radically relativize all of the Hebrew backgrounds of the Christian faith. Then we have a smaller Bible, and we shall be permanently embarrassed by the fact that the New Testament itself generally assumes rather than rejects the authority of the Old. More recent experience has taught us as well that such an attitude can fit into an unevangelical anti-Semitism.

The other approach is to say that when Jesus set aside the model of Moses and David, he did so only for certain realms of life, only within the church, or only for the level of face-to-face relationships. This approach suggests that Jesus let the legitimacy of war stand unchanged as it applies to nations and their rulers, and for those whom the rulers call to serve them. Since God commanded war then, war cannot be sinful now.

On both sides, the argument is legalistic. Neither interpretation places the matter in the concrete historical context of the ancient Near East, nor in the narrative framework in which the Hebrew Scriptures arose.

Historical Narrative of the Hebrew Scriptures: Salvation Yahweh's Way

Beginning with the work of Gerhard von Rad,[5] a sizable accumulation of scholarly analysis has improved our understanding of the wars of Yahweh. The scholars differ in important ways, but they agree on most of what I shall be reporting here. That "Yahweh is a warrior" is the theme of the song of Miriam (Exod. 15), which from a literary-critical perspective may be one of the oldest texts in the Bible. The salvation of the Israelites at the Red Sea is celebrated in military language, but not as a military action of the Israelites. Yahweh is the victor.

Back then, the gods of all the peoples were seen as warriors. Each god defended his own nation; let the best god win. The prosperity or misfortune of the nation demonstrated the power or the weakness of their god. The identity of Israel is defined at the outset by the liberating acts of their patron.

The right way to read the first chapter of Genesis is not to compare it to the accounts that the geologist or the biologist gives of the origin of the earth or the species, but rather to contrast it with the other ancient Near Eastern cosmogonies in order to understand its distinctive message about God as Creator and Provider. In a similar way, the right reading of the accounts of the wars of Yahweh is not to seek in them a comparison to the wars of our time or of the Roman Empire, but to contrast them with the other religious justifications of domination in their own epoch. It is those elements of originality that will progressively define for us a specifically Israelite understanding of Yahweh as different from the gods of the nations.

Yahweh himself gives the victory. It is not that the Israelites did a better job than their enemies of deploying their forces or that they had better weapons or stronger allies. Victory is a miracle. In the most dramatic cases, which critical interpretation suspects may be the most original, the Israelites do not fight at all. That was the case at the Red Sea (or Sea of Reeds), for Jericho, for Gideon, and for Jehoshaphat. In other cases when the Israelites participated in the battle, or came to the "aid" of Yahweh, their contribution was not decisive. The call to the faithful Israelite will therefore not be to fight boldly and even less to fight brutally. It is to trust Yahweh. This trust includes the renunciation of alliances with any of the surrounding (pagan) empires, or the use of their military technology (horses, chariots).

The protection of Yahweh is not unconditional. It cannot be presumed to apply to the interests of an Israelite nation or a Davidic royal house if they do not fulfill the demands of the covenant. Israel does not possess Yahweh. In case of disobedience or idolatry, the Israelites will encounter Yahweh as their adversary, with Assyria or Cyrus taking over as God's scourge.

Another Historical Narrative: Victory the Kingship Way

The holy wars end with the creation of the Davidic state, answering the plea of the elders for "a king to govern us like all the nations" (1 Sam. 8:5). The old histories have saved some passages for us that describe the adoption of kingship as a rejection of Yahweh's lordship and a takeover by tyranny.[6] Other texts describe it as authorized by God. Yet even the more affirmative texts describe a model of kingship[7] with traits that do not fit the real experience of Israel at all. The king must not get horses from Egypt, nor multiply his wives, nor accumulate gold and silver. The king must copy and study the law.

However we resolve the difficulty of interpreting whether God accepted kingship, it is clear in any case that with David, the nature of war changed. There are now standing armies whose officers are foreign professionals, such as Uriah the Hittite. The taxation that supports them and the splendor of the royal establishment are responsible for new oppression. From now on if wars are won, it is by virtue of the shrewdness and the strength of Israel's soldiers. We no longer encounter the rhetoric or the cultic ceremonial of the Yahweh war after the model of Joshua and Gideon. Where we see language like that, it is used to indicate that Yahweh has now become Israel's adversary.

This account has two kinds of importance for later Christian thinking about the morality of violence. The first relates to the perennial debate about the morality of violence. Negative legalism has said that since God commanded those wars back then, war must not be wrong in principle and our wars need not be wrong either. Yet the closer we look at the reports of wars that were commanded back then, the more we see that they are unique happenings, miracles, and sacrifices, in no way comparable to war as a regular instrument of national policy or to the use of an army as an institutional core of national polity. Only if wars today were commended by prophets and won by miracles would the wars of Yahweh be a pertinent example. As it is, taking them seriously would rather count on the other side. Israel was to trust Yahweh for national salvation, rather than using instruments like alliances with Egypt or the accumulation of horses. It is thus blatantly inappropriate to read those ancient stories as a document on whether war is sin, because that is not what they intended to document. What they intended to document is that Yahweh takes the side of his people: they can trust him for their continued existence. If that fundamental truth has any relevance for later times, and for the New Testament community, it would have to be precisely in the direction of trusting God for survival, rather than the lesser-evil arguments for war.

How Jesus and His Hearers Saw Deliverance in Their Historical Narrative

A second level of relevance is the light that this Old Testament story must have thrown on the way Jesus and his audiences looked at their decisions. We tend to assume, because we have been told so, that the Gospel accounts show Jesus recommending patterns of behavior that make sense only if you believe the world is quickly coming to an end. With that assumption in the background, the call of Jesus to love the enemy and renounce self-defense is usually written off as moral idealism, an apolitical tactic of social withdrawal that is intelligible only if society's future has been written off. Either Jesus is practical, and then he will have to admit a certain amount of lesser-evil sin and violence, or he is idealistic and calls for people to behave in a way that cannot "work" in the real world.

But Jesus's audiences were people who knew other accounts of divine deliverance well. The picture is different if Jesus's listeners' minds were authentically formed by the stories of divine salvation in the Hebraic and Jewish experience. Those who were "waiting for the consolation of Israel" (Luke 2:25, 38 NIV) might very well have seen in these stories a model for the way God would save his people again. When Jesus used the language of liberation, proclaiming the restoration of the kingdom community and a new pattern of life, without predicting or authorizing or undertaking any violent means to bring about those ends, he would not have seemed *to his listeners* to be a dreamer. He could simply have been seen as standing in the succession of Hezekiah, or Jehoshaphat, expecting that once more the believing people would be saved despite their weakness, on condition that they "stand still, and see the victory of the Lord on your behalf."[8] To have that expectation in the back of their minds throws a special light on what might have been thought by the hearers of the "kingdom inauguration discourse" of Luke 4 or the "Sermon on the Plain" of Luke 6.

The modern reader is stopped by the seeming impossibility of any such event within history as a generalized jubilee (Luke 4:19); nor can one easily imagine being "perfect, as your heavenly Father is perfect" (Matt. 5:48). The reader then assumes that Jesus must not have been "trying to say"[9] what he says, leaving the reader free to go down the paths of paradoxical or symbolic or spiritualist interpretation. For Jesus's first hearers, on the other hand, the question of whether it would "work" would not have got in the way of the promise. They already believed a history in which the impossible had happened. They could hear the promise without filtering it through the grid of their sense of the limits of the possible.

The sense in which the coming of the kingdom is conceivable for modern listeners seems to be "off the scale" of the real world. Yet Jesus's believing listeners remembered saving events that had taken place within their own history and on their own Palestinian soil. Many modern interpreters of Jesus come to his proclamation considering it as implying a necessary end of real history. Yet saving wonders had been part of the reporting of history in Judges and Chronicles and down through the centuries. Jesus's listeners were not bothered as we are with the fear that the coming of the kingdom that he announced might not happen in reality. They had seen such events before. If they had doubts, it was in the opposite direction; namely, that they would not want that kind of kingdom to come because of its claims on them.

My point here is not to discuss, as a theme in critical Gospel interpretation, exactly what "the historical" Jesus meant, or whether what Jesus meant is credible to modern post-Enlightenment Europeans. I am asking whether *when* the proclamation of Jesus was first spoken it was intrinsically incredible for its hearers. On that subject, the memory of the miraculous deliverances in the experience of the Israelites, which constituted the primary historical memory of Jesus's audience, would seem to be nearly conclusive affirmative evidence.

The Peaceableness of Jews since Isaiah and Jeremiah

Yet the theme of this chapter is not the teaching of Jesus but the evolution of the self-understanding of biblical Israel before him. Centuries of Christian anti-Semitism have established the pattern of thinking that the Jewish faith was warlike and Jesus was peaceable, so that Jesus's announcing a peaceable kingdom was the reason that "the Jews" rejected him. That misreading is a source of continuing confusion in Christian thought. It is made all the more confusing when we remember that Christians, at least since the fourth century, have not been peaceable, whereas Jews have never been violent from the second century until this one.[10] In proper historical reorientation, the reading of the first two centuries would be profoundly different from the standard anti-Semitic reading.

Holy wars and divinely mandated kingship are the beginning, not the end, of the Jewish national story. That story moves ahead so that by the time of the writing of the Chronicles, the model of nonviolent salvation after the style of the stories of Hezekiah and Jehoshaphat is the norm. Ezra and Nehemiah were to restore the worshiping presence of Jews in Judea under the protection of God, but without political sovereignty.

As Ezra set out from Babylon to return to Jerusalem we read:

> Then I proclaimed a fast there, at the river Aha'va,
>   that we might humble ourselves before our God,
>   to seek from him a straight way. . . .
> For I was ashamed to ask the king for
>   a band of soldiers and horsemen to protect us
>   against the enemy on our way;
>   since we had told the king,
> "The hand of our God is for good
>   upon all that seek him,
>   and the power of his wrath
>   is against all that forsake him."
> So we fasted and besought our God for this,
>   and he listened to our entreaty. (Ezra 8:21–23)

That redefinition of national community without kingship or national sovereignty was not a counsel of weakness. It was the culmination of the prophetic critique of kingship as inappropriate for the people of Yahweh. The critique underlying the stories of Judges and Samuel and Kings becomes increasingly clear as the prophets go on. By the time of Isaiah it called for formal renunciation of politics and diplomacy as usual, of alliances with Egypt, and of modernized military technology. By the time of Jeremiah, trusting God had come to entail renouncing statehood[11] and accepting Diaspora as the fitting way for the people of God to live.[12] Jeremiah's letter to the exiles (Jer. 29) called them to take their being scattered among the nations as normal—i.e., as mission. Promises of early restoration are denounced as lying dreams. The prophets who make such promises were not sent by Yahweh:

> Build houses and live in them;
>   plant gardens and eat their produce.

Take wives and have sons and daughters;
     take wives for your sons,
and give your daughters in marriage,
     that they may bear sons and daughters;
multiply there, and do not decrease.
But *seek the welfare of the city*
     where I have sent you into exile
and pray to the LORD *on its behalf,*
     for in its welfare you will find your welfare. (Jeremiah 29:5–7,
emphasis added).

From this time on, Babylon more than Palestine became the base of the continuing Jewish story. The attempts at restoration under Ezra and Nehemiah are not reported as successes.[13]

The violent national uprisings of the Maccabees are reported even less; their stories are not in the Hebrew canon and were not understood by the rabbis as having taken place under the blessing of God. The Zealot adventures of Menachem in 66–70 CE and of Bar Kochba in 132–135 CE are not seen as the continuation of a faithful community, but as mistakes that God judged. The rabbinic communities, whose testimony produced the Mishnah, were the prolongation of the social form projected by the message of Jeremiah. After 70 CE, and definitively after 135 CE, there is no more rabbinic interest in solutions following either the Herodian, Sadduceean, or Zealot models.

Two kinds of Jewish identity were to survive into later history. The Jews who were convinced that in Jesus the Messiah has come were henceforth to be called *Christians*, and the others gathered around the rabbis. Even within Palestine, Jews went on living in a sociology of dispersion, without any need for kingship or sovereignty, heirs of the arrangement established by Jochanan ben Zakkai when he dissociated himself from the Zealots. The numerically dominant Jewish identity was for centuries to be what was defined for and from Babylon. The Babylon community was five centuries old when the generation of Jochanan abandoned the Zealots, and six centuries old when the generation of Akiva fully accepted that lesson. Christians who, in order to understand Jesus, think they should take either the Zealots or the Sadducees as representative of normative Jews thereby misread both the Jewish canon and real Jewish history.

Not only did Judaism, as defined since Jeremiah, forsake visions of kingship and sovereignty for its historical present. Judaism also forsook violence. The rabbinic literary corpus is by its nature complex and contradictory. Some passages reject violence completely, even in self-defense.[14] Others retain the memory of a judicial system qualified to punish people, and of limited wars, since such were there in their ancient histories; but the rabbis' guidance about the moral life of the ongoing Jewish community calls for a fundamentally nonviolent lifestyle, even under persecution. This guidance occurs on grounds not of tactics or weakness, but because that is now seen to be the will of God.

That model of Jewish pacifism was sustained through the Middle Ages, after the Christians had made their alliance with the Caesars, and it continued to be held until our century. Paradoxically, it was thus the Jews who through all those centuries most faithfully represented within Europe the defenseless style of morality that Jesus had taught. Their ways of explaining that stance were multiple:

(1) The sacredness of blood. Blood is life and belongs to God. Even the blood of an animal must not be shed except in a ritual context. The shedding of the blood of a fellow human being is the fundamental denial of human dignity (Gen. 4) from which all other sins against society are derived. Those points in the Old Testament where exception can be made to the wrongness of shedding blood are in the context of the Mosaic provisions for civil administration or the holy war narratives, and *at the most* would apply in a pre-exile state. Even there, however, they would not apply rigorously, if such a Jewish state had not gone into exile, because Judaism assumes an evolving process that moves toward greater grace and humaneness.

(2) The Messiah has not yet come. If anyone could have a right to restore the patterns of vengeance, which alone could justify the shedding of blood, it would have to be the Messiah. Yet we know that when he comes there will be a time of peace. If the time of his coming will be a time of peace, then we participate in that coming while living already in peace. The action of living in peace is a contribution to his coming.

(3) Judaism is marked by the concern to learn the lessons from the Zealot experiences already noted negatively above. This experience came to its final catastrophe in 130–135 CE with Bar Kochba, but the earlier catastrophe is 66–70 CE. These and the still earlier Maccabean drama all represented the same strategy, and all failed. All but the last failed, at least in part because when they took power, they were unable to bring about the righteous and peaceful community they had promised. If anything is constitutive of rabbinic Judaism, in the sense in which historians speak of it as beginning after 70 CE or after 135 CE, it is the concern to be clear about having learned the lesson of the wrongness of the Zealot path, which God evidently had not commanded and had not blessed. In not blessing the Zealot path, God is telling us something he has had to tell us more than once.

(4) The wisdom with which God presides over the affairs of the *goyim* is not revealed to us in any simple way. We do know that God does rule over the whole universe, and therefore over all the nations. But the *way* God rules over the nations is not the same as the way God rules over

us through the revealed Torah. God therefore forbids our drawing immediate conclusions about which things going on in the wider world are God's doing and which are rebellion against God. Since God has given us no revelation as to his judgments in those matters, it would be presumptuous for us to seek to be the instruments of God's wrath, to say nothing of doing violently, ahead of the Messiah's coming, what we think God wants done.

(5) Suffering has a place in the divine economy. That the faithful must suffer is a mystery not yet clear in the Jewish understanding of history. On the one hand there is a correlation between disobedience and consequent punishment, and between obedience and resulting prosperity. If we suffer it is because of our disobedience. Yet this linkage is not automatic, since sometimes the evil prosper.[15] Sometimes the suffering of God's people is beyond explanation. Only those who know little of the past think that the drama of Auschwitz has brought this problem to the surface for the first time. In any case, some suffering at the hands of the *goyim* is to be accepted as *sanctifying the Name* of God.

Though the answers the rabbis give are varied, most of them agree in denying that it is in the hands of the faithful to prevent their suffering or to get vengeance by taking up arms themselves. Sometimes the thought is that we are being punished for our sins; in that case, to ward off the suffering would be to interfere with God's chastisement. At other times the suffering is thought of as discipline or training or refining of the spirit, rather than as punishment; again it would be wrong to prevent it. Whatever the explanation may be, our suffering is within the framework of God's providential control of events. Since God lets these things happen, we should not take up arms to prevent them.

The confluence of all these considerations made the global experience of being Jewish in the Middle Ages consistent and convincing. The stance was viable because between pogroms there were stretches of tolerance during which there were some safe niches in society for such a minority. This stance was self-reinforcing and convincing because the crude, violent, semi-pagan, tribal culture of their "Christian" oppressors was living proof of the moral superiority of Judaism.

European and American Christians are far from completing the penance called for by the centuries of official anti-Semitism in the interest of national and ethnic selfishness. One part of the overdue rehabilitation should be the recognition of the power and profound theological roots of Jewish nonviolence through the centuries.[16]

5

Jesus

A Model of Radical Political Action

I t would be a mistake to assume that my title has a single self-evident meaning and that my task is simply to demonstrate how Jesus lives up to what *radical political action* already means in the reader's mind.[1] The word *radical* has many definitions: some of them fanatical, some angry, some ideological. My task must rather be to describe who Jesus was and how he proceeded, and to leave readers free to decide how to label it.

There was no separation between Jesus's thought or teaching and his action or career as a political figure, just as there was no separation between the *religious* and the *political* in his time. Yet my description may be more accessible if I tell the story twice: once from the perspective of ideas, and once from that of public activity.

The Good News of the Kingdom Coming

Everything about the early chapters of the Gospel accounts conveys a sense of expectancy: the genealogies, the promises to Zechariah and Mary and Simeon, and the recognition by the shepherds and the magi. The very term *gospel* signifies news. The first message of John the Baptist, of Jesus, and of the twelve Jesus sent out as messengers was, "The kingdom is imminent." Thus the first presupposition of *radical political action* is the conviction that a real God is really intervening in human affairs to set things right. Jesus's actions were not mere human idealism; they were defined within a context of promises fulfilled and justice about to be implemented. This conviction undercuts the "business-as-usual" assumptions with which most moral thought begins, on the presupposition (often called *reason* or the *nature of things*) that profound change is not possible.

Jesus's Sermon on the Mount begins with this sense of newness. His phrase "Blessed are those who . . ." marks the contrast between the character of the imminent rule of God and what went before in clearly countercultural ways.[2] His declaration in Matthew 5:20 that "unless your righteousness exceeds that of the scribes and Pharisees, you will never enter the kingdom of heaven" spells out this newness in the form of six specific sample antitheses to the previously dominant moral assumptions about truth telling, loving one's neighbor, and sexuality: ("you have heard it said . . . , but I say . . .").[3] In some cases the radicalizing that fulfills the law might be called *internalizing*: what we are called to renounce is not only killing or committing adultery, but thinking in those ways. In other cases, the *radicality* is outward: loving the neighbor becomes loving indiscriminately, including the enemy; not swearing falsely expands to mean not needing the oath at all to validate what one says.

In both cases, it is a misunderstanding to consider these radicalizing redefinitions as legalistic or morally rigorous in a traditional sense. They are part of the good news of the new world that is on the way in the power of the God who forgives and restores. They are not idealistic about human potential so much as they are realistic about divine power and about the substance of the divine intent.

The phrase "the substance of the divine intent" is a code label for a wealth of detail about concrete behavior with regard to truth telling, sexuality, work and wealth, social organization, and property. It is a mistake, however, to think that Jesus's primary originality was that he changed the rules. Rather, as we saw, what he said was that he was filling them full, spelling out all their implications. That means that a full view of radical social action should envision an agenda as broad as the entire Torah.

If taken alone, part of Jesus's Sermon on the Mount could be understood as tightening the rules; what is more basic, more radical, is the grounding of these new possibilities in the coming of the kingdom. Nonetheless, it is possible that in education or in illuminating hard choices, some of Jesus's "But I say to you . . ." sayings are crucial. "Do not resist the evil person" became for Tolstoy "the key to the gospel" because of all it implied. In our world, "Love your enemy" or "Blessed are the poor" may be the clearest way to articulate the radical nature of Jesus's message.

Action speaks. Jesus's image of the city on the hill or the lamp in the room makes of all behavior a kind of speech. If the world is to learn of the kingdom coming, it will be by observing the law-fulfilling, truth-telling, enemy-loving lives of his disciples (Matt. 5:14–16). Not only does such behavior say that the kingdom is at hand; it also describes God. Jesus says that by loving their enemies his disciples will be like their heavenly father.[4] This is said of no other ethical issue.

The Nonviolent Liberator

The songs that open Luke portray well the expectancy of Palestinian Jews. They expected a liberator who would exalt the lowly and bring down the mighty. The angel instructed Jesus's mother that her child should be named Yeshua, meaning "the Lord liberates." That had been the name of Moses's successor, leader of the original Israelite settlement in Canaan. John the Baptist's preaching in Matthew 3:1–12 and Luke 3:1–17 described the coming change in terms of the *repentance* required of those awaiting it: they would share with the needy. Those of John's listeners who were driven to ask, "What should we do?" were precisely the representatives of Roman oppression: tax gatherers and soldiers.

Jesus did not turn out to be the kind of violent liberator some were expecting; yet neither did he tell his hearers that he was not interested in their oppression. He used the political language of their expectation, speaking of God's kingdom and of righteousness. He offended Herod and the Sadducees who controlled local politics. He attracted large crowds who, when they heard him, wanted to make him king, and he formed a disciplined corps of disciples committed to his cause. He was executed on the grounds—false in detail but credible in principle—that he claimed to be King of the Jews. None of this would have happened if his concern had been to separate the religious from the political and deal only with the "religious."

Jesus faced authentically what the historian must call the *Zealot temptation*, although historians dispute how soon and how widely the actual term *Zealot* was used. Violent revolution, intended to drive the Romans away and to reestablish a righteous commonwealth, was frequently undertaken by rebel groups and may well have been the initial expectation of most of Jesus's hearers, even of many of his close disciples. To reject that concrete political option, as Jesus very pointedly and self-consciously did, both for himself and for his disciples, made sense because of his worldview, described above. He thereby made concrete the relevance of that worldview.

Yet Jesus's rejection of Zealot violence was only important because that violence was, in principle, an attractive recourse. Jesus did see himself as a liberator.[5] He formed a people to be the bearers of the new principles of God's rule. He did not use the violence of the state or of war because that would have been a contradiction in terms, yet he and the community he left behind did incarnate the political newness of enemy-love, sharing bread, and exalting the lowly.

With this account before us, it may be worthwhile to return to definitions. What is called "political" may be almost anything. Candidates for prominent public office often say they are not being "political," when what they mean is only that some particular action or statement is not motivated *only* by calculations of partisan electoral advantage. For others, the "political" concerns only and specifically the state.

The Greek term *polis* means simply "society." The "political" in its root meaning, then, is whatever has to do with power, decisions, and rank. The corporation is not less political than the state; civil disobedience is not less political than unquestioning loyalty; minority testimony is not less political than imperial dominion. Thus, *radical political action* does not automatically mean some way to press for specific state policies, although in some cases (as with Gerard Winstanley, William Penn, Gandhi, the German church struggle, Martin Luther King Jr.) that will be called for—and will also be called forth— by the good news of the kingdom.

The Radical Rabbi and Nonviolent Zealot Is Our Master

No theme is more widely present in the New Testament than that Jesus reveals what God wants of the believer. During his Palestinian ministry, Jesus warned his listeners not to join his movement without counting the cost: they would, like him, have a cross to bear, including social conflict and even death (Luke 14:25–33; see also John 15:18–27). If his fate was the cost of his incarnating a righteousness that the power structures of the world could not tolerate, then his followers should expect to be part of the same process.

Different apostolic authors modulate in different ways the notion of sharing in Christ's life.[6] Some write of dying with Christ and rising with him, or of renouncing "equality with God" as he did and sharing in his being given the title of "Lord." Some say that the Christian's posture in positions of subordination should be like his; others say that Christians in situations of power should become servants. In all of these ways, *following Jesus* is not a rigid mimicry but a participation in the quality that characterized his political being. What is to be replicated in the believer's life is the spiritual and social posture of Jesus. It should not be caricatured by the naive "imitation" language with which later Christians have forsaken marriage, or have gone barefoot, or have begged for a living, or have made an issue of earning their living by manual labor (although any one of these specific paths may in some cases be dictated by the gospel and be politically significant).

The Creative Fidelity of the Next Generation

The standard account of the experience of the early Christians would have us believe that the radicality of Jesus was lost in a generation. We are told that by the time the Gospels were written and perhaps even earlier, or by the time Paul had taken the Palestinian message into the Hellenistic world, the radicality of Jesus had to have been lost. What Jesus proclaimed could not be reduced to the dimensions of a real historical movement.

The postulate of necessary betrayal in the next generation of Christians is philosophically predetermined. It comes neither from the texts of the New Testament nor from the first-century reality. Scholars and preachers have read it into the texts by virtue of their prior philosophical prejudices. Yet to respond to this viewpoint we must review the same data independently.

For some, the early Christian acceptance of the structures of the family and the economy, which several apostolic texts write of as "reciprocal subordination," seems like a betrayal of Jesus's radicality because it did not abolish with one blow the institutions of family or slavery. But upon scrutiny, it becomes evident that such "subordination" was the only authentic way for the tiny Christian movement to undermine oppressive structures. By the same token, the acceptance of the presence of the Roman state (see, for example, Rom. 13:1–4; 1 Tim. 2:2; and 1 Pet. 2:13) represented not social conservatism but extension into the Roman Empire of the subversive strategy of survival in dissent with which Jews since Jeremiah had maintained their moral integrity during centuries of imperial oppression. That God "orders" the realm of "the authorities" does not mean that their authority is unquestioned, but that it is limited and that the criteria that justify their role also condition it.

The most personal way in which the apostle Paul made sense of the power structures in the world, and of the church's testimony to them, was the ancient cosmology of the "principalities and powers." In that set of concepts, which are more solid than metaphor or myth without being as prosaic as what we call social science, Paul contends that the power structures of our world are not devils but creatures, intended for the well-being of humankind, yet "fallen" and thereby oppressive. Jesus Christ disobeys the powers, disarms them, and saves us from their enslavement by dying at their hands. He thereby *tames* them and makes them useable in the service of human dignity. Twenty centuries later, this is what we would call *radical social consciousness*. It analyzes the cosmology of the times and shows how the minuscule community of disciples already participates in Christ's victory when it refuses to honor the idolatrous claims of the fallen powers.

One other oft-maligned dimension of the early church's apostolic witness is the genre of apocalypse. When taken naively, or when abused by modern fundamentalism, visions of coming catastrophe can be used to depoliticize Christian witness. Yet the point of apocalyptic literature in the first century was to safeguard the young churches' confidence in God's ultimate victory. Their present suffering did not mean they were being abandoned. In such a world, apocalyptic literature is historically more realistic than other standard ways of reading history—for example, honorific inscriptions or laudatory chronicles.

The Story, Once Begun, Goes On

This being the nature of Jesus's message and his achievement, the story can by definition not stop there. If Jesus's primary intent and accomplishment had been to create a specific ecclesiastical institution, or to command a specific set of ritual practices, or to impart a precise body of insights about the nature of things, his job could have been done and no more history would have been needed. But if what Jesus came to do was to light a fire on earth, to initiate an authentically historical process of reconciliation and community formation, then the only way for that to proceed would have to be under the conditions of historicity, including the effects of ignorance, confusion, finitude, and fallibility. The ambivalence brought into the Christian movement as a result of numerical growth, crosscultural communication, and the incorporation of non-Judaic religiosity could not be avoided; the occasion necessarily arose for dilution of the vision as well as its enrichment, for apostasy as well as faithful creativity.

Although the original message of Jesus was compromised in other ways, in the course of the processes that created Christendom, the most fundamental apostasy, which enabled and ratified the other kinds of betrayal, was the reversal of Jesus' attitude toward kingship in favor of the Constantinian glorification of imperial autocracy and wealth. Thus the subversive memory of Jesus could not but respond in the finite, fallible, historical movements of radical discipleship that we call *radical reformation*: monasticism, St. Francis, the Waldensians and Czech brethren, Anabaptism and Quakerism, Dorothy Day and Helder Camara, Clarence Jordan and Athol Gill.

These movements of radical discipleship regularly challenged the domination of violence, wealth, social hierarchy, and empty ritual. Each such summons to the retrieval of discipleship confirms the centrality of Jesus in our history. Without the ongoing processes of distraction and reform, we would not know today's form of Jesus Christ's call.[7] We would not be asking the right questions that in every century renew the awareness that his summons retains the same radical substance and mediates the same empowerment.

The Dialogue with Just War

The Case for Mutual Learning

6

Just War and *Nonviolence*

Disjunction, Dialogue, or Complementarity?

The *just war* tradition has dominated Western legal and theological thought for a millennium and a half.[1] It offers a set of criteria for decision-makers (rulers, military commanders, even citizens) to be able (allegedly) to draw a morally accountable line between admissible and inadmissible uses of military violence.

Nonviolence is a much younger term, although some of the attitudes and principles it designates are ancient. It may designate nothing more than the *pragmatically* rational rejection of violence in attitude or action. In this century it has come to be used more often as I propose to use it here, as *nonviolent action*: modes of activism that renounce violence, in order that other kinds of power (truth, consent, conscience) may work.

At first sight the two systems, just war and nonviolence, seem to be incompatible. They certainly are at home in quite different, even opposed sub-cultures. When stated in terms of abstract moral absolutes, they differ on whether "violence" is ever "morally acceptable"—although in view of the variety of meanings of the terms, it is not fully clear that even this difference is fully disjunctive.[2]

My intent here is to project the agenda for a dialogue that would demonstrate that despite their acknowledged *prima facie* contradictions, the two systems belong in the same universe of discourse and are pertinent to one another's integrity. The agenda comprises three components:

(1) Some thinkers have already suggested a complementarity akin to what
I am describing;

(2) Nonviolence can help to make just war thought more honest; and

(3) Just war thinking can help to make nonviolence more disciplined.

Claims that the Two Systems Interlock

James Childress has argued that the moral logic underlying the just war system is the *prima facie* right of everyone not to be harmed (or the correlative
duty of everyone to do no harm).[3] Those who reject all violence consider the
right not to be harmed as inalienable. They believe the duty not to harm is
unconditional. On the other hand, just war theory holds that the rights of
other persons may override that right. Then the several just war criteria are
best understood as determining when and why that overriding may occur.[4]
Nonviolence is thus the *a priori* stance, to which violent action is an exception needing in each case to be justified. One need not be convinced by his
particular philosophical frame of reference[5] to agree that Childress correctly
renders the fact that, according to the mainstream of the just war theory,[6] war
is an evil.[7] Whoever would resort to it has the burden of proof, and it is that
burden that the set of criteria should regulate.

At Harvard, where Bryan Hehir's PhD certification was served by Ralph
Potter, the thesis held by Potter[8] and widely propagated by James Childress[9]
was well established as an intellectual construct. It is intrinsically worthy of
being elaborated as an argument, despite the fact that the bishops' use of
it (or that of their amanuenses) to avoid avowing full responsibility for the
originality of their leadership was formally disingenuous.[10]

In his presidential address to the association Concerned Philosophers for
Peace, James Sterba stated another form of the *complementarity* argument.
Richard Miller has made more of the question.[11]

The seed planted by Potter, Hehir, and Childress bore fruit in a popular setting
in the pastoral letter, *The Challenge of Peace.*[12] The writing was guided mainly
by Bryan Hehir, and was circulated by the U.S. Roman Catholic bishops in 1983.[13]
The bishops sometimes—but not always—equated nonviolence with *pacifism*,
and described it as having been the position of the earliest Christians. They
described nonviolence and just war theory as being complementary, both being
positions a Catholic Christian can conscientiously hold. This affirmation was an
innovation in Roman Catholic thought. No earlier approval of principled pacifism
is found in Roman Catholic magisterial texts in modern times. *Gaudium et Spes*,
"The Pastoral Constitution on the Church in the Modern World," in the Second
Vatican Council, marked the first time that the legal recognition of conscientious
objection had been advocated, and then only conditionally.[14] In *The Challenge of
Peace*, the bishops wrote that nonviolence and just war theory are

distinct but independent methods of evaluating warfare. They diverge on some specific conclusions, but they share a common presumption against the use of force as a means of settling disputes. Both find their roots in the Christian theological tradition; each contributes to the full moral vision we need; . . . each preserv[es] the other from distortion.

Finally, in an age of technological warfare, analysis of conflicts from the viewpoint of nonviolence, and analysis from the viewpoint of just-war teaching, often converge and agree in their opposition to methods of warfare that are in fact indistinguishable from total warfare.[15]

The evaluation of nuclear deterrence constituted the core of *The Challenge of Peace* and its major public witness in the political context of its time. After that evaluation, a section on "Proposals and Policies" returned to the theme of "Nonviolent Means of Conflict Resolution."[16] The complementarity, which had previously been described in abstract terms, was now affirmed pragmatically. To summarize all of the above, the two systems have in common:

(1) A moral presumption against violence (although they differ on whether that presumption may be overridden);

(2) A stake in rejecting total war, and therefore making common cause politically against unacceptable national policies;

(3) Support for maximizing the potential of nonmilitary means for pursuing just social objectives, including national defense.[17]

Not to be outdone, the bishops of the United Methodist Church of the United States also prepared a pastoral letter.[18] On the specific political issue of nuclear deterrence, the Methodists' conclusion is a shade less tolerant than that of their *confreres* of the Roman obedience.[19] With regard to the debate between just war and nonviolence (they prefer the term *pacifism*), they claim to transcend it with a notion of *just peace*[20] rather than to maintain it dialectically. For our purposes, the difference is slight. They retain the claim that the parcels of truth in both the just war and the nonviolence stances can be reconciled.[21]

To bring this first overview to a close, we need to lift up a point that neither body of bishops adequately avowed: the actual rhetoric and the actual practice of modern nations, including Methodists and Catholics in positions of responsibility as citizens, statesmen, and soldiers, have in the vast majority of cases been neither *just war* nor *pacifist*. Total war has in fact characterized our culture.[22] Sometimes what broke through all restraints was simple national selfishness, which some call *realism*.[23] Sometimes what led to total war has been a transcendent religious or ideological claim, which some call *holy*.[24] Sometimes the cause for which blood has been shed is morally even less worthy than that; namely, the need of some ruler to reassure himself and his people of his masculinity. In each of these ways war was totalized, so that there was no effective restraint in most of the Western world's experience of war. Just war theory has not been operational in any significant way in the military reality of the last centuries.

Historical honesty demands that we report that most people who considered themselves to be Catholic Christians—between Ambrose of Milan in the late fourth century and Cardinal Spellman of New York in the late twentieth, including most bishops and most parish priests and a goodly number of moral theologians—looked at the morality of war quite differently, namely in one of two other ways:[25]

(1) For many, the rule has always been "anything goes," including a formal denial of moral criteria that might stand in judgment on what orders a ruler gives, or that might in any way provide grounds for an individual to refuse to kill when ordered. Sometimes that denial has been philosophized by the likes of Machiavelli. Sometimes the imperative to serve unquestioningly has been stated in the name of "the revolution" or of "freedom." Sometimes this understanding has been theologized under the headings of "the divine right of kings." Sometimes its form or foundation has been an oath of absolute loyalty binding the soldier to the sovereign. Sometimes it has claimed to be a self-evident political scientific description of reality, whether by Clausewitz or by Hans Morgenthau. In these varied ways, individuals have been routinely told that there is no basis for resisting the orders of the ruler. Most of the bishops and priests of the Roman Catholic communion have told them this, routinely throughout Christian history, as far as one can tell from the record. The authors of *The Challenge of Peace* know this to be the truth, at least subliminally, but they choose, at least subliminally, not to avow it.

(2) Less often, but no less clearly, there have been times when the affirmation of the moral rightness of war has been even stronger. It has been declared by religious figures to be a duty, even to the point of the individual's expecting martyrdom and the nation's making no calculations of probable success. This kind of thinking for a decade in our own century sent Iranian teenagers to their death on the Iraqi front, and Lebanese drivers of vans to certain death in vehicles loaded with explosives.

In the Middle Ages the Christian version of this was the crusade, and it was specifically Roman Catholic bishops and abbots who proclaimed it a Christian duty to go off to win the Holy Land (or to sack Tunis or Istanbul) for the cause of Christ as interpreted by the church. During the First World War the language of the crusade was still being used on both sides by Christian preachers, Roman Catholic and Protestant, even though the politicians and the generals (and the political scientists since then) knew full well that it was not a war that could be justified according to either moral or technical military considerations.

The logic of the *holy war* is present wherever unthinking heroism is demanded (go down with the ship, fight to the last man) and when surrender is equated with immorality or treason.[26] In short, the holy war thought patterns are still at work, even though the bishops ignore them.

How then can *The Challenge of Peace* tell us that the just war logic and the pacifist position are the Christian tradition? Because their reference (i.e., the reference of Bryan Hehir and Bruce Russett, the scholars in the fields of [Christian ethics and] political science who guided the writing) is to the insightful minority of moral theologians and of religious thinkers, for whom neither holy war nor "anything goes" was respectable. That foreshortening is a peculiar product of the modern Roman Catholic self-understanding—avoiding tacitly the responsibility to recognize that most Christian citizens, most Christians called to arms, most Christian sovereigns, and most Catholic bishops and priests for a millennium and a half were taking the view that war is "holy" or that "anything goes." The readiness of Roman Catholic intellectual leaders to move forward into improved understanding in the present and future does not include overt repentance about the errors and atrocities of the past. We saw this again in the early 1990s around the legacy of Columbus.

Theologians may avow honestly that the criteria of the just war tradition were not respected in the past few centuries, but bishops are supposed to move forward in the mood of fiction according to which future truth is not permitted to "make ancient good uncouth."[27] Some of this development can be welcomed, as a way of letting events teach us the inadequacy of past stances, an openness which Vatican II canonized in the phrase "discerning the signs of the times."[28] Nonetheless, the historical account in *The Challenge of Peace* is simply, statistically, blatantly false. The people of whom that account is true (i.e., those who held to a just war position with teeth, capable of articulating and enforcing negative judgments on particular wars, or particular weapons or tactics) were a slim minority of theologians and prophets. It belongs to the nobility of just war theory *as conceptual construct* that it could provide the mental backbone and the vocabulary for that heroic minority. It did that for people like de Vitoria, de las Casas, and Suarez. But it falsifies history to make those men, who were not supported by Catholic sovereigns or the hierarchy at the time, representative of Catholicism.

That it is a historical fiction does not make the complementarity thesis morally uninteresting. It has an intrinsic logic. Politically, pacifism and just war may well form coalitions against the other less restrained postures. Seen in the context of the usual nationalistic, right-of-state, Machiavellian, and crusade justifications of war, pacifism and just war are more like allies seeking to correct what usually happens. They both reject the uncritical acceptance of violence.

How Nonviolence Can Discipline the Use of Just War Logic

The most obvious intersection between the systems is the notion of *last resort*. Traditionally, every other reasonable recourse to correct for an injustice must have been tried, in good faith, before resort to war can be justified. If the experience of effective nonviolent action now enables us to consider previously unimagined modes of effective struggle for valid social ends, then a society or a nation under attack will not reach the threshold of last resort as soon.

As Gene Sharp has pointed out repeatedly, many of the successful phenomena of nonviolent group action have been spontaneous, or the product of only minimal premeditation or planning. No one would think of evaluating the proportional effectiveness or probable success of a military tactic without extensive prior investment of time and money in planning, training, organizing, and equipping for the conflict. If, then, nonviolent action strategies were made the subject of advance research and training,[29] their potential for national self-defense should be incomparably greater.[30] Last resort would logically demand the development of alternative instruments of conflict. Some would make better use of existing resources: diplomacy, international courts, and sanctions. Others would create yet unknown tools, by extrapolating creatively from domestic experiences in the power of nonviolent alternative strategies.

But *last resort* is not the only intersection of the two systems. The notion of *just intention*, which looks forward to the viability of the peace to be established after hostilities, will be "thickened" by the reminders of the human dignity of the adversary that undergird nonviolent commitment. *Legitimate authority* as a criterion will be tightened by sensitivity to the power of public truth telling. Respect for restraint *in bello* (in the means used in war) will be heightened by an informed and skeptical populace and served by free media, ultimately challenging the use of unnecessary or disproportionate means.

How Just War Thinking Could Help Structure Tactics of Nonviolence

The fact that nonviolent conflict seeks to shed no blood does not exempt its combatants from needing to think about restraint in ways that bear some analogy to just war criteria. The rupture of the normal social flow by a boycott or by a mass gathering, a strike or a march, should be subject to considerations of last resort. Specific lawbreaking (i.e., civil disobedience) needs to be tested to determine whether it is driven by the conviction that compliance with an evil law is intrinsically immoral; or by the thinner and more complex claim that a just law is being applied unjustly;[31] or by the belief that a morally neutral regulation should be violated to make a symbolic statement.

To work through decisions of these kinds there needs to be some kind of *legitimate authority*, legitimated by people's acceptance. That qualification cannot have the shape of the legitimacy of government. Some other mode of validation is needed. Merely claiming ideological correctness (i.e., being on the side of the "people" or the "poor" or the "future") is not enough.

In just war theory, a touchstone of last resort and of legitimate intention is the formal declaration of war, which makes public the conditions under which the adversary may have peace. Nonviolent action as well must have a stated, finite, attainable goal. The demands must not be escalated once the adversary is under pressure. Here too Gandhi and King enunciated this clearly.

For such a decision about stated goal and last resort by some authority to be accountable, there needs to be some definition of the *people* in whose name the nonviolent conflict proceeds. It cannot be the entire nation-state as is the case for war, (until we get to the point, thanks to King-Hall and Gene Sharp, that some national community will freely entertain the nonviolent option). There are ways for such a morally accountable constituency to come together, as we can see in the experiences of Gandhi, King, Walesa, Havel, and in Manila in 1986 and Leipzig in 1989. There are other times when creative and risky initiatives are defeated for want of a way to define *authority*.

The use of nonviolence in settings of great conflict runs the risk of provoking counterviolence; Gandhi and King knew this well. The notion that violence can be easily avoided is always a caricature; the point in nonviolent action is that the resort to violence is left to the agents of injustice. This raises the classical just war considerations of proportion. Nonviolent action runs the risk of doing or triggering damage to property and to uninvolved persons. Boycotts and work stoppages may cause harm analogous to the *innocent suffering* caused by war. In any important clash (although much less so than in war) some such "collateral and unintended" damage cannot be avoided. What matters morally, then, is that the struggle be so structured that all foreseeable damage of these kinds be avoided, and that there be provision for compensation.

Until a century ago, classic just war theory included the criterion of "respecting the human dignity of the adversary as a rational creature," the most specific concretion of which was the prohibition of lying.[32] Gandhi made much of truth telling as the foundation of the power of nonviolence,[33] as did the early Quakers.[34] King sensed the need to justify an exception when planning a campaign required that secrets about strategy be kept.[35] Nonviolent combatants must hold a higher level of commitment to the adversary's human dignity than the adversary does.

Behind this bundle of specimens from the roster of just war criteria, I have tacitly been demonstrating that nonviolent action as a social strategy is a mixed system of moral discourse, combining pragmatic and principled considerations in a multifactored analysis. In this sense too it is like just war theory, which is a mixture of pragmatic and principled considerations. Some considerations in nonviolent action are illuminated by empirical readings of the situation and its possibilities, while others are not. That formal quality should make the two systems able to interact. It also shows why neither by itself can be a univocally convincing religious-moral commitment.

Even though principled proponents of nonviolence can be politically creative and effective, and do pay attention to pragmatic considerations, they do not validate their stance by its effectiveness. Furthermore, some proponents of non-violent action hold that renouncing violence is a personal moral absolute.

Likewise, even though proponents of justified violence reason casuisti-cally, they say there are some things they would never do. Thus they too have a principled ultimate threshold. It must be admitted, however, that in actual practice, their principled threshold keeps slipping. I show that in chapter 7 in this book.

7

The Changing Conversation between the Peace Churches and Mainstream Christianity

I begin by identifying some assumptions I shall *not* be discussing in depth:[1]

First, the peace movement in our culture is much wider than the peace churches. Some of it is academic; some of it is activist. Peace church people lead some of it; some of it is explicitly secular. Much of it is very important, in macro-social terms, but it is too broad for me to try to report on it. The interlocutor that the wider peace movement addresses is the nation, the world, the predominant society. Therefore, the values it must appeal to are so diverse, diffuse, and ephemeral that any account of its church-world dialogue would be more journalism than theology.

Second, meeting at Swarthmore, it is appropriate that I use the shorthand term *peace churches* to name the commonality, both in stance and in activity, which sees Friends, Brethren, and Mennonites standing and acting together to reject war and to advocate reconciling alternatives. The three groups are different in important ways. Only since the 1930s, in the face of the rising threat of national mobilization for World War II, have the leaders of the three groups met regularly to coordinate their representations to government with regard to the draft, and then their overseas service activities. Only since the 1950s did their representatives in Europe begin to work together in addressing a common witness against war to the other churches gathered in the World Council of Churches.[2] Only since 1968 did their conference agencies in North

America coordinate their actual participation in the periodic assemblies of the World Council. Only since the early 1980s did they begin gathering on other than agency leadership levels, in the series of more popular study events and rallies under the name "New Call to Peacemaking," to cultivate common awareness and commitment on a broader common agenda than the antiwar witness. So there is such a thing as the *historic peace churches*, but for most Friends, most Brethren, and most Mennonites, it does not represent a very important identity marker. Many Friends feel more at home among nonchurch peace people than with Mennonites or Brethren. Some Brethren feel more at home among Protestants of the conciliar mainstream. Many Mennonites and a few Brethren feel more comfortable among evangelicals. Nonetheless, there remains a small story for me to tell.[3]

Christians in pacifist minority communities have never had the luxury of ignoring the majority nonpacifist confessions, which in most of our history have dominated society, government, and the schools. That domination has routinely included the assumption, taken for granted almost without a second thought, that war, whenever the government calls us to it, is a Christian duty. No Christian pacifist thinker, no active citizen, could stand by her or his pacifist commitment without needing to take account of the mainstream arguments in favor of participation in the civil responsibilities of military service in an extreme instance. Nonpacifists, on the other hand, need not attend with any care to the pacifist witness. Those major ethicists who took the historic pacifist witness seriously, like Reinhold Niebuhr or Paul Ramsey, were the exception, and even they did not study it in depth. If then there is to be any important change in the shape of the dialogical relationship between the pacifist communions and the others, it will most easily be recounted from the other side, i.e. as a change in the way nonpacifist Christians see us. I can do this best by simplifying and schematizing.

Recognizing That the Moral Issue of War Is *Theological*

For generations, the organized ecumenical movement operated with an understanding of its mission that distinguished between important matters of doctrine and structure (usually referred to in code as *faith* and *order*) that divide the churches from one another, and with an understanding that other differences need not be faced as challenges to unity. This oversimplification was fostered by the fact that some of the historic peace churches did not join the conciliar agencies, and those few who joined felt it would not be good manners for representatives of a powerfully outvoted minority to make much of their dissent.

When the major ecumenical assemblies (Oxford 1937, Amsterdam 1948, Evanston 1954, New Delhi 1961, Uppsala 1968) could not avoid at least noticing the fact that war presented a moral problem, the conclusion reached in their statements was routinely no conclusion. What they offered was a noncommittal description of the variety of positions, a proposed agreement to disagree, and a statement to the effect that there should be more study.[4] But there was no more study.

Only in very recent years, and only in the North American arena, are the conciliar agencies recognizing that the avoidance argument described above will not hold. The matter of war is in fact, and always has been, church-dividing. This is true in more than one way:

(1) Several confessional documents, notably those of Anglicanism, Lutheranism, and Presbyterianism, affirm the doctrine of the just war, so that a convinced pacifism is in principle heretical. There has been no change in these creeds, even though in modern times pacifists within those confessions might not be disciplined as heretics.

(2) Three major communions, those already referred to as *historic peace churches*, are committed constitutionally and historically, to rejecting participation in war, even though in modern times they do not always routinely discipline those of their members who accept military service.

(3) Whenever a war happens, and members of the same communion, who find themselves defined by their governments as enemies, accept killing each other at the behest of their respective rulers, it is a mockery to speak of them as being united by their faith.[5]

The Faith and Order branch of the ecumenical dialogue process, the most careful and deliberate branch, has now recognized this fact. There is now a study process going on, comprising several meetings of different sizes and shapes, and one report volume so far, taking account of the war issue as a matter not only of ethical diversity but of ecclesiology—i.e., raising the question of the meaning of church unity.[6] Yet this process is very modest in scale and little noticed.

Asking Whether the Classical Just War Tradition Can Foster Effective Restraint

If you consult an ordinary ethics manual, the dominant theological position taken in Christian history concerning the morality of war is the just war tradition. Just war theory claims that a series of criteria can be applied to the facts of a particular conflict, with some level of objectivity, in order to distinguish between acts of war that are or are not morally justifiable.

Actually, it is not the case that the just war tradition, in that serious sense, has guided the moral choices of most Christians.[7] Nonetheless, it is important that those who say they hold that view be challenged to be honest with its implications. The operative question is whether, in case a war does *not* meet the just war requirements of cause, authority, intent, last resort, discrimination, proportionality, and legitimate and necessary means, anyone will refuse to participate in that war. Since the 1960s we have come to speak of that possibility as *selective conscientious objection*. Some have called it *nuclear pacifism*, when the particular excess that disqualifies a war is the threat of nuclear annihilation. What is needed to make credible the moral claim of a community is their application of it collectively and to *any* infraction. The notion that such a negative commitment is logically called for goes as far back as Martin Luther and Francisco Suarez. What is now changing slightly is the response to this question, with regard to some (but only some) of the just war criteria.

When young men refused to go to Vietnam, it was in practically all cases a lonely personal decision. With time the Lutheran and Catholic hierarchies came to support it in principle. This showed that the young men in question were trying to be honest with the notion of some war being unjust. It also showed that what the church leaders honored, when some of them supported those men, was the individual conscience, not the objectivity of the just war criteria.

A few voices of protest were raised just after the nuclear attacks on Hiroshima and Nagasaki, but the nation and our allies were in a hurry to move on to organize the United Nations and assure a postwar structure of peace. Only in the late 1950s were major voices again raised to argue firmly that Hiroshima had been wrong, and that future use of nuclear weapons against cities would be wrong, on grounds of the just war standards. This was said at about the same time by a German Protestant group, by an ecumenical one convened by the World Council of Churches, by the premier Roman Catholic moral theologian John Courtney Murray, and by the premier Protestant ethicist Paul Ramsey. For all of them, the criterion that was effective as a basis for negation was the classical one of noncombatant immunity. A quarter-century later, that insight had trickled up from the academic elite to the church leaders. From 1980 to 1983, the U.S. Roman Catholic bishops carried through an ambitious study project, with a broad agenda, including a formal condemnation of any actual use of nuclear weapons and a mitigated condemnation of deterrence. The World Council of Churches took a similar position in its Vancouver Assembly in 1983. Bishops of the United Methodist Church and the General Assembly of the Presbyterian Church followed soon.

The Challenge of Peace, the 1983 Roman Catholic statement, will serve us well as a test case for the question. Can the just war tradition mobilize people to refuse to participate in unjust war?

Early in their 1983 statement, the American Roman Catholic bishops' letter reviewed the history of thought about war, all the way back to Hebrew origins. In so doing they made four changes in the standard account:

(1) In contrast to the account that dominated Catholic thought since the fourth century, *The Challenge of Peace* affirms that pacifism stands close to the position of the New Testament and the early Christian centuries, and is still a possible position for individual Christians to take.

(2) Instead of considering the just war as the polar, disjunctive alternative to pacifism, *The Challenge of Peace* interprets just war thinking and pacifism as complementary. On the level of basic values, both consider war to be an evil, to be avoided if possible. On the level of political practicality, both reject policies which do not meet just war criteria.

(3) Although obliquely and not critically, it recognizes that nonviolent action in the style of Martin Luther King Jr. changes the context for thinking about the situation of last resort.

(4) In contrast to the mentality of the offspring of recent immigrants concerned for acceptance as American, and therefore marked by above-average levels of patriotism, which largely had characterized American Catholics, the bishops followed the logic of just war reasoning for the first time to its logical conclusion: that some kinds of weapons, and some kinds of weapon use—even some kinds of threatened use—are morally unacceptable *even though* enshrined for decades in defined governmental policy. The Reagan administration recognized this as a threat, and went all the way to Rome to try to pull strings to get it stopped.

None of the changes identified here can be thought of as a response to the ecumenical witness of pacifist Christians. Very few important bishops have had any personal awareness of the historic peace churches. As far as I can tell from the record, the most effective pressures that moved the bishops in the direction they took were not listening to Quakers or Mennonites or even to St. Francis, but rather the following:

(1) The moral sensitivity of grassroots Catholics working in arms factories who came to doubt whether the arms they were helping to manufacture could ever be used morally.

(2) The numerically tiny but morally weighty cohort of committed pacifists within the American Catholic communion, mostly admirers of Dorothy Day and her Catholic Worker movement. Day was the only living layperson mentioned in the text of *The Challenge of Peace*. She was a burr under the saddle of her bishop Cardinal Spellman; yet her saintly image, her conservative piety, and her network made it morally impossible for him to silence her.

(3) The rise of an idea on the abstract intellectual level: namely, the notion, already cited above, that pacifism and the just war tradition are not polar alternatives but complementary. This was first formulated by a few Ivy League Protestants, notably the Presbyterian Ralph Potter and the nonpacifist Quaker James Childress, and was widely taken over by others, including Bryan Hehir, the principal drafter of *The Challenge of Peace*. This idea is far from earning the adhesion of mainline Catholic moral theologians, but it was tactically quite helpful in the face of the pastoral challenge the bishops faced in the early 1980s.

Taking these explanations all together makes it evident that *The Challenge of Peace*, although authentically in movement, does not represent a total sea change in thought about war. In numerous ways the 1983 letter falls short of taking just war criteria with full accountable seriousness:

(1) The account of Christian history in the letter avoids naming the place of crusades, of imperialism, and of Machiavellian or "realistic" wars in the history of Catholic pastoral leadership. To take just war logic seriously would demand at least a few words of judgment and repentance concerning what really happened.

(2) The entire discussion of the moral issue of the 1980s centers upon taking seriously only one of the many criteria of classical just war teaching and thought. A few of the others are named, as if it were clear that in every respect but one U.S. policy satisfies them; others are not even mentioned. At least some of those other criteria would call for additional judgments on American policy.

(3) Although the possibility of *selective objection* is affirmed in principle, as it has been since Vietnam, the document holds back from providing any guidance that might lead particular citizens or military to take that position in an accountable way. This is very different from the directive pastoral stance the magisterium routinely takes with regard to matters of sexual ethics.

(4) Just war theory was not taken seriously enough to curtail the Gulf War. Just weeks after the conclusion of the 1991 Gulf War, in the Roman Jesuit journal *Civiltà Cattolica*, an unsigned editorial made the point that the just war tradition had not worked very well to provide restraint in the hostilities against Iraq. Along the way the writer makes the point that although the just war tradition has long dominated writings in moral theology, it has never been promulgated as normative doctrine by a council or a pope. Since this Roman journal is widely thought never to take positions that the pope would reject, that editorial has been widely read as an indication that John Paul II himself had doubts about the sufficiency of the tradition. Certainly, the Gulf War experience would

reinforce that. This does not mean, however, that he, John Paul II, was ready to replace it with something else. Concerning Bosnia he affirmed his readiness to approve of a "peacemaking" use of military force. It is not clear from that editorial whether the author would have preferred a more thorough use of the just war criteria—i.e., asking more and harder questions that would have postponed the onset of fighting or decreased its intensity. Or would he have wanted the United Nations coalition not to be there at all?

Recognizing Limitations of Even a Modified Approach to Just War Theory

The authors of these declarations have taken unprecedented positions, original enough to provoke counteroffensives by governments and disavowals of church bureaucracies by the grassroots faithful.[8] The churchpeople who made these statements, unhabitual and risky for them, were courageous and creative when evaluated from the perspective of what they had thought before on these matters. That is the first measure by which they should be evaluated. Now, however, we must turn to other levels of evaluation. Do these pioneering statements in fact succeed in sketching a new and adequate position? Do they enter the doors they open, answer the questions they raise? The progress they have already made leaves several questions open.

(1) The only just war criteria that The Challenge of Peace implements seriously are the in bello triad of discrimination, proportionality, and immunity. Other no less important classical criteria from the traditional jus in bello (respect for treaties and custom, the exclusion of perfidy, pillage, rape, reprisals, killing prisoners) are simply ignored. Some of these omissions may be justifiable, since one could argue that their application can hardly all be discussed before the fact, in time of peace; yet some of the treaty texts would have something to say to weapons deployment choices. Experience in Korea and Vietnam would warn us about some of them. More significant, perhaps, is the fact that while the ad bellum criteria are listed in The Challenge of Peace, the bishops give no attention at all to the possibility that U.S. policy might fall short of any of them.[9] The bishops give American national righteousness as to ends the benefit of the doubt, asking questions only about means.

In this respect, I fear that The Challenge of Peace is representative. The bishops were driven by their pastoral concerns into taking a morally critical position. They were not led by a thorough or rigorous concern for the integrity of their just war tradition to apply all of its conditions. They were not led, by a renewal of the original medieval vision of Christendom in which all the provinces were part of the same moral family, to transcend provincial Americanism in principle.

Long ago Robert Tucker identified as a special American tendency the idea that just cause—i.e., the righteousness of our national goals—has tended to take priority over the other criteria.[10] America is slow to enter a war, but once we decide it is right, we tend to have less regard for the criteria of fighting fairly or of stopping when we should.

Perhaps in order to be heard when they want to be careful about means, the bishops seem ready to assume that the cause of the United States will always be just. The experiences of two world wars and Korea make that readiness to give ourselves the benefit of the doubt understandable. The experience of Cuba and the Philippines, of a dozen Central American adventures, and of Vietnam, however, ought to have made it harder.

(2) In the bishops' account, there is a significant foreshortening of the history of Christian moral thought and performance. When *The Challenge of Peace* reports that there have been two Christian answers to the war question, just war theory and pacifism, this is correct as far as serious moral teaching by theologians is concerned.[11] But in the actual institutional history of the pastoral practice of the Roman Catholic communion for a millennium and a half, this report is simply false. The wars that most pastors and bishops have blessed over the centuries, in which the baptized have killed without being called to penance and have died with heroes' honors, were not the subjects of serious moral critique by church leaders or bishops. These wars did not meet the just war criteria but were supported nonetheless.

John Courtney Murray is quite right when, commenting that in recent centuries the just war theory has been honored mostly in the breach, he reminds us that the Ten Commandments are valid even when not respected. But my ecumenical question here is not whether the just war theory has integrity as a conceptual system. It is whether the hierarchy's claim to a history of conscientious compliance with an ideal moral discipline has integrity. According to the testimony of their own historians, this "compliance" is not in the record. A call to repentance would have been more convincing than the claim always to have been right.

(3) If it is clear that all-out nuclear war is inadmissible, how far down the scale does that inadmissibility reach? Is half of "all-out" still too much? One tenth? By leapfrogging first to the top of the scale, making the case for moral discipline only from the other end, most of the argument of the past forty years has skipped the discipline of careful proportionality farther down the line. *The Challenge of Peace* bypasses the question by predicting that *any* step beyond the nuclear firebreak would necessarily lead to uncontrollable escalation, so that only the all-out extremity needs to be evaluated.[12] That does not mean that proportionality reasoning is now working. A posture of apparent decisiveness at the top of the scale is thus held without needing to be precise at the lower end of the scale, where present arming, threatening, and planning are done.

(4) May you morally *threaten* to do what you may not morally do? The early discussion among the Catholic bishops assumed that the answer is "no," on the commonsense ground of the unity of intending and implementing. The third draft of the statement, however, left the question to dangle between a credible intention to do mass murder at a point determined by the enemy, and a threat expressed but not sure to be carried out, which some imprecisely call *bluff*.[13]

(5) What may be the price of clarity? *The Challenge of Peace* urges every category of persons to face their duties as citizens, politicians, professional soldiers, youth, etc., yet without spelling out firmly the consistent moral implications that should follow from just war theory in the negative case. If it is not possible to prosecute a war successfully within the constraints of just war theory, the moral obligation of political leaders is to sue for peace. If one's nation pursues a morally unacceptable policy, it is, according to the tradition, the moral duty of citizens to offer opposition and of soldiers to refuse to serve. This kind of concrete pastoral discipline is what the tradition calls for, but it is not provided by *The Challenge of Peace*.

The letter says to every category of person—youth, clergy, politicians, arms industry workers, professional military—that they should be careful, but never does it name the eventual duty of selective disobedience.[14] In that respect, the bishops fall short of the seriousness with which they had recognized selective objection in the later years of the Vietnam War. Nor is that seriousness part of *In Defense of Creation*, the Methodist letter. Even more than the Catholic letter, the Methodist one discusses declaratory national policy issues independently from those of concrete personal decision.

(6) What are the prerequisites of moral clarity? If Christians are to make effective moral decisions on matters in which the right thing to do would be to oppose their government, they would need trustworthy sources of the information on which to base such decisions. Where will we get that information in the crucial cases? For Christians to make such countercultural and unhabitual decisions with moral confidence and staying power, the decisions should not be lonely heroism—impulsive, individualistic, impressionistic—but shared. Have the bishops any notion of what structures of shared moral discernment would be needed for that really to happen, or any serious intention of creating them?

(7) Can a conditional concession be disciplined? The acceptance of deterrence by *The Challenge of Peace*[15] is based, following a phrase from a papal statement, on the claim that the deterrent threat is "not an end in itself but a step on the way toward a progressive disarmament." Is that limitation real or rhetorical? How then does one know when readiness to strike at Moscow is such a "step" and when not? The second draft of the letter had cited a statement with teeth, made in 1979 by Cardinal Krol of Philadelphia to a congressional hearing on Salt II. It stated its seriousness in the form of a concession limited

in time and in function, which would be withdrawn if the use of the deterrent *as a means to real disarmament* should not keep its promise. That statement had involved the possibility of validation or falsification based on fact. The third draft of the statement, however, abandoned that verifiable seriousness.

In sum, to take our reading from its most serious instance, the American Catholic one: the search for a morally accountable nonpacifism is making great strides. If it is to be authentically credible, however, it has a few more steps to go. The relative commonality between just war realism and principled pacifism becomes greater with every step; so does the distance between both of them and the *realpolitik* that usually passes for just war thought. We have yet to see, however, whether this evolving awareness on the part of teachers and pastors in the American Roman Catholic communion will issue in any shift in communal ethos. If so, the shift may need a stronger basis than the increased awareness of the escalation of the risks of war and the continued fine-tuning of the complexities of just war theory. It may need a basis in the discovery of other perspectives. To that we shall turn later.

Challenging the Claim to Effectiveness

As any audience in a town and a college named for one of the holy places of the beginnings of the Society of Friends should know: for several decades Friends thought that it was possible for people who love their enemies to participate effectively in the life of society. This colony began as what historians have called a "holy experiment" in administering a civil society according to the convictions of Friends.[16] There is, however, another view that became powerful among Pennsylvania Friends in the 1760s and that has dominated our conversations since then, most classically formulated for our own time a half-century ago by Reinhold Niebuhr. This view holds that there is an unbridgeable dichotomy between two kinds of morality. There is a morality of consequences, which will sometimes have to do immoral deeds, including killing, for the sake of effectiveness in the service of valuable social aims. On the other hand, there is the stance of purity or absolutes, according to which decisions can and should be made under the sway of rigid *principles* that do not calculate results. Authentic pacifism belongs in the latter category. To think it reconcilable with any concern for civil administration or social well-being is to deceive oneself and others.

A few voices have always challenged the validity of that *a priori* methodological dichotomy on grounds of logic or spirituality. But they have found little hearing in the face of the power of Niebuhr's pragmatist vision. That way of formulating the issue, however, has evoked a reformulation of the pacifist witness in terms borrowed from the adversary. It is possible to accept for the sake of discussion the consequentialist rules of debate, and then to claim under those rules that an ethic of enemy love and truth telling can effectively achieve valid national goals. This argument has been presented especially in two waves, one with and one without religious rootage.

In the 1930s, a young immigrant from India, Krishnalal Shridharani, published a book entitled *War Without Violence*. He meant it as an interpretation of the Gandhian vision in terms that Western pragmatists should be able to understand. Shridharani had studied under the guidance of Tagore and Gandhi, both of whom were running schools in the 1920s. He described the renunciation of violence—historically called *ahimsa* in the several Indian religious traditions and now affirmatively renamed *satyagraha* in Gandhi's own activism—as the outworking of a religious worldview. Yet religious rootage was not a disjunctive alternative to planned social effectiveness, as in the Western consensus cited above. Nonviolence or *satyagraha* can be described as a mode of conflict in settings where the interests of groups clash. It was compared in those days with jiu-jitsu, a mode of conflict that avoids destroying the adversary it defeats.

Recently, the Boston political scientist Gene Sharp, by no means unprecedented or alone, has become the most visible interpreter in our setting of the notion that "the politics of nonviolent action" can be effective in ways comparable to military power. One can train for it; one can develop strategies and scenarios, theories and budgets. One can learn from the many recorded experiences of nonviolent struggle over the centuries, as Sharp's own massive synthetic overview did. Its effectiveness can be compared, usually favorably, on hardnosed pragmatic grounds, with the costs and benefits of armed struggle. "Civilian-based defense" has not yet been taken on as a full-gamut national defense strategy, such that armed struggle could be renounced as a national policy. It is, however, being studied in that perspective by some of the Baltic republics. This position can learn from near approximations in the national struggles of Eastern European nations against Soviet imperial management, or by domestic uprisings against dictatorship from Manila in 1986 to Madagascar in 1990. It can be co-opted by a just war Catholic like Bernard Häring,[17] or by a pacifist evangelical like Ronald J. Sider,[18] as a way to parry the commonsense pragmatism that dominates their respective cultures without resorting to a too-rigid deontological claim.

For both Shridharani and Sharp, the Gandhian experience is the basis for a possibility claim. Sharp, of course, adds many other cases. This fits within the just war rationality in that *last resort* was always one of the just war criteria. The advocate of war cannot say there is no other recourse before weighing nonviolent alternatives.

Shridharani and Sharp, as must be the case with any bridge or synthesis position, provoke challenges from both sides. From the political-activist left or the academic-methodological right, their refusal to reject all violence on exceptionless moral grounds can be called a sellout. It can be accused of avoiding, by claiming to define them away, the hard cases on one end of the scale where martyrdom is the short-range price of deontological or principled fidelity.

On the other end of the scale, this view avoids the hard cases where, for the sake of peace, it seems that someone must kill someone. It fails to denounce the dimensions of idolatry and racism, pride and greed, in the patriotic case for war. It does not *love* the enemy to the point of suffering; it only seeks to overcome the enemy without shedding blood.

The methodological left believes consequential argument to be the only common language available. Therefore, it accuses the appeal to the power of nonviolence of trying in vain to avoid reducing argument to rational consequentialism. The power of nonviolence claims to promise pragmatic effectiveness, yet without conceding that effectiveness is the final moral standard.

From the patriotic/realist right, the promise Sharp projects—that we can achieve selfish national goals with minimal bloodshed—seems too chancy. Even if *in the long run and on the average* nonviolence is *in most cases* more likely to "work" than war, we still do not believe that it will *always* work. How about the exceptions?

Thus the jury is out on whether the transposition of the moral case against war into a pragmatic promise will convince.

Valuing Historical Accuracy about the First Century

From Tolstoy to Niebuhr, the dominant understanding of the specifically Christian case against war appealed to the directly ethical instruction that is most massively found in the Sermon on the Mount. The three antitheses in which Jesus tells his hearers not only not to kill but not even to hate, not only not to retaliate but to go the second mile, and not only to love the friend but also the enemy, have been widely taken as an intensification of the moral demand for unselfishness to a practically impossible level. This, of course, tends to heighten the power of the commonsense dichotomy I have already identified between pragmatic and principled moral reasoning. If Jesus was/is primarily a moral teacher who radicalized moral demands to a utopian extent, the rest of the modern debate follows. His call to unattainable purity writes off all concern for the shape of human society under God.

But what if that is not primarily or exclusively what Jesus was about? Both before and since Tolstoy and Niebuhr, others have seen other sides of the gospel's resources for right living and acting. Before, there were other ways in which Christians came to reject war, none of which centered on the notion of utopian purism. The first Anabaptists, the first Friends, and the first Brethren all came from somewhere else. Each of those movements had its particular renewal agenda and style, and each came to reject war without theorizing about the absolutist hermeneutics of the Sermon on the Mount.[19]

More important ecumenically may be the changes in Christian thought since Tolstoy and Niebuhr. There are new schools and movements in Scripture scholarship that are asking more pressingly about the sociological dimensions of early Christianity. The early movement was much more than a podium for unrealistic moralizing. It was a new and different society in its own right, with regard to matters of social status and ethnicity. It remembered the career of a man who, at the beginning of the Gospel accounts, was looked forward to as a national liberator and at the end was put to death as a rebel. This view wards off the interpretation of his moral teaching as utopian. The same clarification comes as well from the observation that the early Christians considered Jesus to have been a model they were following.

Thus the gospel story itself shows Jesus not as a moral purist but as a social leader. More profound, as a basis for interpreting Jesus in his wider context, is the rising respect scholarship is developing for the fact that the early Christians were Jews, and that Jews since Jeremiah believed that God had abandoned kingship and war as instruments of God's concern for justice within history. The Maccabees and Zealots with their righteous armed rebellion, and the Herodians and Sadducees in their savvy collaboration with the Romans, were tiny minorities compared to worldwide Jewry living everywhere as a powerless faith community. Jesus's pacifism was not an innovation; it was an intensification of the nonviolence of Jeremiah, Ezekiel, and the singer of the Servant passages of the book of Isaiah.

Accepting Realism about the Twentieth Century

At least since the time of Francis of Assisi and Pierre Vaudès, people have been denouncing the relationship of Christianity to political power that became dominant in the age of Constantine. Recent centuries, however, have seen a growing clarity among both religious and secular thinkers about the importance of the waning of the age of establishment. At least part of the reason for theologians' approval of war since the fourth century had been the conviction that the Christian empire was the instrument of God. That Constantinian axiom has been translated in various ways since then, so that particular nations and particular regimes have taken on that theocratic mantle.

Only very gradually and in recent generations, even in the face of the acids of modernity, have Christians begun to retrieve the vision of Christian commitment as a voluntary commitment responding to countercultural good news. This means Christian belief is a minority stance that does not take its signals from the powers that be. By no means does this dictate a critical attitude to national political purposes, but it does enable it. It undercuts the axiom that Christians must always come up with a way to defend their government, or must always give their present rulers the benefit of the doubt in defining moral issues. It re-creates the conceptual possibility that the sociologists call *sectarian*: namely, that Christians might make their moral decisions on other grounds than the assumed identification of God's purposes with their nation's well-being. It cuts the logical link between the "responsible" concern for social well-being and the need to implement that concern by taking over the rule in society. The consequentialist Constantinian logic, mandating war *because* the duty of Christians is to administer the empire, falls away when it becomes clear that we could not rule the world anymore if we wanted to.

Is War a Question of *Spirituality*?

As the ecumenical conversation obligated me to do, I have reported on the ordinary stuff of the standard debate about political ethics. That debate, however, ignores the way that other dimensions of human reality predispose the weighing of actions. *Spirituality* labels for some the weight of the more-than-rational dimensions of personal experience. For others it points toward more-than-human dimensions of moral reality. For still others it pushes us to ask about the moral import of things believers do, such as praying, or breaking bread together, or forgiving. These matters do not correlate in a one-to-one way with the sides of the debate between peace churches and mainstream churches, but they tend to be weightier on the antiwar side. I shall not pursue them further here, but they would not be ignored in an adequate review.

Hugh Barbour's exposition of the subjective religious experience of radical Puritanism in England, under the heading "The Terror and Power of the Light," interprets profoundly the rootage of the renunciation of violence in the inner experience of overpowering grace. What the Anabaptists of the sixteenth century called *Gelassenheit*, or what the early Dunkards called *perfect love*, or what frontier farmer preachers of the nineteenth century called *humility*, or what their Wesleyan contemporaries called *sanctification*, represent closely related but distinguishable labels for the view of human dignity that frees the believer from temptations to feel called to set the world right by force. Probably this commonality is more important subjectively for the peace churches' peace witness than any of the more standard ethical issues I was reviewing before.

The changes I have noted in the conversational scene are those that first come to mind, those most closely related to the classical dialectic between the peace church stance and the mainstream. There would be others, especially as the world changes: replacing the nuclear threat of the superpowers with that of rogue nations, replacing imperial outreach with the ethnic breakup of the USSR, Yugoslavia, and of smaller multicultural nations, replacing the instantaneous destruction of cities with the gradual hunting-down of peasants one village at a time that our technicians came to call "low-intensity warfare." Concerns for ecology, for the epistemological privilege of the poor, for the retrieval of indigenous cultural legacies, and for the dismantling of patriarchal cultural patterns, all have some potential for changing the shape of the conversation. At the same time, other developments continue to drive in the other direction: most notably the renewal of hostilities derived from ethnic self-understandings and reactionary appeals to religion, but also the escalating manipulative powers of money, industry, and propaganda. As far as I can see, these great changes in the dialogical setting complicate the debate since they leave some of our traditional vocabulary behind, but they do not change the basic issues.

8

Gordon Zahn Is Right

Going the Second Mile with Just War

No just war theorists have seriously responded to my argument that if the users of the tradition do not come up with a serious capability whereby responsible actors (church leaders, citizens, government officials, persons in uniform) will effectively implement a negative judgment on a particular war or a particular tactic or a particular unlawful command, the system is not credible.[1] Joseph L. Allen, in *War: A Primer for Christians*, documents with how little seriousness the tradition is taken.[2] Some challenge my right to ask the question.[3] That challenge itself is self-refuting.

The most morally serious way in which majority Christian theologians since the fourth century have tried to think about war was the slowly growing system of evaluative notions known by the intellectual historian as the just war tradition. As a disciple of Jesus Christ, I have never considered that system to be morally adequate. I have, however, considered it part of my responsibility to honor the human dignity of those who hold to it, or who at least say they hold to it.[4] I have invited them to be honest with the restraints that tradition *purports* to impose on the use of lethal force in the extreme cases in which they say conflict is inevitable.

My motives in pursuing that challenge have been multiple. If a handful of responsible actors in the realm of politics and war would refrain from abuse and would authentically respect the restraints they claim to honor, that would probably do more to save lives and to reduce conflicts than all of my own re-nunciation of personal responsibility for violence. Indeed, it would perhaps decrease killing more than all of the individuals whom my testimony might convince that all war is wrong.

But even if they refuse to hear me,[5] and to respect the restraints they are theoretically committed to, I owe it to their dignity as fellow humans, some of whom are fellow Christians, to address them in terms of their moral culture, not only of mine.[6] That readiness to make oneself vulnerable to the language world of the other, as a part of the ecumenical conversational process, is itself a minority view.[7] For many, the only honorable stance in ecumenical settings is a vigorous advocacy of the rightness of one's own orthodoxy. For me, the opposite is imperative on grounds of practicality, ethics, and spirituality.

My use of their language, taking its potential integrity more seriously than they do,[8] is a form of the second-mile response that Jesus taught and lived. I am driven not by the integrity of their position, which is what needs to be proven and which I doubt, but by the integrity of my own position, which is not dependent on results to be valid.

Another side of my multiple motivations is the wager that if I should succeed in understanding and interpreting the just war tradition at its best, it should be possible for me to state more convincingly its shortcomings, and thereby to make the case for what I consider to be the gospel alternative. I make that case not by insisting on preaching my position in its own terms (i.e., my own terms), which people who consider themselves to be "realists" have already *a priori* rejected,[9] but dialectically.[10]

When Gordon Zahn, pioneer Catholic conscientious objector, sociologist, historian, editor, and author[11] was invited by the editors of Orbis Press to contribute a blurb to their printing of the second edition of my *When War Is Unjust*, he questioned the wisdom of even seeming to ascribe legitimacy to the just war tradition:

> I have stressed its consistent record of failure over what, in theoretical presenta-tion, might be considered its promises. . . . The question remains . . . whether a doctrine, under which generations of Christians have found it possible to destroy one another in the belief that by so doing they were serving their Lord, deserves such scholarly recognition or promotion.[12]

Gordon is right. I too question the wisdom of even seeming to imply legiti-macy to the just war tradition. I too have stressed the consistent record of its failure. I too deny that just war reasoning is in fact a serious mode of morally accountable discourse. *Legitimacy* is what the debate is about. I question the doctrine's legitimacy by showing that people who say they hold to it do not in fact honor its restraints.[13]

Yet the dialectical challenge of "seeming to imply" the respectability of the convictions of the other is always at the heart of the ecumenical challenge. I do not take this position on pragmatic grounds because I have any confidence that it will convert people. My position is itself a form of the love of the enemy, turning the other cheek, affirming the dignity of the adversary, which also underlies my refusal of war.

All ecumenical conversation runs the same risk of "seeming to imply legitimacy." I converse all the time with Roman Catholics, thereby "seeming to imply legitimacy" for understandings of the papacy, or of sacraments, or of Mary, which they take for granted, although they do not express much interest in convincing me of them. I work regularly under the name and the statue of "Our Lady of the Lake," at the risk of "seeming to imply the legitimacy" of the doctrine of the Assumption, whose promulgation in 1950 was the only formal exercise of infallible papal authority since Vatican I,[14] or of the related dogma of the Immaculate Conception, formally defined almost a century earlier, even though those dogmas are not of evident existential importance to many of my colleagues.

Such *second-mile dialogical readiness* to honor the interlocutors' dignity, more than they themselves do, does not apply only in the Roman Catholic setting where I happen to have found work. I also visited often over the years, and served once as adjunct staff for a few weeks, among friends in the Geneva office of the World Council of Churches, while on record with my doubts about whether the federative conciliar model of work toward Christian unity which that institution represents since 1937[15] is the most adequate way either to express or to pursue "The Unity We Seek."[16]

Does not all serious dialogue run that kind of risk? Now that Gordon has suggested this, it occurs to me that a very helpful way to interpret the imperative of ecumenical dialogue might be to catalog the ways in which, by its very nature, ecumenical witness must "risk seeming to imply legitimacy" for the positions one rejects.[17]

One of the costs of this ecumenical readiness to converse in the powerful interlocutor's terms is the tendency to let the conversation be narrowed to ethical matters alone, at the cost of ignoring or excluding matters of spirituality and worldview.[18] Another step in the same direction is reducing ethics to consequential calculations rather than attending to other dimensions of moral discourse, such as virtues, eschatology, and divine law.

The riskiness of accepting the interlocutors' terms takes a particular form in dialogical contexts where either numerical disproportion, or something else about the cultural setting, leads one of the parties to claim to be able to include the other. It is part of the self-understanding of the churches which claim to be Catholic[19] that they are inclusive; i.e. that they can handle variety, even dissent, without losing control. Any prophetic minority voice is therefore outvoted without needing to be killed or excommunicated. Labeling it a minority position on a list of voices to be heard sometime, or even putting it on a pedestal, substitutes for listening to it seriously now. This is the theological version of what Marcuse called "repressive tolerance." Gordon Zahn and I are both repressively tolerated, and neither of us accepts being thus patronizingly overpowered and ignored at the same time.

I have been describing second-mile dialogical vulnerability as a normal way to honor an interlocutor. The strength of this call is greater if the interlocutor is, as in the crucial biblical paradigm, an actual enemy, or the heir to enmity. Jesus prayed for his executioners because "they know not what they do" (Luke 23:34). Love of enemy heightens the reason to give him the benefit of the doubt. New Testament cosmology—according to which "principalities and powers" dominate humanity yet can be made humanely useful—might well apply to the core restraining intent underlying just war thinking. If Christ is Lord, then all the components of the value-bearing cosmos, including nature and reason, together with the powers, can become the instruments of humanization. Gordon's note to Orbis suggested that the difference between us might be that he is a sociologist and I a theologian. Hardly; it is that having been born within the Roman family he is free to be a prophetic rebel, whereas I must begin with the ecumenist's benefit of the doubt.[20]

There are two further ways in which I should flesh out my agreement with Gordon Zahn's misgivings. One is to pursue further his statement that "generations of Christians have found it possible to destroy one another in the belief that they were thereby serving their Lord." As a matter of historical fact, Christians over the centuries, when they destroyed one another, were most of the time not respecting the restraints of the just war tradition. Most of the time they were not even claiming to do so. Most often they did not know there was such a tradition. There were of course theologians, in fact only a handful of them, who did elaborate the just war system theoretically, and who get quoted as landmarks.[21] There were confessors who sought to implement the tradition's restraints by means of the confessional. The primary development of the tradition through the Middle Ages was thus in canon law.[22] There were rare theologians who dared to critique their sovereigns' imperial politics on just war grounds.[23] But these voices were always outvoted. None of them projected the empirical social-science claim that soldiers were following their moral guidance. Their position had theological integrity but it was not ecclesiastically authorized, to say nothing of being enforced. No bishop, no council, no pope ratified their call for restraint.[24] What was really going on among the common folk who killed and got killed, or the barons they fought for, whether in Europe on the buildup from the Middle Ages to the Thirty Years' War, or in the Western hemisphere from Leif Erikson on, was an unstable mix of the stances which the moral logician calls "realism" and "holy war."[25]

Cases of serious restraint, exercised by political or military decision makers on just war grounds, are hard to find in the record. Historians are hard put to find a case where officials renounced a military operation that would otherwise be in their interest on the grounds that it would be unjust. John Courtney Murray was certainly right when he wrote in 1958 that in modern times, the just war tradition had never been seriously respected.[26] Since it had not been used, he said, it was not refuted on the grounds of ineffectiveness. Fair enough if by *ineffective* we mean *unsuccessful*. Yet at the same time that record refutes the claim of the just war tradition to have been the normative position on the basis of which baptized princes and their subjects made their decisions about killing.

This failure of implementation did not make the just war tradition simply irrelevant. Critics of a particular war, in the political minority, could still appeal to it to articulate their dissent. This was done by some New England thinkers who rejected the War of 1812 against Britain and by numerous critics of the war against Mexico.[27] The Scottish aristocrat David Urquhart developed a very serious case for commitment on the part of the Vatican to creating an institution in Rome that would rule on the justifications for war, pursuant to which priests would refuse absolution to men having killed in unjust wars.[28]

Critics of area bombing over Germany in World War II appealed to the tradition to give voice to dissent in British public opinion and in the House of Lords. All such restraints had already been overruled *de facto*, however, not only by "Bomber" Harris, but also by Winston Churchill and Archbishop William Temple.

We can thus say that *as a conceptual system* the just war tradition is (or would be) intrinsically capable of formulating limits that *ought logically to be able* to restrain the choices of people planning to wage war. It is capable of providing conceptual ammunition to critics of immoral tactics and strategies. It provides a checklist of relevant questions to help individuals think morally.[29] That makes it all the more important to recognize that that system *has never been seriously respected* by responsible decision makers when respecting its limits would have seriously compromised their chances of winning. It has come closest to being respected by some honest soldiers;[30] it has been taken less rigorously by most church leaders and still less by government officials.

This is one important truth about which the bishops' pastoral letter *The Challenge of Peace* of May 1983 was not clear. The bishops' report that since Ambrose and Augustine some bishops, and since the high Middle Ages some theologians, had articulated a just war argument, was not categorically false; it was, however, deceptive. It left the trusting reader with the false impression that there was a long tradition of *effective* just war discipline governing the real practice of armies. It left completely aside the prominence of the Crusades in the cultural heritage of Europe, to say nothing of the power of Machiavellian realism and religiously sanctioned ethnic pride.

There is another dimension of realism that compromises profoundly the credibility of the entire system. Call it *slippery slope* or *trigger effect*. There are those, including sober military authorities, who say that once you have freed the inherent dynamics of legitimized lethal hostility there is no way to rein it in halfway down the slope:

> All wars carry these painful errors. . . . This is the painful ransom, the inevitable ransom of war. . . . We do not linger on the causes of these unfortunate events because, in truth, there is only a single cause: War, and the only ones truly responsible are those who wanted war.

This was the French General de Larminat, responsible for the obliteration of the city of Royan (in the Bordeaux region), for no possible tactical reason, three weeks before World War II ended.[31] The British Air Marshal Sir Robert Saundby said something similar about the terror bombing of Dresden:

> It was one of those terrible things that sometimes happen in wartime, brought about by an unfortunate combination of circumstances. . . . It is not so much this or the other means of making war that is immoral or inhumane. What is immoral is war itself. Once full-scale war has broken out it can never be human- ized or civilized. . . . So long as we resort to war to settle differences between nations, so long will we have to endure the horrors, the barbarities and excesses that war brings with it. That, to me, is the lesson of Dresden.[32]

We ought to have a special label for this kind of spurious quasi-pacifist rhetoric, used retrospectively in peacetime by generals and politicians, to legiti- mize the claimed impossibility of discrimination once war has been resorted to. When a general justifies an atrocity on the grounds that there was no choice, no possible restraint, a special intensity of moral corruption is at work.

People who are not generals obviously make the same point, but readers take their rhetoric less seriously. Albert Einstein responded to a 1932 Geneva confer- ence on the laws of war, "One does not make wars less likely by formulating rules of warfare. . . . War cannot be humanized. It can only be abolished."[33]

When generals make this kind of argument it should be taken seriously by the journalists, historians, and political scientists who call themselves "real- ists" and yet who go on talking or writing as if the war-making power of great nations, including its propaganda machinery, can first be unleashed and then discriminatingly reined in.[34] The political scientist Robert Osgood has designated as particularly American the notion that being reluctant to enter a war in the first place makes our leaders more self-righteous or unrestrained once the threshold of last resort has been crossed.[35]

There is another point at which *The Challenge of Peace* did move the conversation forward. The bishops' letter built into its exposition the no- tion that pacifism and just war are complementary. Not only do they agree in rejecting unjust war; the letter interprets even the acceptance of war in just war thought as conceptually derived from a prior commitment against harming the neighbor. That presumption can be overruled, in situations that just war criteria define, so that the just war is a special, exceptional subset of the basically pacifist axioms of normal peaceable society: namely, that you should not harm people.

This presumption/exception logic is shared by the bishops' principal drafter Bryan Hehir, and by a generation of moral theologians, beginning with James Childress, Ralph Potter, and David Hollenbach.[36] The dean of Protestant just war thinkers Paul Ramsey challenged it, however.[37] Whatever we think of that point of logic, its presence in *The Challenge of Peace* represented an important innovation of both theological and political significance. The fact that pacifism, although represented by only a tiny minority within the Catholic constituency, was for the first time thus recognized as somehow legitimate,[38] counts as a powerful ratification of the witness of that minority.[39] This is amplified, of course, by the Vietnam drama, which the bishops could not pastorally afford to ignore by mere tolerant inclusion.[40]

That *The Challenge of Peace* roundly condemned indiscriminate bombing, and nuclear weapons with it, merits celebration as an index of the integrity with which the bishops applied the clearest standard just war concept.[41] Yet on the other hand, the bishops' introduction of the complementarity logic is their tribute to the integrity of people like Gordon Zahn,[42] more than it is a validation of the "teeth" of the theory.[43]

In the perspective of time since 1983, it is evident that just war tradition is losing rather than gaining ground. When urban Americans tended to see themselves as potential nuclear targets, they were ready to condemn plans for a massive nuclear war. But now that the illegitimate killing is being done by millions of land mines in poor countries, the rejection is less firm.[44]

The third way to put the challenge is to ask, "Has there ever been a just war?" The utility of the argument as a critical instrument does not depend on having a general answer to that question,[45] but the moral credibility of those who prepare for war is. The moral admissibility of systematically organizing, arming, and training large numbers of people depends on the real possibility that the killing for which they prepare may at least possibly meet the just war criteria. If most past wars have not met the just war requirements, that is not a condemnation of just war tradition as an ideal system. It *is*, however, an indictment of the political and military decision makers who failed to make it work, and *thereby* of their moral teachers, and therefore of their right to call on their citizens to make sacrifices.

If I step back from my broad skepticism to ask whether *any* cases in the record of wars *might* have fit the doctrine, the best I can think of would be Finland's defending itself against the Soviet Union in 1940.[46] But the "proof" I keep asking for, with Gordon Zahn, which is very hard to find in the litera-ture, should logically rather be the test cases that should exist on the other side of the ledger: namely, the honest decision-makers who would respect the rules in serious negative cases, and would reject the actions the rules reject when such actions would be advantageous to their side.[47] I hope I can state this refutation of the just war tradition all the more firmly because, more than Gordon, I challenge the just war system to work, despite my growing doubts about whether it was ever intended to.

Gordon concluded his comment with the suggestion that instead of my effort to make the just war work, Orbis Press might have done better to have a formal debate about the value of the tradition: "It might be well to include 'pro' and 'con' essays addressing more directly the questions of whether the tradition ever has worked and, more important, whether it is likely it could."

I am not very interested in investing more time in putting on paper again, as if it were a real debate with two equal sides, both sides arguing with equal measures of good faith. This is a conversation I have already analyzed more deeply than most people have. I know from having tested it for thirty years *from inside* that the just war tradition is not credible.[48] I don't dialogue with the just war tradition because I think it is credible, but because it is the language that people, who I believe bear the image of God, abuse to authorize themselves to destroy other bearers of that image.

9

Lisa Sowle Cahill Is Generous

Pacifism Is About Conversion and Community, Not Rules and Exceptions

Lisa Sowle Cahill's *Love Your Enemies*[1] walks through the centuries perceptively reviewing the complementary dialectic between pacifism and just war.[2] Her basic innovation in presenting the claims of pacifism is her recognition that what distinguishes pacifism from the majority view is not that it manages the dialectic of rules and exceptions differently, but that it does not do moral discourse in terms of rules and exceptions. It is this insight, seldom before so precisely formulated, that I want to honor. I want to honor it by moving on in the dialogue from the point that she has identified.

Cahill writes that Christian pacifism usually flows from an experience of Christian conversion and community rather than from a theoretical analysis of violence and nonviolence. Just war theorists often miss this point. They tend to see pacifism as an *absolute rule* against violence, the mirror image of just war thinking based on rule-based exceptions. They are not sufficiently aware that "genuine biblical pacifism does not revolve around the absolutization of any human values or rules, but around a *converted life in Christ* that subsumes and often changes every 'natural' pattern of behavior. The incoherence of pacifism and just war thinking lies, . . . most characteristically, in their disagreement about how present and accessible in human life the kingdom, by the grace of Christ, really is."[3]

I am grateful—professionally as ethicist, confessionally as participant in denominational dialogue, personally as one of the people cited and as friend and
colleague within the Society of Christian Ethics and the Catholic Theological
Studies Association—to Lisa Sowle Cahill for her discerning the inaptness of
the rule/exception mode and for her investment in naming the other mode.

She is very right in identifying a contrast of modalities, rather than a debate *within* the rule/exception game. This does not mean that in every way I
consider her formulation adequate:

(1) The bipolar conversation between just war and pacifism, which structures her entire account, oversimplifies. It gives inadequate recognition
to the other modes ("realism," "Rambo") that drive many Christians.
Cahill does take note of the Crusades, though I am not sure that she
considers them seriously to be forms of enemy love.[4]

(2) Her effort to describe generously how pacifists reason resorts to numerous not-quite-identical terms: *community, hope, conversion.* Each of
these might have more than one meaning. For example: does community
mean simply accepting a group loyalty not identical with the whole
society, or does it also mean the distinctive epistemology of dialogue in
the power of the Spirit? Does conversion only mean detachment from
the claims of the fallen world, or does it also mean sanctification and
empowerment? These three terms (with more than three meanings) are
all correct, but which is central? For me the questions are:

(a) Is Jesus confessed as Christ? That is, as fulfillment of the promise
to Israel?

(b) Is Jesus Christ confessed as Lord? That is, as key to the meaning of
history?

Incapability for Dialogue

The exception/rule modality of thought is by definition incapable of dialogue
about its own foundation; every position it looks at must be run through its
grid. It pushes any other position back to the brink of claiming "exceptionlessness," ascribing a rigor that is not there. I can't argue with or against it
in terms it can deal with other than by saying that I allow more or fewer or
different exceptions. A punctual collision once defined is hard to refute.

Nor will it do to argue that there are no exceptions. That is the line of
Finnis, etc., but it is not really clear: if there are two exceptionless rules in
conflict it must choose:

(1) That one of them after all trumps the others, and the others actually
do have exceptions; or

(2) That we can count on a nonconsequential cosmology, which will use miracle/providence and/or martyrdom to enable us to satisfy both; or

(3) That one adds a set of rules which make exceptions without avowing it; a standard maneuver like double effect, or a list of kinds of killing that by definition are not murder.

This game is well-meant but fundamentally dishonest because:

(1) It claims the high ground by positing exceptionlessness and then it affirms exceptions after all.

(2) It brings in under another name the consequentialism it had claimed to reject.

(3) It fails (like most consequentialisms) to define the coefficients used to weigh values against each other, or to test the warrants for each; especially it does not discipline selfishness in value-definition or self-centeredness in epistemology.

Not Accepting the Pattern of Exceptionlessness

Rejecting the adequacy of the rule/exception scheme means I do not accept the "exceptionless" pattern, which is not an alternative to it but one of its subforms.

I neither affirm nor deny in principle that there can be an exception; nor do I refuse to talk about it at all. I affirm that we can handle most of the agenda of ethics without hitting the walls. It is not a question of defining where the walls are, or exactly where the limits defined by rules are and where there might be an exception to the rules; it is a question of witnessing to the shape of discipleship that guides life in the center.[5]

I therefore take the argument in the other direction. I challenge the rule/exception people to show their integrity in their own terms. That means that when a rule is broken they need (for their own integrity) to show that they have a rule to govern the exception-making. This is casuistry in the normal sense. If it is honest, then the application of the rules will be capable of negating an exception that does not meet the requirement. The capacity to negate is the condition of the credibility of the system; if you cannot say "no" to an unqualified exception, you cannot justify the exception-making claim. In the absence of the capacity to negate, the rule/exception rhetoric is a cover-up for hypocrisy in the technical sense of the term, i.e., claiming a rule to whose full claims one is not in fact committed. In other words, what claims to be an accountable casuistry is in fact a slippery slope. While sliding on the slippery slope, one may still claim (a) I use the "rule" rhetoric to drag my feet as I slide down the slope; or (b) I confess the sinfulness of the complicity I cannot refuse.

If I do not utterly refuse rule/exception reasoning, but deny its tyranny, centrality, and priority, what do I then do?

(1) I refuse to center on exception-making as a way to test moral claims;
(2) I refuse to let the discussion of exception-making, as a methodological issue in its own right, become a priority discussion (apart from particular real ethical collisions), as occurred in the high scholastic casuistic debates about probabilism, probabiliorism, tutiorism, etc.
(3) I refuse to institutionalize ahead of time the provision for the actions justifiable only as exceptions; i.e., I do not prepare institutionally for violent self-defense. Not preparing for the far-out exception will decrease considerably the likelihood of its ever happening. If you don't regularly carry a gun you avoid a lot of hard decisions about when to use it.
(4) I refuse to bypass the questions about warrants, coefficients, and egoism mentioned above—in discussing well-meant but fundamentally dishonest games.

Against Consequentialism (and Decisionism or Punctualism)

I will argue against consequentialism because it is a subset of *decisionism* (also called *quandaryism* or *punctualism*). It asks what action in the moment of decision, or the point of decision, or in a moral quandary, will have the best consequences. Decisionism falsifies the calculation of the real consequential stakes:

(1) Decisionism's self-centered point of view or perspective screens out many dimensions/angles of the truth.
(2) Decisionism's self-centered value criteria undervalue the common good in its many dimensions:
    (a) It undervalues the *breadth* of reality: other people's interests, family solidarity, promises made to them, institutional dimensions of the decision process.
    (b) It undervalues the *depth* of moral reality: the dimensions of spirituality, of worldview, of human ontology (new birth, sanctification).
    (c) It undervalues *length* of moral reality: past experiences, habituation, tradition, virtues, and future hopes and objectives.
(3) Decisionism tilts the decision situation against costly and paradoxical modes of decision:
    (a) A mother naturally sacrifices for her child, a soldier for his country.
    (b) Bearing the cross, according to the New Testament, is not the heroic exception but a normal component of fidelity in a hostile world.

(c) Heroic martyrdom is honored by the military.

(d) The power of innocent suffering in the writings and practices of Gandhi and King is a matter of faithful commitment, not consequentialist calculation.

(4) Decisionism places ethics (self-critical analysis) above ethos; it tests not by concretizing but by generalizing.

None of these perspectives, which decisionism undervalues, is unconcerned for consequences. Rather, each of them locates the consideration of consequences within a larger setting where the other dimensions come first and set the tone before weighing the case for the exception.

Those who say that consequential "proportional reasoning" is sufficient all by itself, and who make "Is there an exception?" the first question rather than the last, wrongly ascribe to others a rigidity of means versus ends, or a principled disregard for consequences. Nondecisionist consequentialism (with breadth, length, depth, and paradox) is not less concerned for proportionate reasoning, but rather more richly so.

Effective Peacemaking Practices

The Case for Proactive Alternatives to Violence

10

The Science of Conflict

Some of the analysis that needs to be brought to bear upon the problem of war is "theological" in the narrow sense.[1] We need to ask about Scriptures and tradition, about how the will of God is revealed and interpreted within the community of faith. We need to review how Christians have differed about those issues in ways that must be studied in their own terms.

It is no less the case, however, that debates about moral theology intersect with other debates about human nature and the shape of society. We cannot discuss theology without interlocking with the human sciences that study the same phenomena from other perspectives. The believer says that faith in Jesus Christ makes love of the enemy imperative and possible. Could not a psychologist describe and measure this? If love leads one to go out and make peace with one's adversary, could not a sociologist describe this event? When a preacher claims "Violence is always self-defeating,"[2] is that not a claim that a historian could verify or refute? As we flesh out the realism of the message of reconciliation, it is therefore appropriate, even imperative, that we attend to those other disciplines. There is no room here for the kind of dualism that would avoid such cross-references on the grounds that they would represent unbelief or a confusion of categories.

Sociological Attention to Conflict

People of pacifist convictions have done some of the scholarly research in this area. They have demonstrated that renouncing violence does not mean abandoning concern for the course of events.[3] Other researchers are quite independent of this particular ideological commitment.[4] They merely see conflict processes as an especially challenging object of sociological analysis.

The beginnings of sociology as an empirical science tended to use models of stability or equilibrium. They compared a healthy society to a human body with every organ working well, or to a peaceable village with everyone in his or her place, or to a balanced market with all needs being met. They interpreted society as an organism, so constituted as to seek to restore its balance when it had been distorted. Social changes were then thought of as corrective responses to disequilibrium, tending to restore the balance which some outside force or internal weakness had jeopardized. That approach had its values.

Increasingly, however, social observers of all philosophical schools are finding it more constructive and instructive to describe disequilibrium and conflict as realities in their own right, rather than as a mere phase along the way to restored balance. That way we see how every society has numerous centers of decision and initiative, including numerous definitions of what healthy equilibrium would be.

A parallel development in the kinds of analysis and skills needed for interpreting and guiding social service and political action has gone hand-in-hand with this realism about conflict in sociology as a descriptive science. Here too it is more appropriate to say that a conflict needs to be "managed" in a way that takes account of the valid interests and the human dignity of all parties.[5] This is more realistic than maintaining the heuristic vision of a peaceable order that has almost been established, and that only needs to be defended against the resistance of some who would disturb it.

This shift from models of organic unity to models of intergroup conflict has several values for peace theology. It points toward responses to threat or injustice that can be more effective and more economical in settings where it was thought in the past that violence was the only possible recourse. To say it in the terms of the old just war tradition: even when a cause is just and the authority pursuing it is legitimate, violence is justified only when it is in reality the last resort. Therefore, if we see that serious alternative instruments of change toward greater justice are available and had not been noticed, it changes the fundamental structure of the moral issue.

Images of the social organism as a body needing to have but one will, implemented from above, as a matter of policy, are especially congenial to solutions that endanger the rights of individuals and minorities. They reach quickly for coercion in the defense of "peace" as they define it. By contrast, seeing society as comprising diverse groups with divergent interests—many of them justified, some more valid than others, some unworthy, and others impossible—is more congruent with the biblical vision of the people of God in a hostile world. Christians abandoned the realistic biblical vision in the fourth century, much to their loss, because they began to believe that the kingdom of God could best be served by blessing the "peace" made by Caesar.

Not only is this picture of society as conflictual more realistic; it also helps us overcome the isolation of theology from the social world. Too long the Christian doctrines of reconciliation and forgiveness have been thought of as applying to estrangement between God and the soul, but as relevant only very indirectly to estrangement between God's creatures.

The biblical witness gives us the language of reconciliation, but it should not be understood in a sentimental or wooden way. A process of conflict resolution has not failed if one of the parties is less than joyful and wholehearted in accepting a more just arrangement. Often, accepting a more just solution takes time, as one sees the new arrangement working better. Conflict management thinkers like Saul Alinsky and activists like Danilo Dolci rightly warn against our being so preoccupied with the inner authenticity of the adversaries' "conversion" that we reject positive ameliorative steps short of perfection.[6]

The simplest Christian access to the discipline of processing conflict as a visible social activity is the guidance given by Jesus to his disciples: "If your brother sins against you, go and tell him his fault, between you and him alone" (Matt. 18:15). The intent of reconciliation is served, not denied, by the most direct confrontation. If need be, the circle can widen: "If he does not listen, take one or two others along with you" (Matt. 18:16). The intent is not victory but restored wholeness and common commitment. The passage does not speak of measuring the wholeheartedness of the person's compliance.

Conflict Resolution and Conflict Management

Creative study and theory in conflict resolution as a social science is interdisciplinary. It creates connections beyond the several provinces of traditional academic specialization. Kenneth Boulding, founder of *The Journal of Conflict Resolution* and of the center at the University of Michigan that published it for a generation, was an economist of very broad competence. Anatol Rapoport and Pitrim Sorokin contributed as sociologists of the more philosophical European school. Elise Boulding, Clagett Smith, and James Laue are American sociologists. Adam Curle, who pioneered in developing procedural analysis of how interactions go about "making peace," began as a teacher of teaching. Gene Sharp, whose *Politics of Nonviolent Action*[7] marks the second generation of such studies, submitted that work as a dissertation in the realm of political science. Other contributions come from social psychology.

The work of these researchers has found rootage in public and private universities and research institutes, linked in the International Peace Research Association, the Peace Studies Association, and in North America by the Consortium on Peace Research, Education, and Development. Like any young discipline, it is marked by hot debates about its limits and its methods, about the relations between scientific honesty and technical competence on the one hand and value commitments on the other. Here I can sample only a few of its *fruits*.

Historians' Study of Conflict Prevention

Our capacity to understand who and where we are is conditioned by our understanding of how we got here. Thus a revision of sociology means a revision of history. The renewal of the future demands a revision of the past. The simplest way to do that, but usually not the most productive, is simply to retell our history from the other side. After every war the winners write the history books for the next generation. Later the grandchildren of the victims, or third parties, will find the evidence, if the archives have not been destroyed, for seeing things the other way. So we get underdog history and irredentist history. Thus the 1990s have been marked by multiple revisions of the history of the 1940s.

Yet that kind of revision may still be a part of the old game of telling history as the story of battles, with the writing serving to justify one's own party, so that the battle for sovereignty is in part the battle for the power to interpret events.

A more fundamental revision will not merely illuminate the same questions from the other side but will ask other questions. Instead of chronicling mostly how ruling dynasties clashed over borders and the right to tax, we might ask how parents raised their children to get along with each other and with their neighbors. Instead of combing with ever-greater finesse the documents produced by literate minorities, we might ask how the sages of pre-literate societies communicated the historical depth of their civilizations to their grandchildren. We may find that fluctuating water tables, or rat populations, or mutations in microbes, or the discovery by some blacksmith of a new way to sharpen a pruning tool or shape a plow might make more difference to the quality of ordinary human existence than did the battles about which ruling family should have the right to tax and to punish.

Conventional historiography of violence has often focused on what armies have done. This teaches us that the fate of a nation is in the hands of its army. Now, however, a historiography of the community structures of ordinary people looks for—and therefore finds—other kinds of facts. It teaches us that most of the quality of human communities depends upon the ways they have found to *limit* violence rather than to legitimate it. It shows that truly foundational values are seldom served by those who claim to serve them with the sword.

Tolstoy said long ago that progress in history was made by the persecuted. If children grow to fruitful adulthood, if fields are cultivated in a way that preserves fertility, if carefully coordinated labor achieves large goals, it is because ways have been found to hold violence to a minimum. Finding those ways is the object of sociology and psychology. There are better ways and worse ways to handle conflict. The differences can be studied. We can generalize from them, extrapolate from them. This is a descriptive science, challenging the best intelligences to observe and analyze.

The actual management of conflict is a skill, or an applied science, derived from those insights. In a healthy society it may also be a vocational specialization. Working between small groups as in family disagreements, or between medium-sized groups as in urban neighborhood conflicts, skilled professionals are achieving impressive results.

Nonviolent Direct Action and Civilian Defense of Democracy

On a larger scale, the study of conflict management merges into analyzing nonviolent direct action as in the thought of Gandhi and King.[8] On a still larger scale, on the level of international peacekeeping or international conflicts, or the defense of the national values of peoples without state sovereignty, the search is in its infancy; yet there is every reason to expect that the lessons will be similar.

It is a scientifically and therefore theologically realistic projection to suggest this: in the long run, the defense of values that people assumed could be protected only by lethal violence will be seen to be defended more economically and less destructively by nonviolent means. Thus the demonstrable advantage of nonviolent means is growing, while the destructiveness of weapons is increasing at a much greater pace, and the controllability of those weapons is diminishing.

Commander Sir Stephen King-Hall of the British Royal Navy, editor of a specialists' newsletter and lecturer in military science for the Army and Navy War Colleges, may have been the first expert to say clearly how Hiroshima had changed his world. In his *King-Hall Newsletter* for August 16, 1945, he wrote of the first two atomic bombs: "those two bombs . . . may have been and I think will prove to have been the last explosions of consequence in the history of large-scale war. Total war—large-scale national war—is at an end. . . .Total War . . . has made political and economic nationalism a meaningless thing and so Total War has abolished itself."

This statement was not idealism: it was pure, pragmatic military science. If the likely effect of the use of your weapons is to destroy yourself, there is no context in which their use can be justified. But King-Hall went on from that negation to a set of affirmations about how the Western democracies might defend their values nonmilitarily. He called it *psychological warfare*, but he did not mean by that any kind of manipulation or deception. He meant that the foundational social values of free and open communication, popular initiative, noncooperation with evil laws and administrations, and shared social values should work in defense of the democratic system, rather than suspending such values for a time in order to defend those democratic values. Beginning with Gene Sharp's studies of the power of organized nonviolent action, the anecdotal record of scores of similar actions from the past can be synthesized inductively into usable patterns for future tactical creativity.

In weighing the claims routinely made for necessary violence, the first logical demand is for a rational assessment of the evidence that counts as proof of what can and cannot be done. An example: since the Sharpeville massacre of 1971, in which some seventy demonstrators were killed, the rhetoric of the armed wing of the African National Congress says that "nonviolence has been tried and has failed"; yet no one uses the same standards to measure the many more lives sacrificed by violent means. The Hungarian resistance of 1956, the Czech resistance of 1968, and the Solidarnosc movement of the l980s all took off spontaneously; yet their critics compare their effectiveness with the power of adversaries profiting from long-range planning, staffing, equipping, training, financing, and celebrative legitimation. As Gene Sharp said (yet again—he had already been saying it in less dramatic settings) after Manila's February revolution,

> In the past, most nonviolent struggles have been improvised, without large-scale preparation or training. Thus they may be [merely] prototypes of what could be developed by deliberate efforts. It seems certain that a combination of scholarship and preparation could make future nonviolent struggles much more effective. It is possible that this technique could become a full substitute for violence in liberation struggles and even for national defense.

What Sharp's "Program on Nonviolent Sanctions in Conflict and Defense" at the Harvard Center for International Affairs continues to elaborate anecdotally and theoretically is the theme of the sciences of the management and resolution of conflict, which I have been describing as new branches of sociology and of psychology. What Sharp meant by "preparation" might have been anything from his own War College lectures to the creation of "Peace Brigades" for foreign intervention:

> The presence of a body of regular World Guards or Peace Guards, intervening with no weapons whatsoever between two forces combating or about to combat, might have considerable effect. . . . As an example, if a few thousand of such World Guards had been parachuted into Budapest during the five or six days Hungary was free, the outcome of that struggle might have been quite different.

Or it might mean the training of domestic populations in resistance techniques for the eventuality of a hostile armed invasion. Between the "study" and the "preparation," what might be the most needed would be another set of resources on intermediate levels: the development of community structures, value consensus, living patterns, movement literatures and celebrative styles, particular stories, confessional identities, etc. These are matters that Sharp avoids, not wanting to be accused of unscientific pacifistic special pleading. They are not matters that we need to avoid in our study of Christian ethics and of the Christian contribution that might be made to the wider social process. *If* we have not attended to these possibilities, we not only cannot claim to be in the situation of last resort; we are delinquent with regard to the specific contribution that ought to be the specialty of communities of faith.

From his wide knowledge of the science and politics of the arms race, Freeman Dyson has drawn a modestly promising interpretation of how the virtue of hope might lead us past the tragic impasse as we have defined it. Dyson is one of the most perceptive interpreters of the impact of the nuclear age as a global cultural phenomenon. The very same close reading of the intractability of the polarized world, which makes it look tragically insoluble in Dyson's initial description, on further attention opens the scene to a more flexible, more patient, ultimately more promising grasp of the same hard facts. That vision includes some attention, though less spelled-out than Sharp's, to the potential of nonviolent resistance, and (partly following George Kennan) to the potential of nonnuclear resistance.

United Nations Peacekeeping

One reasonable way to test the thesis that the moral case against violence can be translated into terms understandable in the civil community would be to ask soldiers under the constraints of military obedience to obey rules that forbid them to use their weapons. This can be done: the command not to shoot can be explained, and trained soldiers can obey it even at the cost of some risk, just as they can be asked to run other risks in fighting according to the rules or in obeying any other command. This has been happening, off and on, under United Nations auspices. Interposition of buffer forces, for a while in Zaire, in the Sinai, in Cyprus, has in general been very effective. They do not win wars or impose peace: they can and do maintain the distance between hostile camps willing to be held apart long enough for a peace process to begin again. UN peacekeeping forces in these locations have been able to keep hostile camps separate precisely because of the consistency with which they hold to the commitment not to shoot, even if armed. As Brigadier Michael Harbottle and Dr. Rosalyn Higgins unfolded the lessons to be learned from the Cyprus experience, "The UN's record in containing hostilities has been a good one." Such holding operations do not replace the properly political and economic tasks of bridge building for which they gain the time, but they do less damage than does anything else that people might do under the same circumstances. They do it by finding it quite possible to impose restraints on the use of violence even much stricter than those of just war theory, within the chain-of-command ethos that works for the military, and in so doing to increase the chances of peace.

International Networks of Interdependence

Next we turn to the vision of an alternative political theory. Janice Love, a political scientist named by the United Methodist Church as delegate to the World Council of Churches, which in turn named her to its Central Committee, expressed her appreciation of the Methodist bishops' statement *In Defense of Creation*. She called attention to the work of several of her colleagues in the discipline of political science who see their discipline as not only a descriptive but also a normative science. Following her suggestions, we may take the studies of Robert Johansen, the first writer whom she recommends, as representing a beginning school or a trend in political science. Johansen does with disciplinary generalities something like what the UN "blue line" had begun to do gradually with soldiers, or what Dyson was doing with the nuts and bolts of social psychology. Johansen's major book *The National Interest and the Human Interest* explodes the uncritical assumption that only the most amoral or selfish definition of *national interest* is "realistic." Any definition of "interest" includes components of the "self" in question, which are never without moral or normative dimensions. To see that the "self" of the nation is but part of the larger human community's self-interest is not idealism but a deeper realism, which Johansen spells out in full disciplinary detail. From his perspective, by challenging a too-narrow concept of national interest, Johansen is able to illuminate the specific alternatives to war as a global system. In his 1978 pamphlet *A Proposal for an Appropriate Security System*, and in his 1983 update entitled *Toward an Alternative Security System: Moving from the Balance of Power to World Security*, he projects a possible path from the present nonsystem of mutual menaces to an authentic system of reciprocal interdependency. He describes a doable process of depolarization and transnationalization, beginning from where we are, bringing down to earth the moral power of the world federalist vision, without its visionary thinness.

Janice Love then proceeded beyond her sympathetic recommendation of Johansen to a yet more basic critique of her own, attending to the ways in which the military assumptions of our culture are specifically masculine. For our world, that analysis convinces. Yet much of the alternative orientation that in our setting is called "feminist" would from farther away be simply "Christian." As "positive feminine values" Janice Love's contemporary analysis names "cooperation, caring, equality, fairness, love, and the affirmation of diversity." The New Testament describes such values as part of participation in the nature and work of Jesus, no less mandatory for men than for women.[9]

Aggressivity in Human Nature

Two questions arise in the disciplines of psychology and sociology when more attention is given to conflict resolution. In the sociological field there is the challenge of interpreting the place of aggressivity as a basic component of our nature, which we share with other animals. In psychology *aggressivity* is also the word used to denote an ambivalent component of our behavior. Recent research in zoology and anthropology has extended that approach to human nature, accentuating the continuity between us and the rest of the animal kingdom, especially the other primates. Scientists derive characteristics from the study of other animals that are then projected into human nature to throw light on some shared characteristics.

The scientist whose name is most prominently associated with the development of this subdiscipline is the Austrian zoologist Konrad Lorenz, followed by a wide range of zoologists and zoologically inclined anthropologists publishing since the 1960s. Lorenz described "aggressiveness" as a mark of all the kinds of animals that one can study. A defensively intended aggressivity is socially necessary. Animals do not attack each other randomly, but they do attack one another at certain points. Those points are the borders of their "territories," where each animal defends its "turf." This is not an imperialistic drive, but a necessary defense. Some of the higher primates do try to extend their turf, but generally the intent of aggressivity is not imperial. There is a defensive aggressiveness built into social animals, which contributes to survival, according to a Darwinian understanding of viable animal nature. Then one extends that same observation to humans. You say that war is a natural expression of something that is unavoidably part of what it means to be an organism that evolved out of the earlier history of the animal kingdom. Fighting is our nature; why fight it?

Some people draw antipacifist conclusions from this line of argument, saying that the notion of reconciliation and the notion of a wider human community, the idea that you could learn from your mistakes, or from your faith, or from Christian education, to turn the other cheek, are counter to nature and therefore bad or sick.

Others derive alternative conclusions from the same data, saying this just tells us more about the shape of the problem we have. What we need to do is to find ways to channel our aggressiveness in nondestructive patterns. This part of our nature can be sublimated, or guided fruitfully, so that it will apply to other adversaries rather than each other, and be used for other causes than just defending our own turf. We can then accept this reading of the human constitution and still not be driven fatally away from the ability to relate nonviolently.

With regard to conflict viewed sociologically, I already said that the answer of the Christian peace message is not to dichotomize or to reject "worldly wisdom," but to incorporate all reasonable insight in the promise of global reconciliation. Similarly, for this animal/anthropological vision, we must say that it cannot ultimately be alien to the peace for which God made us. Some components of basic animal aggressivity may be seen as fallen or destructive; others can be viewed as fundamentally wholesome and ready to be used in giving power and structure to the renewal of human community. There is nothing to fear in the encounter with improved information on this dimension of human nature.

The other cross-disciplinary challenge relates to the psychological disciplines. Aggressiveness is a part of the constitution of the individual person, as seen by personality theory or the counseling professions. A person who has no aggressive will is a sick person. You must be self-affirming. You must therefore push at the borders between your personality and the neighbor's. If you completely internalize your mother's pressures on you to be nice, and to give in, and not to offend people, this will in the long run keep you from growth into responsible maturity. Too much emphasis at the wrong time on giving in to others and loving your enemies is psychologically dangerous. It will undercut the growth of normal, wholesome self-affirmation.

It is possible to interpret a nonviolent ethical commitment in a way that makes it contradictory to wholesome personality development. Even more may this occur if the preferred term is *nonresistance*, as used by Tolstoy, Garrison, Ballou, and some Mennonites. Obviously it then becomes possible for teaching about the moral imperative of nonresistance to have a stultifying effect on the development of an adult sense of self. But does it need to have that effect? I cannot see why it should. Certainly there will be situations of conflict where to be consciously nonresistant, to say nothing of being actively nonviolent in a purposive way, will require more personality, more self-awareness, more self-control, more self-understanding, and more self-acceptance, than just to run along impulsively with a conflict that has been structured for you in a brutal way.

As we have seen in the sociology of conflict and also in the anthropology of aggressivity, the disciplines concerned with the psychic wholeness of the person should also be welcome allies in elaborating a theological perspective on peace among humans. There is no clash between psychic wellness and love of enemy. To love the enemy is not masochism or self-hatred but the widest kind of self-acceptance, the most inclusive way to receive one's self as a gift from God and to share that selfhood with one's fellow creatures who are no less loved and gifted by God.

11

Creation, Covenant, and Conflict Resolution

In previous chapters, I have chronicled cultural changes within Christian moral thought on two levels:[1]

(1) We have observed rising levels of Christian thinkers' concern about war, as they have been provoked by the facts of the arms race and as the uncontrollable destructive potential of present strategic assumptions has become more visible. Part of the reaction, we saw, is mere pragmatic survivalist realism, in the face of the danger of self-destruction. Part of it is also pastoral moral realism, seeking to retrieve the potential of the justifiable war tradition.[2]

(2) We have noted briefly how new initiatives from the gospel have bypassed the old paths: for example, Tolstoy's Jesus, Gandhi's truth power, and King's dream. We have seen the praxis of hope in the authority of the incarnation beginning to bear unprecedented fruit, enabling a different angle on the interface between faithfulness and effectiveness.[3]

Our next step is to move behind reporting on current events to identifying their possible import for the logic of Christian moral discourse. You might say that I will be seeking to illuminate the current changes in thinking about war from the vantage point of a basic question of how to reason morally; you might also say it the other way around. Which of those you prefer may be a matter of taste, or it may be generational. Whichever way we prefer to say it, we shall seek now to look past the war question to some of the perennial issues raised by the ways we have been taught to reason morally.

The academic technicians among us will call these questions of methodology in moral discourse. Yet the rest of us reason more or less the same way: we just call it common sense, or think it self-evident.

Creation and Covenant

Just over a half century ago, Reinhold Niebuhr laid down the ground rules that have since dominated American debate in social ethics. At the time, he called his own view *realism* or *tamed cynicism*, over against views which he had previously held and which he now began to call *idealistic*. Niebuhr had begun his argument as a midcourse correction within his own liberal Protestant establishment, but then he went on to retrieve older underpinnings that had been sustaining Western thought ever since Luther, or Augustine, or Paul. It is those older underpinnings, a dominant account of the shape of moral epistemology, with which we must here come to grips.[4]

As I indicated by using classical terms in this chapter's title and this paragraph's subtitle, what is at stake here is by no means only the moral issue of war, although in modern Protestant experience it has been especially around the war issue that it was brought back into focus. The question bears on all of Christian morality, and in fact on all of Christian identity.

Ernst Troeltsch described the debate down through Christian history as a debate between two concepts of the law of nature. One of them means by *nature* the way things *should* be, according to the original divine intention. The other means the way things *really* are when you go out to look. The former sees nature as forbidding slavery, challenging private property, transcending tribalism, and excluding war. The latter takes things as they are, and accepts all four.

H. Richard Niebuhr, Troeltsch's American interpreter, restated the same tension in terms of a difference of priority between knowledge attributed on the one hand to God as Father, whose will is accessible to us in the orderliness of creation and known to reason, and on the other hand knowledge attributed to "Christ," whose way is revealed in the particularity of Jesus, seen in the work of redemption.[5]

Troeltsch and the brothers Niebuhr are merely rephrasing a far older, even classical structural question. They rephrase the question in their own slightly different but essentially parallel ways, but each is asking a classical question. The classical question is about the tension between two contrasting approaches to knowing the will of God.

One side of the tension claims to be rooted in the orders of *creation*. It counts on a basically manageable epistemological scene. The world "out there," as anyone can observe, still bears for us the revelation of what God wills that we should be and do.[6] We can know this by our human reason, though we are fallen and our reason is marred by sin. It is accessible and credible to all reasonable persons.

The social demands of that divine will, being known from within things as they are, cannot be radically discontinuous with present arrangements. The major movers of human affairs, evidently, are the nation-state and the marketplace. Within the given framework it would be wrong to tell people to hope for salvation: there can be relative healing, preservation, consolidation of the social order in its own terms by its own means.[7] But there can be no fundamental change. There are no resources for change—no criteria, no perspectives, no strength—from beyond the system's own intrinsic potential. Salvation, then, belongs in a realm qualitatively other; whether that other realm be discerned in the sacraments, in the hereafter, in personal self-acceptance, or "before God."

What makes a moral position or decision *Christian*, by this account, is not substance but form. It is not that it is "right" in any original way. Only natural reasonableness can determine that. What makes a position Christian according to this account is the provincial theology, the subcultural setting, the denominational affiliation, or the piety of the agent, not anything specifiable or significant that could be said about the action or the reasons for it.

From this perspective nothing is less acceptable than the notion that Christian moral truth might be *particular*, known, and validated first in some other way than by public consensus.

The other side of the tension I will designate as rooted in *covenant*. "How odd of God," the dictum ran, "to choose the Jews." That gracious oddity which we call *covenant* or *election* represents an irreducible surd in the face of a worldview claiming the authority of nature and reason. It is as irreducible for rational discourse as the existence of Jewry since Jeremiah has been among the nations.[8]

The Christian cipher for the particular is *evangel*: gospel, good news. Functionally defined, good news bears something new, or news about a particular occurrence that was not known previously by natural law because it had not occurred previously.[9] It is an event about which it is fitting to speak of news: something new has happened. For that we turn to the Scriptures, and to the gospel or good news about Jesus of Nazareth, Lord and Savior. The gospel does not avoid conflict; it is full of conflict, and it faces conflict head-on.

Conflict Avoidance and Conflict Resolution according to the Gospel Covenant

Conflict is a part of all human experience, and yet we tend to prefer not to deal with it directly.[10] There are some good reasons for fearing conflict.

There are societies in which conflict has a very important part in the way decisions are made, and it works out destructively. Some groups are constantly at war with each other, to the disadvantage of both. Some cultures provide for ritual conflict between representatives of different groups, as in the duel. In some societies it is by destroying competitors that a leader becomes a leader. A certain readiness to honor the self-sufficient leader, even the brutal "strong man," the *caudillo*, may be found in many cultures. Conflict is enjoyed ritually. It is praised as ennobling. The outsider, the enemy, has no rights. These uses of conflict are destructive—physically destructive when the violence is physical and psychically destructive when the violence is psychic. Since decisions are made on the basis of power rather than of truth or fact-finding, the decisions reached are often not for the best welfare of all the parties involved.

The gospel adds to the pressure against letting decisions be made by battles. The gospel tells us to ask about what is true instead of about who is strongest. We are instructed to love our enemies, and to accept persecution or abuse without complaint. We appeal to the model of Jesus himself, who suffered unjustly because of his love for those who wished to destroy him. This is true, we confess, because God wants to pay the price so that no one, not even the most evil and unworthy, should perish. Christians affirm that in the power of the Spirit, quiet truth may prevail. Christians understand the social value of peace and order as the basis for personal wholeness and social productivity. So it should be no surprise that some Christians believe that avoiding conflict is a universal imperative. They believe that one should resolve any clash either by giving in, or by indirect ways of getting things decided.

So the analyses of personality and of society have come to speak of *conflict avoidance* as a particular pattern of behavior. Some believe it is a Christian duty, the same thing as loving our neighbor. Others criticize it as unwholesome, and as condoning social ills. This danger arises especially in two situations:

(1) Some believe that Christians should place such a high value on social peace, or order, that to avoid its being troubled by conflict we should be willing to accept the continuation of unjust and oppressive arrangements in society. Other times, the effect of conflict avoidance is that decisions are postponed, or that they are made invisibly.

(2) For others, the abhorrence of conflict is for use on the small-group or personal level. The individual seeking to be gentle and to avoid offense may bottle up emotions, may leave important arguments unstated, and may accept destructive humiliation and deprivation.

In both of these cases, the spiritual foundation of the Christian's willingness to suffer has been lost sight of, and conflict avoidance has become an end in itself rather than a servant. Against this danger we need to be warned.

It is therefore important that our subject here is the *resolution* of conflicts, not their avoidance.

(3) Still another tactic of conflict avoidance is what we sometimes justify as *tolerance* or *pluralism*. We call someone else's position or action a "difference of opinion" rather than an offense, thus releasing ourselves from the duty and privilege of reprimand and reconciliation.

Without retracting the gospel's judgment on the wrongness of ritual and destructive conflict, we need to restate the rightness of conflict of some kinds in some circumstances. While much that needs to be said here is not true only for Christians, I shall be speaking first of all as a Christian and in a Christian context.

It may be helpful to remind ourselves of one particular debate of central importance for the early Christian church. It is directly described in Acts 15 and Galatians 2, with indirect echoes at other points as well.[11]

The early Christian community had to face the question of whether or not a Jewish lifestyle was imperative for Gentile believers in Jesus. The reason the issue arose was the success of the early Jewish Christian mission.

Conflict is a sign of life and growth; it is inevitable because in any living organism, and especially in an organism like the church that is charged by the Lord with proclaiming a message, new persons will be encountered and new questions will need to be resolved, not by accident or by default but by the nature of the case. Not all conflict is the result of successful mission or creative cultural growth; defensive societies and contracting cultures can also have conflict. It is a sign of life in most cases, however, and a source of life when correctly handled.

Conflict is provoked by God's righteousness. Not all conflict is between people who have irreconcilable selfish interests, or between right and wrong. Yet often the form a conflict takes, and the degree of urgency of its resolution, are linked with issues of morality or interest, where there needs to be a reprimand, or a demand for change. The prophets of God and the prophetic community in our time proclaim the wrongness of sin. They proclaim the demands of the kingdom of righteousness, which cannot be separated from a negative judgment upon unrighteousness and disobedience. This kind of conflict cannot be avoided except by unfaithfulness to the proclamation of the righteousness of God. Yet what the God of the gospel does with the unrighteous is not the same as in the age of Saul or of Joshua. God's intention is not destruction but repentance and restoration. God takes upon God's self the costs of that restoration, through costly means, which neither sell short the demands of justice nor exact from the unrighteous the price of their sin.

Jesus is the prophet proclaiming that greater righteousness in whose light we all stand condemned. He is also the priest bringing the acceptable sacrifice that works our reconciliation. And he is the king who establishes a new order. Which of these aspects of the work of Jesus, as of ours, do not call forth conflict?[12] But in each, the end and the means are not ratifying our rightness, nor our victory, but the justification of the godless, the forgiveness of sins, and the creation of a new people.

So what did the believers in Acts do when they discovered a difference of conviction about whether the Gentiles needed to keep all the law? They faced the issue, rather than hiding it or postponing it. Those whose work had raised the issue—Paul, Barnabas, and their supporters at Antioch—went more than halfway to enable a conversation. They told what God had been doing as they saw it. Others, like Peter, also recounted their experiences. They listened to one another until there was nothing more to say. Then James, the mediator, the conservative peacemaker, proposed an arrangement well calculated to resolve the original offense. They confessed that that conclusion—reasonable and practicable compromise as it was—had been given them by the Holy Spirit. The other biblical guidance for conflict is in Jesus' words. "If your brother sins against you," he says simply, "go and tell him his fault, between you and him alone. If he listens to you, you have gained your brother" (Matt. 18:15). Thus the scriptural method for dealing with conflict on the personal level is direct, personal confrontation, with readiness to forgive. The apostle Paul describes the same procedure thus: "You who are spiritual should restore him in a spirit of gentleness" (Gal. 6:1).

There is *also* scriptural provision for conflict on the level of powers and institutions. Believers are called to refuse to participate in evil patterns of life. Then it was called *nonconformity to the world* or *refusing to be unequally yoked*. Today we would call it *noncooperation*, or perhaps *civil disobedience* or in some cases *boycott*. There is public denunciation of evil, as the prophets often did.

12

Conflict from the Perspective of Anabaptist History and Theology

We have been taught that conflict is bad.[1] I do not intend to challenge the correctness of this sweeping summarization as a description of American culture, American Christian culture, or American Mennonite culture, as we could empirically observe it.

Yet we would learn more by challenging it. It would be worthy of much more study if we could determine exactly what is meant, and what is not, by the prevalence within our culture of this axiom, "Conflict is bad." Does it apply to all kinds of conflict? What elements of our personal and social life is it meant to apply to? What does "bad" mean? Where does the idea come from? How is it taught to us?

I do not plan to project such an analysis here. I merely say it would be fruitful, and that it should not be taken for granted that we know the answer to these questions, or that the answers are what they might immediately seem to be.

It suffices for my present purpose to point out that that assumption that conflict is bad does not come from Jesus or the Anabaptists. (By "Jesus" I refer to the central ethical testimony of the New Testament writings as they gather around the proclamation of Jesus as Lord. By "Anabaptist" I refer to the heritage of radical reformation that began before the sixteenth century and continues to break through in every century up to the present. My concern is not with the sixteenth-century Anabaptists in particular, by virtue of their being the fathers and mothers of American Mennonites—which they are not really—but rather with the radical reformation stance. That stance can lay claim to a particular relevance in every age, and some Mennonites, and others, appeal to it as a program for renewal.)

Not only would it be fruitful to take some time to ask about the origins of the slogan "conflict is bad"; it would also be fruitful to dissect its semantics. What is assumed that you do with that person who is guilty of conflict? What kinds of tension are identified as conflict? Can you really say generally that conflict is good or bad, or must you not rather ask which kinds of conflict are to be dealt with, and how? Even straight semantic analysis would probably push us away from the simple generalization.

But for the present we must leap over the piecemeal analysis to a direct affirmation: namely, that conflict is in itself not unequivocally evil. The word rather identifies a category of challenge that must be dealt with. Perhaps some kinds of conflict are bad and perhaps some are good; either way, it makes more sense to focus on how conflict should be dealt with.

Conflict and Congregation

The first phase of my discussion deals with conflict within the Christian community. Here I may well take my point of departure from a lecture presented on November 8, 1969, by J. Lawrence Burkholder at Conrad Grebel College. His second lecture in a series of three bore the title "The Ritualism of Conflict." Burkholder dwelt on the obvious fact that the New Testament prescribes patterned ways of dealing with conflict in the Christian congregation. Most precisely we find this in the instructions of Matthew 18:15–20, which later were referred to by Martin Luther and the Anabaptists as "the rule of Christ." Other expressions of the same concern and the same procedure are found in the writings of Paul.

"It is possible to resolve conflicts," Burkholder observed. "Growth in understanding and growth in love results from such resolution." Thus the thing to do with conflict is not to hide it or to say that it is bad, but to resolve it in particular ways.

The proceedings called for by "the rule of Christ" have about them the following essential ingredients:

(1) The initiative is personal. If your brother sins against you (both pronouns are singular), then you go to him alone. This church discipline is not something that can be delegated to a disciplinary officer of the church (to say nothing of the way the Reformed tradition used to delegate it to an officer of the state). It is the immediate responsibility of every Christian, who is to take each question to the party presumed guilty. This forbids gossip and excludes the centering of this kind of moral

responsibility for conflict resolution in the hands of official functionaries or specialists.

(2) The overture has a reconciling intent. The purpose is neither to scold the brother nor make him suffer or exclude him, but to win him; to resolve the conflict by the restoration of fellowship. This may come through his admitting that he was wrong, or it may come through my learning that I was wrong in thinking him to be wrong. Such a resolution can come only by taking the conflict with full seriousness and casting upon it whatever light we can, by way of moral insight or factual information. "You have won your brother" is the expected outcome of the overture. Only in exceptional and regrettable cases must the procedure be referred further to a widening circle of responsible fellow Christians.

(3) The procedure is rooted in the Christian community. The reason I go to my brother is not my own hunch or complaint, but the common responsibility we have as members of the same community. Thus the ultimate recourse, if my brother and I cannot come to terms, is the congregation, passing first by way of a leadership segment within its membership. The basis of the mandate to go to the brother, and the mandate of the brother to listen, is the baptismal commitment that constituted the congregation in the first place, whereby I committed myself "both to give and to receive counsel."

(4) The action is binding. Once this procedure has been undertaken, its results stand as historically valid. What is "bound on earth" through this procedure stands "bound in heaven" and what is loosed stands loosed in heaven. This is to say that history is to be taken seriously, and that the positions we take, whether affirmative or negative, become a matter of record, and are to be dealt with as decisive in the future. Individuals who, by closing themselves off from the recurring overtures of the congregation, make clear that they have withdrawn from the fellowship, are to be treated seriously as ones who have withdrawn, and either remain outside or must once again be won. The person who has accepted the reconciling overture must now definitively be dealt with as one who has no bad record and is under no shadow of guilt but is fully restored to the community and can count on this restoration to divine favor. But it is most significant that this reconciling concern is not stated simply as an attitude or a concern but rather as a prescribed procedure—what Burkholder called a *ritual* and I call a *practice*.[2] "Even as in the church God's salvation and man's response are ritualized in worship, in baptism, and in the Lord's Supper, so the ritual for dealing with conflict resolution comes about not by accident but by design. It must be structured so as to avoid the view that dealing with conflict is peripheral or regrettable. If there is no ritual, there will be an explosion. The form for the ritual is found in Matthew 18, where the conscious, deliberate dealing with

conflict is set in the context of forgiveness." Conflict is not a discredit to a small group, for the closer the relationships, the more likely there is to be conflict. Burkholder wrote that it is "because of the concern for community that Mennonites have had so much conflict."

If I may make one exception to my earlier promise and fall for once into sixteenth-century archaeology, it should be pointed out that the first theologian of Anabaptism[3] provided three liturgies for his young churches: one for baptism that constitutes the community by the voluntary act of each member, one for the Lord's Supper that sustains the community by the sharing of bread, and one that restores the community by dealing with offenses. Conflict resolution liturgy or sacrament is just as important to the identity and the survival of Christian community as are the other more frequently observed rituals.

Now how does this prescription for conflict resolution by Jesus and the Anabaptists differ from the modern preoccupation with openness and communication, sensitivity and the like, which is currently so widespread in our society?

One element of the difference is what I would like to call *objectivity*. We modern, psychologically concerned westerners tend to locate both conflict and its resolution within the person and on the level of feeling. Jesus and the Anabaptists would rather have placed these realities on the level of truth outside oneself and based their claim to authenticity not in feeling but in revelation. My brother or sister and I can be reconciled partly because we recognize an authority sovereign over both of us. We are not simply negotiating a middle position between the two of us, to which we can each move without too much loss of face. Each of us is in principle open to radical change on the ground of a genuinely superior authority whose will is known. This is not democracy making decisions on the basis or the preference of a majority. It is not letting the strongest parties act the way they feel. It is not salesmanship; it does not expect to be accepted by most people. What my sister or brother and I do is not to bargain about our different tastes or preferences or interests. We study together whether there is a truth bigger than both of us, under which we must meet, whatever the change it demands of us.

Without this objectivity, the concern for conflict and its resolution can very easily lead us to an unhealthy exaggerated respect for the self, whether my self or yours or hers. We think of the demands or rights of selves as being what needs to be respected. We even talk about the honor and the dignity of the self in such a way that it would be a kind of sin to accept something that is not congenial to my tastes. This makes it possible for me to use the label *self* to cover what in reality might be an unwillingness to obey. There is likewise a possibility of too great a respect for the freedom of other parties, if it means a refusal to take responsibility for addressing and challenging them. Certainly there are types of pressure or coercion that I must not impose upon my neighbor or my sister or brother; but Christian fraternal concern is also a kind of pressure that is often neglected out of unbelief or weakness.

Modern respect for the freedom of the other party may wind up as creeping relativism, which means leaving my sister or brother at the mercy of other pressures, whether open or occult. The Anabaptists and Jesus would have another kind of respect for the neighbor's dignity, namely the renunciation of coercion, or what is technically called voluntarism. Yet within my respect for the freedom of the other party to make his or her own decisions, I am still responsible to put issues to her or him.

The other formal distinction between modern concern for conflict resolution and the style of Jesus and the Anabaptists is the element that I would call *covenant*. I am responsible for my fellow believer and she or he is responsible for me because we have committed ourselves to this pattern of responsibility. This means first of all that the procedure of conflict resolution has something to build on. It is the outworking of a contract we have made with one another. Secondly, it will be the case in any given cultural context that such a covenant will not merely mean staying in touch, but will bind us to live together in a given time and place according to a given style. Thus the covenant understanding in that place will include at least certain minimal understandings of the criteria by which obedience or disobedience is to be measured, and the procedures though which conflict is to be resolved. Not only that there is obligation, but also what the obligations will be: these matters are at least partly defined by the substance of the covenant.

Conflict in Society

We move now to our other somewhat distinct topic. It is distinct not in the subject matter, or in the acuteness of the clashes, but in the social presuppositions with which one can seek to work at it. What is the Christian style of involvement in the social conflicts of contemporary society?

The traditional name for the position taken by Jesus and the Anabaptists is *nonresistance*. If we had time to develop our own semantics, I would be ready to argue that this is still a good term. Yet its immediate meaning to someone with no background of usage or with particular Mennonite usages in mind is open to serious disadvantages. It projects an image of apparent retreat. It focuses attention on specific Mennonite privileges such as exemption from military service in certain countries, and it fosters misunderstanding about concern for what happens to my neighbor.

A recently more popular term is *nonviolence*, or *nonviolent action*. This is not much clearer, however. There is real difficulty in defining how far the word violence goes. And there is real concern about other kinds of injustices that are not characterized by physical abuse. In addition to suggesting that the basic moral line to be drawn is between that which is violent and that which is not (the line that I have just said is hard to draw), it also hides the fact that there are two other lines that are more important to draw.

One line comes well on this side of physical violence; it is the point at which one begins to despise one's neighbor and not consider him/her as a person. According to Jesus, this is in one sense morally just as bad as seeking his life (Matt. 5:21–22). But then on the other side of physical violence there is the act or intent of taking life, which is qualitatively one serious step worse than physical force that shocks, insults, or wounds, but does not kill. Thus *nonviolence* is not much better as a precise label for Jesus's attitude to conflict. Rather than seeking to fix on a third term which I would claim is a better definition, I propose to come at our question from the other end: that is, by identifying some of the most original or particular characteristics of what Jesus tells us about the Christian style of conflict in the wider society. These are all concordant with what is traditionally called *nonresistance* or with what is coming to be called *nonviolence*, but they are more precisely characterized, more definable, more identifiable, and more specifically linked to the person and/or the teaching of Jesus. They must then be essential to the definition of what we are looking for. I shall use phrases that need definition, rather than assuming that we can ever find automatically self-explanatory phrases.

Jesus says that his disciples are to be perfect as their heavenly Father is perfect (Matt. 5:48). Few dimensions of the ethical teaching of Jesus have been more fundamentally and destructively misunderstood than this call to perfection. Most theologians have taken it as a dramatic overstatement (hyperbole being a trait of the culture at the time [as in "if your right eye causes you to sin, tear it out and throw it away"—Matt. 5:29]) that shows that this and many other imperatives of Jesus should not be taken literally. Obviously we cannot be perfect. By definition, perfection is that which we cannot attain. So when Jesus says we ought to be perfect, this is an indirect symbolic and Hebraic way of saying that we always stand guilty before God, that we never do enough, and that we therefore must not be proud of even our best deeds. Now that is a good point in its place, but it is not what Jesus was talking about when he said "be perfect like your heavenly Father."

Another strand of Protestant thought says that Jesus would not ask this if it were not possible. Therefore we must trust God to bring about the perfection that the former group said is impossible. A doctrine of *sanctification* is developed to describe how God can do that. This has been followed through the most thoroughly in the wake of John Wesley, and especially in the Wesleyan Holiness movements of the nineteenth century. This is a good point in its place, but this too is not what Jesus meant.

It is fully clear from the context that the phrase has a much more precise and more modest meaning than any of those explanations. Jesus is asking his disciples to be indiscriminating. They should love their enemies as they do their friends. They are told to do this because it is what their Father does. God loves God's enemies as well as friends. God does not discriminate. God's love is not conditional. ". . . so that you may be children of your Father in heaven; for he makes his sun rise on the evil and on the good, and sends rain on the righteous and the unrighteous. For if you love those who love you, what reward do you have?" (Matt. 5:45–46).[4] Thus the point is precisely that we emulate the quality of the love of God, not by being flawless or impeccable, but by renouncing discrimination and loving the enemy on the same grounds and in the same way as we love our friends. This means in practice a preference in favor of the adversary; it takes a built-in preference to correct for our natural predilection for our friends. Thus the first foundation of the Christian style of conflict—call it *nonresistance* if you will—is derived not from an interpretation of the stakes in a particular conflict but from an understanding of the nature of God.

After perfection the next trait is servanthood, or renouncing lordship. In all of the Gospels, in different ways, Jesus tells his disciples to be servants. In the first three Gospels this teaching is given in very parallel ways, although reported in different places within the story: Jesus says, "You know that the rulers of the Gentiles lord it over them. . . . Not so with you" (Matt. 20:25–26). Jesus does not say that the fact that rulers exercise dominion over their subjects is a bad thing, as if it could be done away with through some kind of anarchistic development that his followers would promote. Neither does he say that it is a good thing, so that it should be blessed and supported by Christians in an active way, as they did beginning with Constantine. Jesus merely says that it *is* the case: rulers do dominate. We might call him *positivistic*. But while not saying it is either good or bad, he says that it is not for his disciples. They have a different task, namely to be servants. The reason they are to be servants is that he is servant. Thus this second mark of the Christian style of involvement in conflict is derived not from an analysis of the stakes or the setting but from a reflection upon the style of Jesus as a person in society. He did not avoid conflict. In fact, he sometimes even provoked it. Yet within it he renounced, intentionally and not merely out of weakness, the temptation to impose his will upon others through superior power.

The third trait of the style of conflict that is at home with Jesus and the Anabaptists is what the early Quakers called the *War of the Lamb*. We normally assume that weakness will be defeated, and therefore we look for explanations to help us face defeat. But from the perspective of faith in a God who raises the dead, Jesus and the early Christians and Anabaptists believed that their death was itself the victory. Their willingness to suffer the full costs of faithfulness in a society that turned its hostility upon them was not a prerequisite of the victory or a result of the victory but was itself the triumph of the love of God over that hostility toward him. The point is not that if we suffer and do not lose faith, then some time later God will win. It is that "in our suffering we do not lose faith; it is the beginning of God's victory."[5] This is a vision with solid New Testament grounding. It gives to suffering-in-conflict a meaning very different from the kind of pragmatic understanding that certain modern approaches to nonviolent technique may try to give it.

How does this vision differ from the standard meanings that Mennonites in the past have had in mind under the label *nonresistance*? First, it does not filter the problem of evil through a dualistic framework of assumptions, whereby one set of moral standards applies to the Christian and another set to the outside world. This dualistic framework was a reaction against the optimistic kind of pacifism that spread widely in the 1920s and then died very suddenly in the 1930s. This optimistic pacifism had assumed not only that a world without war was possible, but also that pacifism based on Christian assumptions could be commended to everyone, including the bearers of political power. This pacifism was destroyed both intellectually, by the inadequacy of its non-Christian view of human nature and history, and practically, by its failure to find the hearing it expected. Mennonites then joined with some nonpacifist interpreters of ethics in concluding that war is wrong for the Mennonite Christian but may be right for certain other kinds of persons or agencies. This was an understandable correction for the optimism that had gone before, but it is a position that the New Testament avoids, and that the earliest Anabaptists acceded to only in a very restricted way under very peculiar circumstances. Jesus avoids both the affirmation that power-bearers outside of faith can have a world without war *and* the affirmation that they must have any particular war or exercise any particular kind of violence or injustice. He neither deplores nor condones the violence of the existing authorities. He simply recognizes its presence and says that it is not for his disciples (as it was not for him) to take that path.

One of the places at which traditional Mennonite dualism is uncritical is its granting to the militarist or to the statist-realist the assumption that superior physical power or coercion does work. As a matter of fact, violence can never work on both sides of any given conflict. It always fails to attain its objective in half the cases. It can never work against all the people, and, by definition, it cannot work all the time. To grant the assumption of omnipotence in the calculation made for the moral justification of violence is therefore a concession that neither logic nor Jesus would grant.

Jesus does not simply pronounce a moral judgment on what is wrong with some particular line of action. He presents a concrete, saving alternative. He does not side with the violent Romans or with the violent Zealots, but neither does he withdraw. He condemns them both by creating, within the arena where they both operate, a new option: a voluntary Christian community with its own character independent of the promise of effectiveness. By its very presence, this counter-community constitutes a more profound condemnation of injustice than that which can be represented by either party in the existing conflicts. His counter-community is not dependent, for its identity or self-confidence, on an ability to take over the situation; thus, it is not destroyed by ineffectiveness. This is the originality of the Anabaptist approach: that the reformation that we need cannot be imposed from the top, since imposing from the top is part of what is wrong. The error is not that someone is using coercive power toward the wrong end, but that it is used at all.

But Why Renounce Coercion?

In the context of traditional moral judgment, the renunciation of coercion or of the threat to kill is based upon the simple postulation of a rule that forbids killing, and that tells us that if we break this rule we will be guilty, or God will not love us, or we should hate ourselves. Much has been said recently about the unhealthiness of that form of moral discourse. The unhealthiness attaches not to the violence or coercion, however, but rather to the framework within which it is to be understood.

In the sacral roots of culture, the provision for violence may well be rooted in some magic or superstitious understanding of the divine significance of blood. We may have culturally outgrown this spooky respect for blood, but that does not say that what it forbade should be any less forbidden.

The social contract rootage of a moral imperative or legal provision, to which modern thought usually resorts in order to explain when something is right or wrong, would lie in calculations about what kind of society you get if life is protected or if it is not. This kind of thinking generally calls for the protection of the life of the good, and of those who protect others, but it usually also accepts sacrificing the lives of those who are judged to be evil.

The humanism of Jesus, or his "perfect love," is rooted in respect for the personhood of the neighbor, even if he may be the bad guy. He is respected not because of his goodness or productivity but for the sake of his self as person, as image of God. A creative force is an alternative way to find one's path through ethical discourse. One rejects force not to keep one's hands clean or to keep one's conscience confident, but for the sake of the personhood of the neighbor.

In a sort of concluding marginal comment, it remains to take note of one significant question that is often thrown back at the advocates of nonviolence. Is not nonviolent action itself coercive? The campaigns of Gandhi or King exercised power; they made things happen. They caused people to do things against their will. The social disciplines of a Mennonite rural community in the early twentieth century imposed life patterns on persons who did not always have real freedom to entertain other alternatives. Thus renouncing physical force is by no means a guarantee that personhood will be respected. Is not the pacifist's condemnation of coercion compromised by the willingness to exercise other kinds of pressure in other kinds of contests of wills?

One way to answer this question is to draw careful lines between degrees of coerciveness. Coercion that takes life or threatens to do so is qualitatively distinct from any kind of nonlethal pressure. Police power (even if lethal) in the defense of civil order is qualitatively distinct from war. Is the person on the other end of the tension thought of as a person to be won or as an object to be overcome? Is the conflict subject to third-party observation or adjudication? There are numerous such qualitative distinctions to be made, but doing so may seem evasive. Thus it cannot be the entire answer.

It would be more important to clarify that there are different ways of pressing people to change. Reinhold Niebuhr can call them all *coercion*, because in the several cases the other party yields. Yet they vary in their structures and their sanctions. The coercion by the sword, which majority Western moral traditions consider legitimate, says to the adversary, "Do what I say or you will suffer." The adversary, in order to avoid the suffering, does what I say, if I am stronger. If he does not, I impose on him the suffering that I threatened.

The coercion I apply by nonviolent techniques is of a different kind. Gandhi or King says to the adversary, "Do what I say is right or I will suffer." If the adversaries concede to my moral pressure, it is because of their unwillingness to impose on me the suffering I was ready to bear. This act is itself an honor to their self-respect and heightens their own humanity. If, on the other hand, they refuse to concede, then it is I who suffer at their hand, as I had said I would be ready to do. It may well be that the persons who concede to my pressure, out of the humane self-respect with which they hesitate to hurt me, will still be dissatisfied or unconvinced about the issue that was at stake. There are Americans who still believe that the concessions made to the civil rights activists were mistakes. To the extent to which the adversaries are unconvinced of the rightness of what I have been asking of them, they may be of the same opinion still. I may have failed in the purpose Gandhi and King had, in which they also often failed, of converting the adversaries. But even then the quality of the coercion is fundamentally different from threat of the sword, because the sanction would have been *my* suffering and not theirs. The exercise of that sanction debases them but does not destroy them; it rather might have destroyed me. Avoiding this sanction saves me, ennobles them, and serves the just cause.

13

The Church and Change

Violence Versus Nonviolent Direct Action

I cannot simply leave the Christian case against violence without analyzing how for centuries, and especially in modern times, this issue has shaped and been misshaped by some standard patterns of argument.[1] These patterns must be criticized analytically if we are to move forward.

One very regular, and very misleading, way to handle the question of violence and nonviolence is to pass it through the filter of a discussion not of ethics but of method in ethics. The issue may be labeled as *ends versus means*, or as *principle versus pragmatism* (or *prudence*), or as *rules versus utility*. Each of these polar conceptual pairs has a slightly different shading, but each is used to move back a step from the substantial question of violence's justification to the formal question of how to think about justifying anything.

Very early in any discussion of social change, the question arises whether those who reject violence are doing so on moral or practical grounds. Is it "always wrong" or is it wrong "only because" it is usually counterproductive? Many will grant a *tactical* renunciation of violence as recourse in certain kinds of conflicts, yet want to keep an exceptional last resort open. Sometimes the concern is *pastoral*: i.e., a safeguard against a wooden absolutism that recognizes no hard cases. Sometimes it is a simple, honest *pragmatism*, for which all morality is a calculation of optimal effectiveness.

Thus the debate is set up: either you want to be righteous by keeping the rules, or you are willing to do good to others by whatever means are necessary, even if that means breaking some rules and hurting some people. In our age of pragmatic progress, in which the major ways of being righteous are "being effective" and "not being self-righteous," this way of stating the question is hopeless, it is confusing in its semantics, and destructive in its impact on the cause of change. I cannot here unfold the full debate as an exercise in the semantics and logic of ethics, with due attention to the advocates of the various views, but I must at least show why that is not a helpful way to put the problem.

Without pretending to semantic sophistication, both Gandhi, whose liberation movement began in South Africa, and Martin Luther King Jr., have denied the ends/means split as a way to evaluate violent action. Both argued formally, Gandhi repeatedly, against the notion of an evil means serving a good end. For each of them this is partly a matter of an organic religious worldview, whether evangelical black Baptist or neo-Hindu, in which path and goal, character and behavior cannot be separated. Its moral appeal is part of the power of nonviolent direct action. That action can never be *only* the pressure of demand, noncooperation, and challenge. There must be some way to claim that what the adversary is doing is intrinsically wrong and must stop. The weight of the moral appeal in nonviolent direct action and conflict resolution is such that, in distinction from violence, it can be seriously held that these means can only be used for a good cause.

Not only is moral language indispensable to appeal to the adversary. Subjective moral certainty is a necessity if any person or group is to stand in a posture of costly opposition.

What Gandhi and King said in terms of a religious worldview, their more secular heirs can say in terms of social process. Evil means poison the social system and vitiate the very ends for the sake of which they were resorted to, by creating uncontrollable cause/effect ripples beyond what was intended by or can be controlled by their authors.

Or we can say it in terms of psychic process. Creativity works within the bounds of reality, including respect for the personal dignity of the adversary. Readiness to justify an easy resort to unworthy means cuts short the search for better means.

But not only the activist/advocate like Gandhi or King must reject the conceptual polarity. The logician in ethics must object as well. The self-labeled pragmatist or realist may be willing to relativize one value: namely, the life of the adversary. Yet he or she does this for the sake of other goals that are all the more absolute by virtue of the sacrifices made to them. The *nation*, or *justice*, or *socialism*, or *liberty* are such absolutes. *Why* the adversary's life and/or dignity should be sacrificed to that cause is seldom seen to need justification. When the person who claims to be relativist about violence is not relativist after all about other values, and when he or she is in fact willing to kill for them, then it is a disservice to dialogue to grant that the issue is one of relativism versus absolutes or of pragmatism versus principle. It is rather one of *which* principles are to dominate our pragmatic decisions. Often the claim that one is thoroughly pragmatic indicates only that the person making it is committed ideologically—i.e., in a way incapable of dialogue beyond one's own frame of reference—to a position held without examination on emotional, provincial, or sectarian grounds.

Sometimes the claim to be pragmatist goes even one step farther from accountability into what some call the "Masada complex" or the "Laager mentality."[2] Here the conviction is that one must go down fighting even though it is for a hopeless cause. Then, despite the explicit claim to that effect, the appeal is not at all to prudence or effectiveness but to the transcendent rightness of the side one takes, the "heroism" with which one sacrifices to that cause even if hopeless.

Other times the flaw in the pragmatic argument for violence is not absolutism about the cause but irresponsibility about the means. What are the available possibilities? Prince Buthelezi said correctly at the South African Christian Leadership Assembly: "Efforts towards nonviolent change are now increasingly being portrayed in many quarters here and abroad as puerile and naive efforts, which have no chance of achieving any results."[3]

That is quite correct, as a report of what people generally think. But it is not true, in either fact or logic, that all the possible recourses have been studied deeply, and weighed over against the violent alternatives in terms of cost and benefit, before reaching that conclusion. As a World Council of Churches study report in 1973 concluded,

> We are convinced that far too little attention has been given by the Church and by resistance movements to the methods and techniques of nonviolence, in the struggle for a just society. There are vast possibilities for preventing violence and bloodshed and for mitigating violent conflicts already in progress, by the systematic use of forms of struggle which aim at the conversion and not the destruction of the opponent and which use means which do not foreclose the possibility of a positive relationship with him. Nonviolent action represents relatively unexplored territory. We must stay with the question, by what standard one may fairly test when "enough attention has been given" to alternative techniques.[4]

Often those who lean to the conclusion that nonviolent alternatives have been tried sufficiently and that we can therefore now give up and resort to violence think only of:

(1) Nonretaliation, concerning which the underdog often has no choice; or

(2) Specific civil disobedience tactics, which in some situations seem hopeless.

This is not only an unfair foreshortening of the positively nonviolent resources that are available; it also tacitly fails to critique the promises made
for the good that violence can do.

The pragmatist who shortchanges nonviolent direct action with the accusation that it is not effective has often not done any serious comparative calculation of all costs and all benefits. The just war criterion of *last resort* demands
comparison with all other means. The criterion of probable success forbade
any recourse to violence for lost causes, however desirable the cause might be
morally. Haste to justify violence skews these measurements unfairly.

When preparing for violent conflict, time, training, and equipment are
necessary: we pay for the Pentagon, war colleges, research centers, arms in-
dustries. Yet people reject nonviolence for its failure to "work" without any
comparable investment.

It can be argued, it is true, that nonviolent direct action may sometimes be
effective spontaneously, whereas armed conflict always demands lead time and
organization. It can also be argued that nonviolent direct action is a weapon
the poor can use. These considerations do count in favor of nonviolent means
where there is nothing else available.[5] But we are confused if we compare the
prospects for success of planned and budgeted armed conflict on one hand
with those of spontaneous, poor nonviolence on the other.

In violent conflict, one expects casualties. The combatant is prepared to
face death, and responsible military strategy will plan to run serious risks.
Sometimes it will even call for sending some people to certain death. Yet in
evaluating nonviolent alternative means, the risk of casualties is seen by many
as grounds for rejection. For some, merely to mention the name of Sharpeville
counts as proof that nonviolence is sure to fail; yet many more have died
with gun in hand without our concluding "it does not work."[6] The victims
at Sharpeville 1960 and Soweto 1976 were numerous, yet fewer in the long
run than the guerrilla fighters fallen along the borders. Who can weigh these
deaths against those in terms of "effect"?

In advocating violence, the effectiveness promised is often short-range and
often negative, like toppling a government or killing a tyrant. But that is in
itself not liberation, to say nothing of establishing a more livable order. Many
recent "liberations" have broken their promises of greater freedom—not only
in Iran or Indochina. How soon and by what criteria can we know a regime is
well established, and is better than before? *Free* can mean different things:

(1) Sometimes *free* means simply "no longer under colonial administration."
    But an indigenous government can be just as oppressive.
(2) Sometimes *free* means "committed to a particular view of human dig-
    nity" (whether that vision be socialist, or liberal, or some other).
(3) Seldom does *free* mean "providing effective safeguards for the dignity
    of all the subjects."

Freedom in form (1) may be achieved by violence; freedom (2), perhaps; but freedom (3) is more likely to be destroyed than to be served when freedom (1) or (2) is won at the point of a gun.

I well remember an Argentine student in 1971 arguing that violence can liberate. The reason he gave was that South America's original nineteenth-century "liberators" had been successful. But they had won freedom (a); certainly not (c) and hardly ever (b); otherwise Buenos Aires in 1971 would not have been looking for yet one more liberation. The rights of the poor and indigenous people of South America would have been better served in the nineteenth century if the Spanish and Portuguese empires had lasted just a little longer. Madrid and Lisbon by then were becoming more careful about the human rights of their subjects than were the "liberating" feudal warlords and landowners who swept across the South American continent, creating locally managed (freedom (a)) but oppressive regimes.

Behind the simple claim that only violence is effective, there is a power of deception deeper than mere illogic. One of its most extreme forms is what I have called the "King-Che discrepancy." The thought pattern is widespread. I was first struck by it in 1968, when Martin Luther King Jr. had just been assassinated. Many leaped to the conclusion that nonviolent alternatives had thereby been refuted. At the same time, all over Latin America, the fact that Che Guevara had been gunned down in the Bolivian mountains did not mean that guerrilla violence had failed. Why not?

The incongruity is even more striking when we remember that King, like Gandhi and Jesus before him, had expected to be martyred. This was true both in the general sense of the knowledge that nonviolence will be costly, undergirded by the Christian's readiness to "share in the sufferings of Christ," and in the more precise sense that King gave voice to ominous premonitions in the weeks and days just before his death. Che's defeat, on the other hand, was not in the Marxist scenario. On the general level, for the Marxist the victory of the revolution is assured by the laws, as sure as those of mechanics, of dialectical materialism. In the narrow sense as well, Guevara, just before he was captured and killed, was still expecting to win as head of the violent insurgency in Bolivia.

Is there not some flaw in the logic here? Of a man who predicted his death, who explained why he accepted it, whose work did not perish with his death, the critics argue that his view is refuted by that death. Of the other man, who promised victory and whose campaign did collapse with his death, his faithful proclaim his resurrection ("*Che vive*"; "Che is alive"). The Marxists believe that their hero's death is powerful on some other level than his military defeat. Whatever that reasoning may be called, it is not standard Marxist pragmatism, but some kind of apocalyptic myth.

Another Dichotomy

A second misleading debate, which intersects with the first, is the disjunction between *involvement* and *withdrawal*. This line of argument is clearly established in our time. Among social critics, it divides those who call themselves liberal and those who call themselves radical. On the one hand, it is held that one position "gets involved" and can "take responsibility," but, by the very nature of the case, is "compromised"; i.e., it takes willingly upon itself substantial moral guilt for the imperfection of the system in which involvement is accepted. The other clean logical alternative, we are told, is to say that "the system is all wrong," and that the only morally respectable thing to do is to reject it so fully as to have nothing to do with it. This "clean simplicity" language of wholesale systemic rejection tends to prevent some from noticing that it can lead to quite different actual options. It may lead to a *zealot* commitment actively to smash "the system" (which then is a very important and also morally compromised involvement after all). Or it may lead to *quietism*, which although verbally disallowing the system, lets it stand unchallenged. But there is also the possibility that it may lead to emigration and the construction of an *alternative structure* in the desert or in the ghetto. Those three strategies—zealotry, quietism, and ghetto—are so different from one another that to group them under the heading "noninvolvement" is seriously deceptive.

Right now this debate is especially focused upon the conditions under which it might or might not constitute realism or betrayal for black community leaders to serve in the new Koornhof community committees.[7] You know better than I the other forms in which that same debate rages, around other ways of opposing apartheid while still operating within South African society. Despite the widespread consensus, to the effect that involvement and compromise (on one hand) versus rejection and purity (on the other) constitute an either/or choice, I submit that that is a false debate. There are always elements of both, even in situations of almost apocalyptic tyranny.

Nonviolent action is in any case involvement and not withdrawal. It is a form of involvement to maintain a broad range of pressure within the existing order at the same time that one seeks to replace it. All serious nonviolent activist strategies have maintained such pressure. The work of Martin Luther King Jr. included a very strong affirmation of the use of the American courts and appeal to the American Constitution against specific injustices within the American system. Likewise, King's activity presupposed strong investment in obtaining and using the vote, and in calling the courts to implement the Constitution.

Gandhi had his reasons for trusting less to litigation than King was later to do, but he created his own political party, which ultimately became the governing party. And before that, he brought into being (first of all in South Africa) the powerful educational instruments of the ashram and popular journalism. Both Gandhi and King, without embarrassment or sense of compromise, made use of the money and connections of friends in high places.

A second form of involvement that always keeps nonviolent action from purism or quietism is that wide sweep of activities that might be gathered together under the heading *building the alternative culture*. Both Gandhi and King invested in sanitation, in education, in the development of skills and self-esteem, in journalism, in respect for one's own distinctive cultural history, and in a high view of the place of one's present effort in the history of the world and the nation. Both were committed to developing economic resources in the underdog community. Both linked social action with liturgy, celebration, and telling the story of how God had helped his people before.

Part of the community-building concern that Jesse Jackson's work most dramatically exemplifies is the celebration of the dignity of what is already present. "I am somebody," Jackson's listeners respond when he leads them in celebration. That is of course also a part of the need here in South Africa as well. Nonviolent life and witness, both nonresistant suffering and aggressive direct action, are already going on. "We are doing something" should be the litany. My thesis is not that South African Christians should reverse themselves to accept something they had rejected or not known of. The call is rather to recognize, clarify, and then be in a position to deepen and extend what is already at work.

Last, but not unimportant: both Gandhi and King, like Jesus, invested in developing and proclaiming an intelligible theory to interpret and justify what they were doing. They offered this theory in terms both of traditional religion and of contemporary debate. For much of this kind of activity, which I have referred to as building the alternative culture, there is no more impressive specimen today than the prolongation of the work of Martin Luther King Jr. by this conference's eminent guest, Jesse Jackson.

These two headings—maintaining pressure within the system and building the alternative culture—help only in a very vague way to deepen our awareness that those particular symbolic or trigger gestures that people often think of first under the heading of nonviolent direct action (the marches, the civil disobedience, going to jail) are only the tip of an iceberg. They are only the exceptionally visible part of a much larger unity. They are in fact, as is the case with icebergs, only visible and effective in proportion to the size of the hidden block below the surface. The integrity, the credibility, the intelligibility, and the actual social impact of specific tactics or techniques or dramatic direct action, whether within or against the law, will be proportionate to the size and the solidity of the floe beneath the waves.

If the use of nonviolent techniques or tactics is to be more than episodic or sporadic, then both in our projections of how it must work and in our evaluation of its chance of working, we must be more attentive to those deeper dimensions below the water line. Among the most important requisites are, then, the following:

(1) There must be a readiness in principle to enter into a position of resistance. That it is possible to stand against the powers is self-evident in some social situations and unthinkable in others. In segments of the Christian church, the idea that Christians should ever really have to make the choice whether to "obey God rather than men" is only theoretically imaginable (Acts 5:29). From that perspective, it is not possible to think further about the prerequisites of nonviolent resistance.

Such readiness to oppose the powers that be has both psychological and theological components. In the early church, it was self-evident. In Reformed theology, it is a classical extreme possibility under the heading of just revolution. In the lived experience of Lutheran and Catholic, Anglican and Baptist churches, it has only rarely even been thought about, and never thought through or practiced regularly. The notion that there exists a possibility of knowing the will of God concretely, with sufficient clarity that it is one's duty to refuse to obey the authorities, even at the cost of suffering, does not come easily.

(2) For nonviolent resistance to be more than episodic or sporadic, there must be a committed body of people. Such an action may sometimes be sparked by spontaneous individual initiative, but it will never be a solid movement if there is not a wider base in a group of people who know each other. The individuals in this group know that they can count on each other because each knows that the other has freely and responsibly made a commitment to the posture of the group, and because they can listen to one another and advise one another in decisions about timing and policy. That commitment must be voluntary, because holding to it will be costly. For the earliest Christians this commitment was correlated with the meaning of baptism. That can no longer be assumed in most Christian communities. Therefore, there needs to be some surrogate experience in order for us to know that we stand together in a common resistance to oppression, correlated with a common refusal to meet the oppressor on his own terms.

(3) It is obvious that both of these first two requisites are most easily met when it is clearly affirmed that the rootage of the rejection of violence is principled and not only pragmatic, moral and not only strategic. That distinction between "moral" and "practical" rejections of violence is a morally harmful one. Here we see why. It is not possible to see the growth of committed communities, viable in terms of common decision making in internal discipline, if the several members all retain their individual liberty to determine at what point the costs of discipline are too great, or the immediate pragmatic payoff has not been delivered.

No Marxist, no guerrilla "freedom fighter," no patriot, lets his or her commitment be conditioned by the promise of short-range success.

(4) A community that genuinely exists has a story to tell. Its members remember and tell one another, and tell their children and their neighbors, the stories of victories and defeats, sacrifices and successes, heroes and renegades. Any significant resistance community has its own distinctive way of reading not only its own story but the story of the wider society, against whose stream it affirms its criticism. It has a reading of the past with the evident implication of an alternative future. Every solid resistance community has its own songs, stories, and distinctive humor.

(5) Harder to describe than the other marks, and still harder to work at, is the need for every effective resistance movement to have personalities. Recent social theory has established the pattern of talking about this function under the label *charisma*. This is regrettable phraseology, in the sense that in the biblical vocabulary every person has a charisma, the mark of charisma not being flashiness or claims to be more gifted than others. The fact remains that nonviolent resistance cannot be bureaucratized and routinized as can military strategy. Martin Luther King Jr. was the first to say that his movement would have been nothing if he had been alone; yet his distinctive spark and character were indispensable. Many of the failures of specific nonviolent efforts have been due to the lack of that creative spark, the sense of appropriateness in timing and gesture, which is more an art than a science, more a skill than a technique, more an event than an institution, more a gift than a rule.

In thus describing the characteristics of a community able to sustain a nonviolent liberation struggle, I have not been talking about anything abstruse, or imaginary, or anything specifically religious. I am simply summarizing solid social-science wisdom. Some equivalent of these characteristics is also indispensable if one wants to have a good college, or a good athletic team, or an effective business. They apply even to some extent in violent struggle. If a military institution needs to depend too much upon conscription or routinization, in the absence of creativity and personality, and if there is no sacrificial commitment to a value system opposed to the values of the other side or of the general course of human events, then even an army will be ineffective.

My attempt to exemplify the point has gone beyond the initial question. The issue is the inadequacy of the disjunction between involvement and responsibility. If we criticize our society at all, we are always doing something of both, and doing each only as we also do the other. If someone says he or she will have "nothing to do with" any particular contemporary social structure, that is one very visible way of having something to do with it. It must be interpreted in terms of witness or social impact, and it may need to be debated. But the debate cannot be about whether the refusal to cooperate is itself a form of involvement. Similarly, when one does consider it "realistic" to help the present system solve a few of its problems or be less destructive of some of its people, that should not be evaluated first of all in terms that either affirm or deny moral guilt as itself the meaning of involvement.

I make this observation of course as an outsider, and in terms of logic. It is not my prerogative to try to show with more specimens how much the debate among South Africans is hampered by the legacy of that disjunction.

Continuing the Conversation

Following the opening lecture at Hammanskraal, there was a very open exchange. Some of what it helped to clarify has already been woven into rewriting the above text. Yet a few additional worthwhile perspectives remain that may more fittingly be appended here piecemeal.

(1) The call for positive initiative in direct action was not stated emphatically enough in my first oral presentation at Hammanskraal. In the later discussion, a strong accent was centered on the passive absence of violence, on turning the other cheek, on again and again repressing the urge to retaliate.

Now it is true that "turning the other cheek" appears in the Gospel of Luke. That is, in one sense, passive. But that act of restraint is an expression of strength, not a recurrent defeat.[8] The aggressive "cleansing of the temple," the "woes" of Luke 6, the predictions of the temple's destruction, and the formation of a group proclaiming a new regime are *also* in that Gospel. It is precisely the call for nonviolent direct *action* that replaces the passivity of "we have no more cheeks to turn" with the dignity of "I am somebody," with the self-affirmation of "we can do this," and with the victim's move from victimization to initiative. If empowerment can only be done with guns or money, only a few can ever enjoy it; but empowerment can also be achieved by alternative ideas.

I was struck that, in the discussion at Hammanskraal, the expressions of doubt about whether anything more can be done did not take the form of the confident advocacy of violence either on the borders or in the townships. There were rather testimonies of extreme frustration of continuing to be victims, while identifying that victimization with "turning the other cheek" and with nonviolence. What I had not been able to make adequately clear was that nonviolent *action* is a more accessible alternative to resignation and frustration than is talk about how violence is unavoidable. Arguing that nothing can be done deepens the frustration and hobbles creativity.

(2) We saw in our meeting that saying "violence is not the issue," as several did, can mean a variety of quite different things.

Some meant "we agree already, without needing discussion, not to use violence, both on Christian and on practical grounds, but what we need is to know how to respond to the violence of others." To this at least three responses are needed:

(a) It makes a great difference whether the *Christian* grounds given for not responding violently would still stand if the apparent practical impossibility of doing so were to change.[9]

(b) For others, especially black youth, the meaning of the phrase is to say the option of violence is open, if not to those at Hammanskraal. "It is not an issue" then means that it is considered a dependent variable, to be used or not according to the situation, not an issue in its own right.

(c) Nonviolent *action* is a response to the violence of others; it is not only the absence of retaliation or vengeance.

Others in the meeting used the same phrase, "violence or nonviolence is a nonissue," to say something very different. They meant that, by the fault of others who are in control of the situation, no options are available to us that are free of violence. Violence is systemic. Suggesting that it can be avoided is unrealistic. This observation is factually correct, but it changes the subject. What is called *nonviolent direct action* does not pretend to avoid violence or to ban it, but only to avoid willingly and wittingly inflicting it. Some nonviolent action will actually provoke violent response, knowingly and with full moral accountability. Some nonviolent action self-consciously takes responsibility for deciding when and how one shall suffer the system's violence.[10]

Still others, under the same phrase, "nonviolence is a nonissue," meant to say that concern for the dignity of personhood, especially love of enemy, must not be permitted to stand in the way of other political values: ends are what counts, and all means, even violent ones, must be left open to be determined pragmatically. This is a theme dealt with elsewhere in the body of the paper. Violence *is* an issue, they mean, but we retain the freedom to resort to it when other values are weighty enough.

(3) In the later discussion, it became clear that I had given too little attention to the human issues of haste or frailty. Some said, "When the oppressor strikes me, I have no time for a Bible study about how to respond." That is why the accent needs to be placed not on hoping to be surprised by nonviolent spontaneous responses to occasional abuse, but on the development of character. No military or guerrilla power trusts spontaneous response. In all serious settings where armed conflict is planned, there must be training, practice, and drill, so that the fitting (violent) response becomes second nature. No one expects effective violent combat to be possible "with no time for study." Likewise, the community discipline of Gandhi's ashram or King's Southern Christian Leadership Council trained people ahead of time to face abuse or failure without being surprised. Responsible decision or action is not usually a quick response to an unfriendly challenge. Most challenges are foreseeable, and most responses are

the product of pre-existent expectations, attitudes, and promises. Fortunately, family life, school, and wholesome sports are all laboratories in which one learns by experience to respect the dignity of the adversary.

(4) I should have said more strongly that there is a serious dishonesty at work when nonpacifists (usually white, living at peace in independent nations) call others (often not white, living in unfree societies) to be nonviolent in seeking justice for their people. This was brought out at Hammanskraal in comments made by several, especially Dr. Gqubule and Bishop Tutu, with whom I agreed. It applies as well to much of the European outcry against the "Program to Combat Racism of the World Council of Churches."[11] Some comments at the South African Council of Churches (SACC) seemed to accept the assumption that whites are against violence while blacks have no choice but to be pro-violence. This is demonstrably not a correct descriptive reading. To wit:

(a) Most white Christians are not, and since the fourth century, never have been, against all violence.

(b) Black Christians, past and present, though often not by choice, have often been closer to Christian nonviolence than whites have been.

(c) The *arguments* that some pro-violence blacks use are the same as those most Europeans have always used. Calvinists used them from the Huguenots to the Voortrekkers. Neither the black experiences of oppression, nor the conflict-management resources of African culture, have made the distinctive contribution to the form of that argument which they could have.

(d) The experience in Western culture of the *positive* potential of nonviolent direct action has largely been the product of the creativity and sacrifice of nonwhites. Both Gandhi and King brought into their work specific resources from their nonwhite cultures, interlacing them creatively with Christian and Occidental values. In terms of objective cultural history, the idea of violence in the cause of justice is European, and the idea of nonviolent direct action is nonwhite.

(e) The most dramatic experience in the Hammanskraal conference session was the testimony of a recent survivor of police torture, whose concern as he recounted his experience to Secretary Desmond Tutu was not for vengeance, or even for respite, but for saving the human dignity of his torturers and their kind. To affirm that one's oppressor is a child of God is one of the least frequent and most profound expressions of commitment to the crucified Christ as Lord and as hope. That was not an alien, European perspective imposed on the local victim. It was the authentic expression of that brother's discipleship.

This skewed picture of nonviolence as an alien import, which I here seek to correct, keeps many from recognizing that nonviolent action is even now at work. Steve Biko, the martyrs of Soweto, and the others recently dead in detention, are even now changing the face of South Africa. Those tragic deaths, compared to other tragic deaths under arms in the bush and on the border, are doing something. How much more would their impact have been if, instead of being unplanned when they happened, and disavowed afterward, such events of martyrdom had been framed within a more conscious theology and strategy in which sacrifice would be expected before it happens (as it is in violent conflict) and celebrated in song, legend, and prayer afterward? Non-violent direct action is going on right now in black South Africa, within and beyond SACC programs, without being so named and without being thought about in those terms. What is needed is not to argue for it as if it were an alien import, or an odd excrescence of moralistic rigorism, but to take note of it, to name it, to celebrate it, for more white Christians to join it, and for strategic thinking to be more conscious.

This presentation has been mixed in style and mood. Some of it has been simple description of the nature and potential of nonviolent action, some of it has been direct advocacy, and some has been in between the two—namely, a discussion of what constitutes a fair test for an unfamiliar idea. Beyond advocacy, I have expressed my grateful recognition that the potential for creative ministry in this land is greater than in many other times and places, sufficient ground for my testimony of gratitude for the hearing this exposition was given.

A certain argumentative dimension to the description on all three levels is the unavoidable mark of the ecumenical recognition that what I have been invited to describe is a minority view, and that some of those who think they have dealt with it, or that they are beyond it, have in fact not yet deeply understood it. That is not a complaint on my part, but simply a description of the state of the unfinished discussion. That is why my gratitude for the open hearing granted me at the annual conference is so profound.

14

Politics

Liberating Images of Christ

Three characteristics of the current conversation define the task before me.[1] First is the present pervasiveness of a certain trendy pluralism in constructive and pastoral theology. Rigid dogmatism has lost credibility because it cannot engage the manifold challenges of modernity in authentic dialogue. Since the fourth century, traditional piety had been in tactical coalition with dogmatism, but urbanization has robbed it of its self-evident base in village culture. The discipline of theological articulation has broken loose from its traditional structures of accountability, whether dogma or hierarchy. Theology has borrowed something of the mood of nondirective pluralism fostered by psychotherapeutic humanism and free-market ideology. The sellers of soaps and Subarus have accustomed us to assuming that innovation is the *prima facie* mark of creativity. Deconstructionism as a critical fashion has tended to free the literary disciplines from what being a *discipline* used to mean. As a result of all these changes, space has been opened, not only for creativity, but also for fad and whimsy. For some, it seems that the word *Christ*, designating the object of human activity—as in the phrase "imaging Christ"—functions as a kind of empty cipher, pointing to a malleable mass and subject to any sculptor's whim, which any one of us is free to model at will. *Imagination* thus signals to some a loosening of the discipline that a rigid ontology used to impose on Christology, in favor of a great freedom to reformulate, whether flippantly or pretentiously.

At one end of the spectrum of open options within this mood of stylish pluralism, a system as monumental and traditionally stable as Eastern Orthodoxy will still be held to be worthy of respect. It must make its case in the marketplace like anyone else, however, rather than simply claiming that the truth has never changed. At the other end, Matthew Fox or Thomas Berry can submerge all the old landmarks in a new wave of nature mysticism, baiting the traditionalists with the brashness of their reformulations, yet still claim that *Christ* is what they are about. Everyone has the freedom to pay his or her money and take his or her choice of Christ images.

That is, of course, a game anyone can play; precisely for that reason, it is not really an interesting game. If everyone is right, then being right has become meaningless. If imagination is unaccountable, it has lost its right to a hearing.

As I thus take note, by way of preface, of the confusing panoply of imaginary possibilities, I do not mean to blame anyone in particular for the confusion or to suggest that it could have been avoided. Nor do I mean, as some of my stagesetting description may have suggested, that the problem is only modern. Modernity makes it less avoidable, but it was present in the first century, and it properly has to be present in any missionary situation.

The second characteristic of our current conversation is the specific testimony of the Jewish tradition, which is not only anti-iconic but iconoclastic. It not only does without images; it says images are wrong. It is not enough to say that other gods should not be *worshiped*. Since other gods are unreal, and making their images is a human activity, we are commanded not even *to make images*.[2] The gods do not make images of themselves; people do. But they should not. Yahweh does not make images of himself (with one exception, to which we shall return). The human activity of image making is named and is forbidden.

Early Israelite culture did not live up to this anti-iconic vision. That is one of the reasons some historians doubt that the Ten Words existed in the early period in the shape we know, as text or as fixed ritual formula. Yet the experience of exile and the ministry of the prophets clarified not only that image making is prohibited, but that that prohibition, in a way qualitatively deeper than is true for the other Words, is permanently foundational for the identity and mission of the Jewish people.

This anti-iconic stance underwent no change in the birth of the first-century messianic movement within Jewry. The witness of Acts 14:11–15 (Paul at Lystra), and Acts 17:24–29 (at Athens), of apostolic allusions to idols like those in 1 Thessalonians 1:9 and 1 Corinthians 8:4, and of the direct polemics of the Apocalypse (Rev. 13–20), make it obvious that the Jewish monotheistic polemic was assumed unchanged by the first Christian generation. (I mean this in both senses of the verb *assume*—both "taken for granted" as a presupposition, and "appropriated" as a legacy.) There is no trace in the first centuries of any sympathy for the Hindu solution, which, in the face of icon-rich polytheism, says "the more the merrier," letting the many gods fight it out in the free market of vitalistic religiosities. It is all swept away, explicitly, in the name of the jealous honor of the one true God.

The third fact that orients my task, after I have noted the mood of undisciplined imagination in our culture and the Hebrew prohibition of image making, is the presence of a very clear and *very much limited* pair of usages, rare but univocal, at foundational points in both testaments. Some might take these usages as exceptions to the anti-iconic thrust I just mentioned. Others argue, I think more correctly, that they presuppose and undergird it:

(1) At four points in the early chapters of Genesis, *and only there*, it is said that humanity, *adam* in the generic sense, a noun carrying with it the aural echoes of "earth" (*adamah*) and "blood" (*dam*), is made in the divine image. Yahweh forbids image making. Elohim does image making, but just once. What Elohim makes is not a statue, but a race.[3]

(2) At four points in the Pauline writings (1 Cor. 11:7, 2 Cor. 4:4, and Col. 1:15 and 3:10), Christ is called "image": the visible icon of the invisible God.

(3) At two other points in the Pauline writings (Rom. 8:29, 2 Cor. 3:18), it is written that believers are in the process of being conformed to the image of Christ.

(4) Just once (1 Cor. 15:49 RSV, modified), the two "images" are juxtaposed: Paul writes, "Just as we have borne the image of the *adam* of dust, so we shall also bear the image of the man of heaven."

(5) Just once (Col. 3:10), the two are telescoped into one: our new (nature) is "being renewed in knowledge according to the image of its creator."

And that is all. All other uses of the word *eikon* in the New Testament designate prohibited idolatry.

Thus, the pattern from both testaments seems to be clear: there is no place for any human activity of making images. We may speak of God's image only in one of two concentric senses. The larger circle is Adam, humanity as such, specifically in the context of the creaturely sacredness of human life as a racial whole. The smaller circle is the normativeness of Jesus, whom believers are in the process of coming to resemble. The larger circle is our status as creatures; the smaller, our calling as believers.

A few paragraphs ago, it was helpful to illuminate the anti-iconic edge of the Judaic critique by contrast with Hinduism. This humanization by divine initiative, designating by grace two "images" after the general prohibition, shows that the biblical iconoclasm differs also from the Buddhist corrective for idolatry. Buddhist insight turns its back on the whole Hindu pantheon, though without rejecting it; it turns toward that particular kind of absolute whose ultimacy is defined by its very ineffability. The Mediterranean gnosticism with which Christianity soon had to dialogue did something similar. The apostolic commitment to Jesus as divine image, on the other hand, is incorrigibly and unapologetically effable. The key event in the cosmic drama is a Word, and that Word became human.

This *tour d'horizon* should serve to focus my present task. I will investigate the way the political realism of the Gospel testimony to Jesus as the Christ can respect the primordial Hebraic prohibition of human image making and the precedent of God's humanism.

This needs to be a normative activity, not a whimsical or arbitrary one. It will not suffice to say, "If you are looking for a political message, we can speak to you in those terms." Much of the search for contemporaneity in modern theology does that, trying to serve any identifiable "market." That motivation does not suffice. The political shape of God in Christ is not one option on a menu. I need to demonstrate that what Jesus in fact was and did must not be interpreted apolitically, on pain of being guilty of heresy.

The Normativeness of Jesus as Image of God

When the first lines of the Gospel of John speak of the Word becoming flesh, that is far from an invitation to do late Hellenistic ontological speculation. When Paul spoke of Jesus as image, or when the authors of Hebrews or the singers of the hymn cited in Philippians 2 used similar expressions,[4] they were practicing the opposite of freewheeling image making. They were affirming the abiding normativeness of the work and words of the man Jesus as revelatory of God's being and will.

Two decades ago, when I wrote about Jesus's work as political, my usage was atypical, although it was not original.[5] What the Gospel accounts say, whether we take them straight as texts or read them through the grid of some critical discipline, is that Jesus's originality was not that of a gnostic guru or cosmologue, but that of an anointed heir to the role of announcing and inaugurating God's kingdom. The substance of his vision is nothing if not political. It is unconcerned with general speculative religiosity.

Jesus calls his followers to share their bread with one another. He calls them to be reconciled with one another, and tells them in detail the way to go about it. He tells them to love their enemies and to honor the underdog and the outsider. These definitional marks are more political than they are ritual or speculative.

This new political style is not laid on Jesus's listeners as an arbitrary or heteronomous ethical obligation; it is really lived (*imaged* would be too thin a verb) before us as historical reality. Hearers are called not to understand or to contemplate, but to follow, to be incorporated in that same lifestyle. The basic category is not insight, but obedience and solidarity. This is the reason that the good news we need, which we receive in him, must be the narrative of a real person's life, servanthood, death, and life. The life was political; the servanthood and death were political; and the new life was political. All of this is part of the meaning of *polis*, with the structures of living together, exercising power, and making decisions. This is not only a part of the picture, but it is the *critical* edge from which we can and must be vigilant against the menace of trendy, unaccountable "imagination."

What Jesus calls his hearers to do, most fundamentally, is not a cognitive act but a political one. They are called not to understand him, but to follow him; not to master a mantra, but to join a movement, to proclaim news, and to bear a cross. In the life of that movement, elements of cognition, statements in an ontological mode, both straightforward and paradoxical, are not missing; but they are not the heart of the challenge. Some texts (especially the parables, the apocalypses) intend to jolt the hearer into a new way of seeing, but this seeing is not an ahistorical gnosis; it is a new way of living, a walk (*halakah*).

I need not repeat here the thesis of my text of a generation ago as if it were novel.[6] What then seemed to some to be a dangerous or even irreverent formulation has since become commonplace, not because of my synthesis but because of the growing scholarly consensus on which it was based. To see the Jesus of the Gospel accounts as a political figure is not hermeneutical acrobatics, like what is done by the genre experts who play with the paradigms of tricksters and wonderworkers. A straightforward reading of the Gospel texts as they stand tells us that Jesus came to people who were expecting a liberator, that he attracted people who were hungry and thirsty for righteousness by promising the imminent irruption of God's reign, and that he was condemned to death by his society's rulers for threatening their rule. A straightforward reading of the rest of the apostolic writings tells us that it was that cruciform career—and not only his parables or his moral wisdom—that shapes the life of believers. What we observed at the outset in the special use of the word *eikon* is present elsewhere in the metaphors of head and body, shepherd and flock, vine and branches. "As he is, so are we in this world" (1 John 4:17) cannot be said without including reference to the earthly work of Jesus.

The Recent Development of Theologies of Liberation

This brief characterization of the meaning of Jesus both is and is not what most of us are used to understanding under the heading of *liberation theology*. Since liberation theology is a decentralized and people-based phenomenon, any effort to characterize it simply, as if all instances of it were alike, must be unfair. Since it is by the nature of things an enterprise that challenges the way things have been going, it should be no surprise that it provokes defensive criticism, both fair and unfair.

In a few summary pages, I must seek to distinguish among the various arguments milling around along this contemporary frontier, and to determine which ones correlate and which do not with the normativeness claimed by the apostles for the Jesus of the Gospel accounts. A large part of what needs to be clarified arises from oversimplification, sometimes well-intentioned.[7]

Any theological system ought to be classified as theology of liberation if that system considers *unfreedom* to be a necessary way to describe human perdition and *freedom* to be a necessary way to describe salvation. Within the broad stream of people and systems that fit that formal definition, however, many of the perennial questions of the rest of theology are still open. Among the many stances fitting that formal definition, not all are equally thorough or equally original.

(1) One set of advocates links *liberation* as a master conception with the political strategy of violent revolution. Obviously, violent revolution is about liberty in one sense. What needs to be discussed is whether the violent replacement of one regime by another is the most apt, and the most fundamental, way to describe the freedom God promises. It is odd that so many consider the notion of a morally justified revolution to be novel, or to be threatening, when most legitimate governments, including our own, are the product of such revolutions.

Precisely because of the testimony of the Gospels, I have reasons to doubt the adequacy of this vision of liberation, but we must be fair to it. It represents a consistent variant of the just war tradition, which has dominated Western moral theology since the fourth century. *If* you reject all war on moral grounds, then you can consistently fault liberationism for its acceptance of violence; if, on the other hand, you grant that war can sometimes be morally justified in the defense of some causes, then it is not the openness of this kind of liberation theology to violence that can be faulted. The openness to possible recourse to violent insurrection under certain circumstances is, in any case, not what characterizes a position as liberationist; that has been the mainline position for centuries, and still is. The debate is only about which causes and intentions may justify violence and which authorities legitimately represent those causes. Nor is the notion of justified revolution as a subtype of the just war in any sense new; it was represented by the Taborites in the Czech Reformation of the fifteenth century, by a wave of peasant movements within the German and Swiss Reformation of the 1520s, and successfully by the army of Oliver Cromwell in the British Reformation of the 1640s. These wars too were for liberation. They happened in parts of the world that entered little into the education of those thinkers who today have developed the notion of violent revolution in the interest of the poor. It was thus a new idea for them, even though not unprecedented in history.

This is not the time or the place to run through the details of the application of the just war tradition, as a set of political criteria for justifying violence, to the case of revolution. Our topic is not the several settings where radical political change seems to be imperative as prerequisite to establishing a social system compatible with the human dignity of the underdog. This is the time and place to observe that the more clearly one brings into focus the notion of a morally justified armed insurrection, the more it becomes clear that Jesus was tempted by such an option and rejected it. He rejected it, not because it had no attraction for him, and not because he was concerned with religious and not political matters. It *was* attractive to him; it was a concrete temptation that he did not reject easily. From the testing in the desert, just after his baptism, to the testing in the garden, just before he was taken captive, the role of zealot liberator was the alternative with which Jesus had to struggle. Had he been the apolitical mystic that most interpretation since the fourth century made him, the zealot option would have been no temptation. Yet it was one.

(2) Many are morally offended that some of the definitions of liberation make use of categories of analysis that are derived in more or less direct ways from the impact of Marx on social thought in the West. By no means are many liberation theologians philosophically Marxist, in the sense of dialectical materialism and atheism. More of them are vaguely Marxist, in the sense that categories of class struggle fit the world they know and the exploitive capitalism that they have seen at work. As José Miguez Bonino, the most widely known Protestant within the Latin American liberation theology movement and former president of the World Council of Churches, has described it, this commonality of perspectives is pragmatic. It is a coalition in the face of a problem which both Marxists and Christians care about: how to understand and then to transform the oppressive structures under which they suffer.[8] It is no more a betrayal of Christian theism than it was when Augustine borrowed from Plato or Aquinas from Aristotle.[9] It is less a betrayal than it is when our contemporaries borrow their visions of economic justice from Milton Friedman or their vision of personal flourishing from Freud.

What cannot be wrong is recognizing that the commitment of Jesus to the cause of the poor was not marginal, nor derivative, but constitutive of his ministry. The Magnificat and the preaching of John demonstrate that economic redistribution was part of the salvation expectation of the suffering people to whom Jesus came. His desert temptation and his first "sermon" in Nazareth confirmed that intention. As an anticipation of its fulfillment, he made his disciple circle an itinerant commune, and, as high point of his public ministry, he fed thousands in the desert. If by "Marxism" we mean that an elite will impose a new order by the violence of the state, that is wrong, just as it is wrong when Christian patriarchalism, Christian imperialism, and Christian nationalism have done it.[10] If by "Marxism" we mean an atheistic materialistic determinism, that too is wrong, in the same way as is the commitment of

Reaganomics to the sovereignty of the laws of the marketplace. If, however, by "Marxism" we mean sobriety about the reality of class interest, if we mean the recognition that where one's treasure is there one's heart will also be, and if we mean a moral bias in favor of the underdog, then that cannot be what is wrong with liberation theology.

(3) A third axis along which liberation visions vary among themselves is the extent to which they promise quick success. *Triumphalism* has become the code label for visions of God's victory that shorten its time frame and narrow the circle of its beneficiaries. That "we shall overcome some day" is simply not true, if by "some day" we mean tomorrow and by "we" we mean only ourselves. That distortion of the promise has sometimes been fostered by a too-simple application of the exodus metaphor. It is clear that the event at the Reed Sea was foundational for the identity of ancient Israel. Our texts of the Decalogue and the rest of the self-definition of the Hebrew people arise from their having been brought forth by the mighty acts of God. But there was only one exodus. It is not a paradigm to be replicated any time we wish. It would not have happened in the first place without prior people-building events in the land of bondage, and it would not have been remembered had it not been followed by many other people-building events at Sinai, in the wilderness, and in Canaan.[11] Had it not been for the failure of kingship and the new mission of Diaspora in the age of Jeremiah, the exodus would not have been transformed from the mission of Israel into the mission of Judaism for the blessing of the nations. All of this *together* is the shape of liberation. If our reference to the metaphor of exodus refers to all of that, in an authentic synecdoche, that is fine. If, however, we foreshorten the image, concentrating on our survival at the cost of drowning the Egyptian cavalry and slaughtering the Amalekites and assorted Canaanites,[12] then we have made of the imagery of liberation a new engine of oppression. The only use of the word *exodos* in the Gospels is to refer to the fate Jesus was to encounter in Jerusalem, as he spoke of it with Moses and Elijah on the mountain.

Crucifixion and diaspora, not conquest and revenge, are thus the shape of the liberty through which Jesus's victory frees humankind. When the apostles use *eikon* language, it is of the crucified Messiah that they speak, not of some other kind of hero or victor figure.

In sum: Jesus as unique bearer of the divine image cannot but be a liberator, since Yahweh is a liberator. Yet, in our conformity to that image, we shall be mistaken if we assume that freedom can be the product of coercion. We shall hold lightly any of the human sciences whose language we borrow, whether it be Marx's or anyone else's. We shall proclaim God's freedom as imminent and incipient, as present in Jesus and in ourselves and in the victims of our world. We shall provide no timetables for its final victory, however, and we shall not repeat the mistake of the twelve in the upper room, debating about which of us belongs at the head table.

Any Further Need for This Iconoclastic Perspective?

I said above that the danger of arbitrarily loose imagination is not a new phenomenon except in degree. Another form of the same challenge was foundational for first-century believers. They faced the challenge of putting their testimony to Jesus within the frame of a wider religious imagination repeatedly, in various settings. At least five important New Testament passages testify to this challenge, quite independent of one another and yet strikingly parallel in their shape.[13]

The author of the Gospel of John faced the challenge of describing Jesus in terms of a *logos* cosmology that was ready to hand. The writers to the Hebrews and to the Colossians were challenged to locate Jesus among the angels. John of Patmos was challenged to put Jesus on a ready-made apocalyptic timetable. The poet behind Philippians 2 faced the challenge of passing Jesus through the grid of the Prometheus/Adam myth.

Each time, the apostolic writers refused; they placed the human Jesus above, not within, the proffered wider frame of some extant Jewish or Gentile gnosis. They used creative intelligence *not* to come up with a new way to talk about Jesus that a given public would buy, but rather to restate their confession of his lordship: that his humanness, his Jewishness, his cross, and his call to costly following would be the last word.

These texts are not marginal or incidental in the New Testament. It is from these passages—one could almost say only from them—that the development of the notion of the pre-existence of the divine Son, as undergirding the normativeness of the incarnation, began. Trinitarianism evolved historically from this argument, *not* as a "constructive" or "imaginative" elaboration of a speculative metaphysic, but as the defense of the normativeness of Jesus.[14] When understood in the context of the polemic of the time, that development, which ultimately led to the notion of a Triune God, is, not a dilution but a defense of the radically anti-iconic Mosaic monotheism within which it was born. It is not a mental *tour de force*, stretching a hard-to-believe mathematical miracle. It is, rather, a lexical rule to defend at the same time as Hebraic monotheism and the normativeness of Jesus. Only later, when *incarnation* and *trinity* were taken over by Hellenistic speculators and alienated from the Mosaic heritage, did those notions take the shape that was later to seem to Jews, then to Muslims, and more recently to Western Unitarians and rationalists, to sell out the prophetic monotheism, as it seemed to others to constitute a precedent for unaccountable speculative reformulation.

I suggest that the experiences of the early centuries retain a certain prototypical value. While we should be modest about how far the classical typologies of the early centuries can reach, there is something perennial about them.

(1) On the one hand, there is the perennial power and threat of the Arian heresy. It claims the capacity to posit a pure rational monotheism, epistemo-

logically prior to Moses and to Jesus. As it was said then, it claims to possess a way to know about some pretemporal, not historically conditioned nature of things, accessible by reason to everyone, so that we can make statements such as: "there was when he was not." In the face of that rationalism, the gospel witness calls us to affirm the abiding normativeness of God's having made humankind in the divine image and of Jesus's particular first-century Jewish humanity. Jesus reveals what it means to be human, what it means to be prophet, priest, sage, and king.

(2) On the other hand, we cannot but observe the perennial power and threat of the gnostic/Docetic/Eutychian heresy. Here, we find those who claim privileged access to an apolitical religious metaphysic, of which Jesus is merely one instantiation. The really operative revelation for such persons is in the mind of the contemporary interpreter who puts it all together. In the Middle Ages, the people doing this found cosmologies in antiquity into which they inserted Jesus. Official trinitarianism sometimes fell into this game without knowing it. In our day, people who enjoy being innovators make a similar move. The market value of innovation versus conservation has shifted; yet the priority of the game of speculative cosmology over the struggle of political concretion is the same.

The above tension is not somebody's fault. It is given in the nature of things. It arises from the tension between "make no image" and "divine image in humanity/Jesus." But if my thesis is to stand, yet another dimension of jeopardy/heresy arises *by virtue of the political* substance of Jesus's work. This new dimension makes the picture more difficult, but considering it may also help to move us toward a more adequate understanding.

(3) This third temptation is not found overtly in the apostolic writings, since it came to full flower only centuries later. It is the Constantinian heresy of denying the political thrust of Jesus. That heresy began when people like Eusebius, grateful for the privileges given them by Constantine after centuries of being socially disadvantaged, identified the work of God with a political project that does not favor the underdog, does not share bread, does not reconcile Jew and Gentile, does not share power, does not reach beyond the limits of empire, and does not love the enemy.

The normativeness of Jesus, in other words, created the possibility that a new heresy could be identified over against it: making Constantine, rather than Jesus, the norm of political humanity under God's sovereignty.[15] It is not coincidental that the enormous cultural attractiveness of the Arian alternative in the fourth century was correlated with those courtly circles where Constantine and his heirs were considered to be special instruments of divine historical intervention, not subject to judgment in the light of the words or the work of Jesus.[16] The notion of Jesus's being *kurios*, or "king," was relegated to another world. For opposite reasons, both the Arians and the Eutychians were willing to let that heresy happen and, by adjusting to it, to aggravate it.

We might follow the Arian danger through later instances. Martin Luther used the phrase *theology of glory* to designate the notion that one can have general information about God's nature and purposes for which the cross of Christ is not the key. Arianism, without the royal house on its side, is less destructive than it is when it has political backing. The alliance with the court makes it qualitatively worse. One prominent form of that alliance occurs when the monotheistic purge—repressing one's enemies by accusing them of unbelief—is implemented by a "Constantinian" power strategy. The strongest early example of that was Mohammed, but the Crusades and the Inquisition soon emulated him.

We might also follow the gnostic danger through later instances. It arises wherever a thinker claims the ability to construct a new synthesis, accredited by the claims of its own inner coherence, of which Jesus is a mere instance; whether this be done by Hegel, Paul Tillich, Thomas Altizer, or Matthew Fox. It allies itself with the ruling party not by blessing purges but by depoliticizing the prophetic thrust of the call for justice and replacing the coming of the kingdom with the privilege of vision.

We could also follow the third heresy further through history; namely, dominion in the name of a more-than-historical righteousness. Its most prominent modern Western instances have been Cromwell, the French Revolution, American manifest destiny, Wilson's "war to end war," and Leninism. What all of these have in common is the way they differ from more modest visions of politics. They are new versions of the Constantinian hope, identifying a political regime's victory with the cause of God. We could survey, on the basis of experience, their promises and their limits. We could itemize and critique their axioms. Here, however, I must limit myself to tracing something of the growth of the critical alternative to the Constantinian idolatry.

In the last very few years, our age has begun to see in a new way that the alternative to the politics of dominion in God's name is not political irrelevance but an authentically creative politics of imagination: i.e., of humanization after the model of Jesus.

When, in the nineteenth century, William Lloyd Garrison, Adin Ballou, and William Ladd in the United States, and Leo Tolstoy in imperial Russia, argued that the word and works of Jesus constituted a political example that his followers were called to emulate, it appeared evident to everyone else that their "idealism" was irrelevant.[17] When, long before that, the Franciscans and Waldenses of the late twelfth century, the Czech Brethren of the fifteenth, the Anabaptists of the sixteenth, and the Quakers of the seventeenth retrieved the pre-Constantinian vision of the suffering Messiah, everyone who mattered was sure that such radicality was both inhumanely rigorous and unrealizable.[18]

Mainstream critics perceived the notion of *nonresistance* (Tolstoy's and Garrison's term[19]) as purist withdrawal, rather than as a way to break the vicious circle of evil begetting evil. It was too far from the consensus for its originality to carry the day. Garrison was written off as a journalist, not a political realist. Tolstoy was written off as an artist, not a bishop. Yet, in the ensuing century, there has been a powerful evolution, leading from Tolstoy through Gandhi through Martin Luther King Jr. to Benigno Aquino and Lech Walesa. Some of the bearers of this alternative vision are still, without apology, socially marginal, like the Catholic Worker or Thomas Merton; yet, the marginal is not irrelevant. The creativity provoked or enabled by that marginality is more relevant than is trying to fix the system on its own terms. It is on the margins that the search for alternatives prospers. In the past decades, and especially in the past five years, it has borne new fruit.

Christ Crucified: The Wisdom and Power of God

How renouncing righteous violence contributes redemptively to the course of history has been interpreted in social science by Gene Sharp, by some westernized Gandhians,[20] and in other ways by the late Saul Alinsky. For our purposes, it may be more helpful, original, and imaginative to draw into our conversation the recently widely noted work of René Girard, a literary critic turned cultural anthropologist and interpreter of the place of violence within social order.

Girard finds the same phenomenon in anthropologists' reports on exotic tribes and in the subsoil underlying classical mythology. Answering violence with violence is a natural phenomenon of the primitive primate's nervous system and of primitive human cultures. Girard calls it *mimesis*; I imitate an evil deed by striking back as I was struck, by killing my enemy as he killed my brother. Later cosmological visions assume that by violence the world is somehow set right; that God or the gods exact vengeance and, if satisfied, will bless us with restored peace and well-being. Thus, retaliation is the bulwark for peace in the clan.

Yet as societies grow, this mechanism works less well. Retaliation tends to escalate beyond equal measure, as we read already in the boast of Lamech (Gen. 4). All of society is threatened by degeneration into chaos, an unending spiral of retaliation for retaliation. At some point, society must and will turn a corner and find another solution. Girard believes that this did in fact happen, prehistorically, at the roots of every viable civilization. Through a primeval social compact, it came to be decided that, instead of everyone's avenging every offense, there will be one foundational ritual killing; in each society, perhaps one per year. One person, a kind of scapegoat (though this is not what the scapegoat meant in the Mosaic ritual of Lev. 16), is charged with the sins of the entire community and immolated for the sake of the peace of the entire community. This ritual atonement vents the pressures that otherwise would demand endlessly escalating acts of retaliation, and lets the rest of life go on.[21]

This is not the only origin of ritual sacrifice in ancient and primitive cultures. A different kind of mimesis applies to fertility. The firstfruits of the field and the flock are sacrificed so that the gods will further bless. The firstborn child is sacrificed so that the mother will remain fertile and later offspring will be protected from the curse. That too is a kind of mimesis. But the socially mandated killing that Girard is concerned to interpret preserves the health, not of a field or of a womb, but of a society.

When later legal cultures prescribe retaliation in terms of civil punishment, attributing to God or the gods the demand for recompense and positing thereby the notion of a retributive divine order, Girard helps us understand the etiology of that moral vision. It extrapolates the primeval mechanism of atonement into a juridical frame of reference without sacrifice. In that setting, it becomes more deeply visible how the willing death of Jesus, accepting innocently the role of victim, destroys the fabric of justifications whereby the victimizing powers were claiming that he bore a curse. The juridical language could be used in the Middle Ages to explain the need for the cross, as the metaphors of ransom and sacrifice had served before; but the history behind the metaphor is the love that leads an innocent man to lay down his life for his friends. Caiaphas spoke more truly than he knew, saying that it was expedient that one man should die for the people. That was the old law of ritual purgation; yet Jesus's voluntary assumption of that role reversed its meaning. Instead of cementing the Sadducees' social power, Jesus unveiled its injustice.

Tolstoy had said much earlier, in a simpler way, that the refusal to return evil for evil would break the vicious cycle of violence for violence. Girard provides a deeper anthropological interpretation both of the imperative for retaliation and of the way the cross breaks the chain.

Girard's theory is probably wrong in many ways. Such a brand-new synthesis, projected with such Gallic brilliance and omnivorous competence, has to be too simple to be true. Nonetheless, Girard has created a new and illuminating way to understand violence as a spiritual power, not reducible to equal legal retribution or deterrence.

When Jesus, the nonviolent Zealot, accepted death willingly and innocently, that was far more than merely one more martyrdom to add to the many others before and since. It was the end of the sacrificial system, as the Epistle to the Hebrews had already said in a more narrowly ritual frame of reference. No more can a society claim that its peace demands the blood of a scapegoat. Enemy love—the cross as a way of life and of death—is not merely a moral ideal. It is more than love of neighbor raised to the nth degree; it is participation in redemption. It is "the key to the gospel" in a far deeper way than Tolstoy had in mind when he used that phrase.[22] If Jesus, accepting the cross, is the icon of the invisible God, then our participation in that same love is at the heart of the transformation of humankind into that same image.

The Power of the Cross as Real History and as Social Science

Violent dominion cannot govern those who refuse to honor its idols. This truth was celebrated, in late 1989 and early 1990, as concrete political realism all across Eastern Europe and in Cape Town. The long-range effectiveness of that commitment gives the lie to the self-styled "realists," from Machiavelli to Hans Morgenthau to Reinhold Niebuhr to Breshnev. According to them the only power of nonviolence is the moral rigor of its claim to purity, whereas real power comes only from the barrel of a gun. The gun has one kind of power; the conformity of peoples to Jesus's renunciation of the zealot temptation has another kind of power. The use of the gun requires no creative imagination; the creativity of Gandhi and King, Walesa and Havel, does. They found answers that were not previously available.

You will note that I just used the word *imagination* for the first time in a favorable sense. The reason that is fitting is that what Gandhi, King, Walesa, and Havel did was *not* arbitrary or whimsical mental playfulness, but the creation of a new inclusive peoplehood around the model of Jesus's humanity, whereby the renunciation of violence defined the integrity of the new way.

These new answers to the political problematic are so strong and so pertinent that they can be effective politically; i.e., they can "work," even when their bearers do not avow their historic derivation from Jesus. They can work even when their bearers do not know that they come from rejecting the Constantinian temptation. The African National Congress, which in 1960 explicitly renounced its previous principled rejection of armed rebellion, celebrated in 1990 the beginning of its accreditation by the Afrikaner regime—*not* because of the success of their recourse to arms, but because of the moral power of their vulnerable populism. They succeeded, not because of the armed struggle they theoretically affirmed, but because of the fact that the bulk of South African blacks lived a suffering struggle. When Nelson Mandela was freed, Coretta Scott King described it as another proof of the power of unmerited suffering. "Unmerited suffering" does not quite say it all, but it is certainly correct that what President de Klerk yielded to, what moved him to free Mandela, was not the machine guns brandished by ANC youth.

The *intifada* on the Palestinian West Bank, although not literally nonviolent, is winning a moral victory because it is, with surprising consistency and persistency, enormously less violent than the Israeli occupation.[23] Fighting tanks with stones is far more like nonviolence than it is like war; that is the reason it is strong, as a performative celebration of underdog empowerment.[24]

Gene Sharp can exposit, in terms of profane social science, the reason the anti-Constantinian way of Jesus "works." In other words: once the idea has been let loose in history, it enables an unprecedented vision of the people as bearers of the meaning of history. What is this new idea? It is the humanism of the image language of Genesis, rejecting any image of the divine except the macro one of the human race as such and the micro one of the martyred Jew Jesus. Gandhi can translate this vision into Hindu. Martin Luther King Jr. can reformulate it in a unique fusion of black Baptist hope and the American dream. Lech Walesa can do it in Catholic Polish. Nor is its pertinence, once discovered, limited to those who share the believing cosmology from which it sprang. Gene Sharp can distill it out of the faith setting and translate it into Ivy League social science.[25] It works even for people who have not studied it or who do not believe in it. How can that be? The reason is that what is known, when human life is conformed to the image of God in Jesus, is not a knowledge experiment, but a revelation of the way things really are. The cruciform life "works" because it goes with the grain of the universe.

Effectiveness without Consequentialism

The simple reference I have just made to effectiveness does need to be protected against a misunderstanding that recent American moral thought has made more likely. The particular variant of consequential reasoning, which Reinhold Niebuhr called realism, made its case by arguing a profound dichotomy between moral purity and effectiveness. Niebuhr could honor both the "purity" of the principled "nonresistant" love of enemy, which he saw in the teaching and the fate of Jesus, and, on the other hand, the assumption of civil responsibility by those who abandon purity for the sake of finite but very important political causes, such as the defeat of Hitler.

Those who accept responsibility are not morally pure, Niebuhr says. He is thinking in Kant's terms—that only actions purely motivated by a principle and not by any other aim are morally valid. The nonviolent position is pure, in the style of a Tolstoy or the Amish or the Franciscans. It is good to have a few of those holy perfectionists around to keep the rest of us humble. But what the world needs more is the dirty-handed realist. A former proponent of liberal pacifism himself, Niebuhr needed the deep dichotomy between purity and responsibility to make his case for a new national militancy in the defense of democracy in the 1930s. His classic, "Why the Christian Church is not Pacifist," made this argument strongly.[26]

Niebuhr's categories were widely accepted without much criticism. William Miller, the pacifist author of *Non-Violence: A Christian Interpretation*,[27] divides all the history of nonviolent action down the middle. On the one hand, there are cases of pure nonresistance, unconcerned for effect, and cases of effective action. It might seem to follow, from my attention to effectiveness and to the consequentialism of Gene Sharp, that I accept the terms of debate set out by Niebuhr, beginning with the duty to save Western civilization, but then argue that you can be both pure and powerful. By no means.

When I report, as a matter of recent historical record, that strategies of conflict that respect the life and the dignity of the adversary can, in fact, be politically effective, I do not mean to be accepting either Niebuhr's dichotomy or his "realism," or to join him in making the Allied cause in World War II a moral absolute.[28] I rather argue, as did the apostles, that if Jesus is confessed as both fully human and the icon of God, then the axiomatic dichotomy between necessarily sinful, politically effective human life, and necessarily powerless, apolitical moral purity has to be a pair of category mistakes. The renunciation of violence is not right because it "works" (sometimes); it works (sometimes) because it is right. If and when, in a given frame of time or place, it did not work, it is still right. Particular tactics of nonviolent action may be more or less fitting on pragmatic grounds, but enemy love is not. It is right because it unfolds out of the divine nature that became history in the public ministry and the cross of Jesus.

The Abiding Mandate for Vigilance

My subtitle was phrased: "Liberating Images of Christ." It can be read more than one way. If "Liberating" is adjectival, I need to conclude from the above that images in general do not liberate. Not even images of Christ liberate. Not even the image of Christ as liberator necessarily liberates; it may enslave. Any image that we can fabricate enslaves. We must reject the notion that we should have or should take the freedom arbitrarily to reimagine Christ so as to hope to serve some market, even the market of people whom God wants to liberate. What can liberate is only the authentic image of the Genesis vision, i.e., humanity as a whole. Who can liberate is only the authentic image of the gospel vision: Jesus the nonviolent Jew, confessed as revelatory, God enfleshed.

If, on the other hand, "Images" in the title is the object of the verb, and "Liberating" is our action, then there may be something modest we can do. We may be able to help liberate the divine image. We can renew the Mosaic iconoclasm, directing it against the images of our own age, within which Jesus has been taken prisoner, against the familiar ones as well as the far-out ones. Like the thinkers of the apostolic generation, who refused to let Jesus be squeezed into the wider cosmology of their age, perhaps we can find new ways to let Jesus's Jewishness and his openness to the Gentiles, his attraction to zealot revolutionary violence and his rejection of it, stand in judgment of all our autonomous idol making—including when we make some specific recipes for freedom or peace or justice into the idol to which we will sacrifice others—and let him spark our authentically theonomous creativity.

15

A Theologically Critical Perspective for Our Approach to Conflict, Intervention, and Conciliation

One of my colleagues, whose academic field is the Bible, regularly complains that in the standard pattern of structured study meetings, the deliberations start with a paper on the "biblical basis" for whatever is being discussed.[1] Then conversation goes on to all the other papers, which of course have all been prepared ahead of time by experts on other parts of the subject matter, without any reference to that "basis." Like the text on the "basis," the other texts have had to be written before the meeting. Thus, the Bible is given a tip of the hat at the same time that it is declared structurally irrelevant.[2]

Our meeting here in Kansas City avoids that pitfall, at least, by getting around to theology only at the end, where my assignment comes, and not letting it get in the way of the serious studies at all. Instead of beginning devotionally, I have been assigned to look back on the dialogue, and thus to end our conversation by letting our experience help us to ask the right questions.

I take my long assigned title as meaning simply that we should not leap to the head of the subject too soon, rather than what it would require for theoretical thoroughness if a German scholar had chosen that title. It means that we are aware of the need to ask broad questions of orientation. My understanding of what we can do in this kind of framework sees *theology* not as a normative discipline, above and outside other disciplines and dictating to them, but as the way to work at how we can be consciously critical of our perspectives, in the context of real problems.

In the last two decades we have seen much of what the technicians are coming to call *genitive theology*: the theology of power, theology of liberation, theology of ecology, theology of women's liberation, etc. You decide first of all what you want to do, what basic meanings and values are at stake, and then you raise it to a higher power by giving God the credit for it. That is a very selective and arbitrary kind of undertaking, at least the way some people do it.

My understanding of what we ought to do here is precisely the opposite. Instead of baptizing our own predilections, we should rather try to get some distance. We should do that partly by analyzing concepts, partly by questioning whether we could think otherwise, and partly by referring to history. We should especially attend to the story of the community of faith, reaching back through history all the way to canonical times. That is the frame of reference in which I have been assigned to operate.

I was tempted to try to apply Jim Laue's typology to my task,[3] and to classify theology as a conflict-resolving intervener. Sometimes its role is advocacy, sometimes assessment, and sometimes moderation. But I don't know which of those I was asked to do, so I'll just do them all together.

This way of thinking critically, theologically, after the fact, is itself a mark of the way our meeting has gone on, in contrast to some of the earlier material on the subject. The pioneering Mennonite paper on the theme of conflict resolution, written by Bill Keeney several years ago, had a sizable theological "front porch."[4] It began by asking why it is fitting that Mennonites should be concerned in this area. At that time, that background survey was functional, because of the reticence among many people in our church constituency about any kind of special social intervention or involvement.

Conflict among Christians Requires Processes for Justice

Since conflict is normal, not only in the world but also among God's people (as displayed in both testaments), we need processes for reaching judgments about justice. One of the turning points in the story of Moses is reported in Exodus 18. Moses was not only a prophet; he was also trying to be the community manager, which means the judge. He spent all day troubleshooting his people's conflicts until his father-in-law (interestingly enough an outsider—not a Hebrew, but a Midianite) told him, "That's a silly way to try to do this. Why don't you decentralize your judging process?" Moses thought that was a good idea. He named seventy elders, or *judges*. Dealing with conflict in the midst of the community is part of the structural agenda of being a community. That is true not only in the fallen world but also in the process of redemption.

In Deuteronomy 17–19 we read a projection of the structures that the people of God will always need. They will always need *priests*, obviously, and God will repeatedly raise up *prophets* for them. They won't really need a *king*, but they'll want one, and finally God will let them have one.[5] Therefore, Deuteronomy also gives rules about how kingship should work and how it shouldn't work. Then, fourthly, there should be *judges* "in all thy gates."[6] Consistent with its pattern of providing legislation, Deuteronomy gives a prescription for how adjudication should take place in the life of the covenant people. The judge is not an intervener without a mandate; he or she is an adjudicator, a decision-maker who has a defined authority. The judge is assigned by the people's structure to solve their problems.

There is some possible carryover from that ancient process for understanding the conflict management process. Deuteronomy 17–19 makes it clear that this judging process is not to be delayed: there is to be no long postponement of justice for fact-gathering. The detailed legislation of the rest of Deuteronomy, which the judge is to apply, is marked by a general bias in favor of the poor and the victim, the widow and the orphan and the sojourner, and by suspicion toward the bearers of institutional power.

Conflict management is also linked to the holy place. In fact, sometimes the Levitical priests, servants of the sacrificial cult, share in the judgment process. Judgment is pronounced within a ritual and a worship event. It is not a worldly chore that has to be done outside the tabernacle so that you can come to God clean; it's done in the presence of God. Speaking about justice is one of the things that God desires. There is, as I said, special reference to the need to care for widows and orphans—that is, for society's victims. They have special standing before the judge. It is therefore clear, even from Deuteronomy, that God's people ought to have a vision of the normalcy of conflict management procedures.

In the New Testament—again this is all superficial, and a reminder rather than instruction—the only two times we find the word *church* reported as from the lips of Jesus are when he tells his disciples in Matthew 16 and 18 that they are to judge. They are to "bind and loose": that is, by their deliberation, they are to open and close the fellowship of the community.[7] The process is described at greater length in Matthew 18. "Binding and loosing" is a technical pair of terms from the rabbinic process. The rabbis gave guidance in matters of moral discernment. Jesus says his followers are to do that, and that when they do that, the Holy Spirit does it. "Where two or three are gathered in my name, there am I in the midst of them" is not a mandate for very small prayer meetings.[8] It is a statement about the justice process. "Two or three witnesses" being together is the standard Old Testament term for the attestations necessary for an accusation against a respected person to be heard in court. When Jesus speaks of "two or three witnesses" in Matthew 18:16, he is using standard language to talk about due process. "When due process happens," he says, in essence, "it is happening in my name. I am the judge. What you do, what you decide, you decide in my name; it is to stand in heaven." So the basic definition of the church, in the words of Jesus, is a conflict adjudication process in which, when your brother or sister has sinned, it is your duty to reconcile him or her.[9]

In 1 Corinthians 6, regarding one particular conflict, we observe that the very young church to which Paul was writing was already organized to carry on the function Jesus had described. Somebody in the church in Corinth had taken another member of the church to the secular court—the Roman courts or the Greek courts—about some financial conflict. Paul reprimands them on three grounds:

(1) You shouldn't take the secular world that seriously. Don't let the fallen world judge you, because in the long Christian vision, in Christian eschatology, we're going to judge them. You shouldn't trust pagan society to speak justice on your behalf.

(2) The Christian ought to be willing to suffer. "Why not rather suffer wrong? Why not rather be defrauded?"[10] This is the ethic of the cross.

(3) The argument that concerns us here, made between the other two, is in the form of a question: "Is it possible that there is nobody among you wise enough to judge a dispute between believers?"[11] In other words, you must have somebody among you who can handle this; you should have within the congregation a conflict resolution person. It is understandable that this kind of resource could exist in the church, because the same thing was done in the synagogues from which the Christians took over many of their patterns.[12]

So the idea that "Christians don't confront," which is in the back of many of our minds and which has been referred to repeatedly in the past few days, is a recent, nonbiblical cultural pattern. That idea is not biblical; it arose later in modern Western Protestant culture. The idea that "Mennonites don't confront" is not historically descriptive of the sixteenth century. The people called *Anabaptists* at that time were part of a quite disorderly movement. One of the most striking expressions of their conflictual initiative then was interfering with other people's sermons.[13]

The other day, Jim Laue described the view that conflict is natural a Marxist view: that is, it isn't merely a sign of pathology in some person but is in the very nature of things. That view is also biblical. There might be other things about how Marx describes that conflict, or how Laue describes it, which the Bible as I see it would differ with, if we spelled it out. Yet we must affirm first of all the naturalness, the normality, of conflict. We must also affirm, therefore, the conflict management process as belonging not only in the life of individual Christians as they deal with the evil world "out there," but inside the life of the Christian community. That is part of the Christian experience of the Holy Spirit. The Holy Spirit is present when we are doing real business with each other on matters of differences and offenses and reaching reconciliation. So if we had needed, at the beginning of the meeting, a *theology* to say we ought to be doing what we've been talking about here, it could have been provided. It would not have been unfair to the story to lay that foundation.

Our Human Failures Do Not Mean We Have No Gospel Way

My second set of comments do not fall in the realm of theology in the abstract sense but more within the domain of *practical theology* in the context of what congregations regularly do, their practices. The theme has surfaced often in our papers and in our oral comments. It is noteworthy that contemporary or recent Mennonitism, as a given cultural phenomenon in white North America, has not shown any special level of success or moral authority in conflict resolution. We have generally been weak in handling conflict on the local congregational level. We have not been successful in handling dissension in the life of the local church. We are weak in community leadership development, problem solving, and in choosing, mandating, supporting, and governing our leaders. We have relatively little experience, creativity, or victory to report in those matters.

With regard to the wider social agenda, we have no special successes to show in challenging our own overidentification with the white-majority social and political establishment. Some of our members react on racial issues or on economic justice issues the way mainstream white established America reacts. We have resources in the radical reformation heritage, in the Bible, and in experiences of revival and renewal—from Wesley to Finney to *The Other Side* and *Sojourners*[14]—that can enable us to offer better, more critical judgment. Modern intellectual disciplines can also contribute. All of these resources sometimes do help, and they could help more if we would reach back and use them. Mennonite efforts toward conflict resolution thus far have not drawn seriously enough upon these abundant, relevant resources.

If our whole community had had recent experience of victories in locally effective redefinition of social sensitivity, we may have had a special momentum and confidence as we moved into our subject for this week. We might then have been able to envision intervening in other conflicts with new ideas. But the converse does not follow; that is, the mandate for Christian witness or Christian service is not invalidated by our lack of past successes in Upper Grass Roots—our own congregation back home. Our lack of a proven track record may weaken our self-confidence, and our failures may teach us what *not* to do, but the mandate to intervene comes from beyond us and cannot be set aside by our failing. It is the call of the one true God as known in Jesus. If we haven't had many past successes, that properly makes us modest, a little less confident, and a little less credible; it does not, however, change the mandate.

The fact that we have not been successful in community reconciliation before, especially in our segregated ethnic communities, is no grounds for not trying. Our ethnic communities were set up self-deceivingly in such a way as (our ancestors thought) not to have the problem of needing community reconciliaion. More involvement in "mobile troubleshooting," such as we've been talking about here, might have constructive feedback into our older "home" communities, among those who think that there is no need for change, or that there are no resources for the change they need. It might well be that the involvement of some in conflictual events of a home community, or in a not-very-coherent suburban community, would be one more aid toward renewal.

We fall short of gospel faith when we overdo our sense of failure—as if our message depended on our goodness instead of God's. We need some theological distance to remind ourselves that our own internal hang-ups and feelings of inferiority at having a strongly ethnic social identity are not a basis for negative theologizing. The mere fact that we feel guilty—that when we go from the farm to the city or to the Ivy League, we have to learn a new language—doesn't mean that our sense of inferiority must be the filter for the question of whether the gospel has anything to say to the modern world. That's what we often do. We say, "Because in such-and-such a country town the Mennonite preachers can't get along, therefore I have nothing to say about conflict," or "Therefore the gospel has nothing to say." That is a shortsighted perspective. It ought to be seriously questioned when we are trying to get some theological distance on how we are delivering our message.

We Do Have Some Resources and Gifts

Now I'd like to respond to some of the issues that came up during our meeting. It was clearly said that there are certain personal qualities, certain characteristics of skill and style, that not every human being has, but that Christians *should* have. These qualities, which correlate with the Christian message, are embodied by some Christians and also some non-Christians. Therefore, we should find in the church a predisposition, a readiness to be concerned with conflict resolution procedures, that shouldn't be expected in the same statistical probability from society as a whole or in a church of a completely different style. Jim Laue was certainly right in saying that the problems of conflict must not be boiled down to personality problems. It denatures valid process on real issues to limit it to that. But Jim also talked about the personality resources needed in order to function in some specialized roles, especially as nonindigenous interveners:

(1) Vulnerability, readiness to be shot at from both sides.

(2) Willingness not to get the credit.

(3) The long-range holding power that comes from having one's psychic self-acceptance rooted in something other than immediate success.

(4) A network of understanding people with the same language and the same values to whom to turn for morale, encouragement, and also for acceptable criticism.

(5) The commitment of Christians to the *dignity of the other party*. This is not necessarily a commitment present in all other humane value systems. In strict biblical language, we say this as "love your enemy." If you say it in Quaker language, you talk about "that of God in every human." There are different ways of saying it, but a substantial Christian commitment is that the outsider—the different one, the one not yet in our realm of concern, the "enemy," the one to whom we do not have a given relationship of pride and culture and language—is *in a special sense* the test of whether I love my neighbor. The neighbor I must love is not my near neighbor; it is especially the enemy, the adversary. You don't have to be Christian to think that, but it is a distinctive part of the Christian message. It is one of the prerequisites for the kind of process we have been talking about, especially in a culture in which the leaders of many groupings have a vested interest in not affirming the full humanity or the equal dignity of the other parties to a controversy.

(6) One other resource is the pertinence for resolving conflict of the doctrine of gifts—although we haven't drawn all the conclusions from it that we might. It is a part of the richness of God, working through the Holy Spirit, that we have been given different things to do, and for that reason different capacities and different personalities. The complementarity of those gifts means that we should expect that we have different things to do, under God's empowerment and blessing, in different places. I shouldn't ask you to be like me, and I shouldn't feel badly when I'm not like you. The inventory of the variety of roles that are needed in a conflict management process, and that have been mentioned during these days demonstrates this. It doesn't help to merge these roles into one person's work, and it doesn't help to decide that one is more important than the other. What is important is that they all be there, just like the members of the body. *Complementarity*, or the valuing of each distinct role, is what the apostles were stressing when they used the image of the body.[15]

One question discussed yesterday was whether Christians belong in all the various roles of society. If you have come from an Amish perspective, you probably won't think we belong in a lot of roles. To some others, reacting against that much restriction, that may look like a legalistic way of solving the problem. You want to get free from Amish restrictions by saying, "yes, we can do everything." Then there's John Adams's story about the Methodist bandit: it was good to have a bandit be a Methodist because although he would exercise his vocation of thievery on some people, at least he wouldn't take the preacher's money.[16] The joke points to the question of whether the Calvinist vision of the whole society being furnished with a Christian in every slot is adequate. When a slave owner was a Baptist, did it help? Should it rather have been a pagan? A Ku Klux Klansman? I don›t know. Should Christians occupy all roles in a social structure, even those of oppressors?

On one level, that's a flippant question. Obviously, you don't want a Christian to be an aggressor. Yet on another level, if we consider conflict as natural and not just as a dirty trick that the nasty establishment played on us, perhaps the oppressor can play a positive role. Might some situations need a Christian to be the "boss," because reactions that are indispensable for getting an issue resolved won't happen unless people can direct reaction against a power figure?[17] We did hear some tactical descriptions yesterday, referring to times when the intervener properly had to withhold certain insights that would have been helpful in the short term because they would have been dysfunctional in the long run. Had the participants known everything the intervener knew, they would have bypassed necessary learnings along the way. John Adams said he did not tell the AIM people (American Indian Movement) that he thought one of their important colleagues was an informant, until they would find it out on their own. He spoke of "letting the conflict mature": to develop organically in terms of a life of its own. Does that analysis not already begin to suggest that *all* of the components of the conflict, even the oppressor, are in some sense functional, because even the oppression contributes to the maturation of the group needing to assume power?

Some people say that a weak or absent father makes for a weak adolescent; that is, the father has to be paternal so that the young people have something to kick against. I do not know whether that is true. I'm merely suggesting that *if* we really believe in the great variety of roles in the body politic, and in the believing body politic, then sometimes somebody has to take the unpopular role. Maybe for some within the church, that means becoming a bishop or a bureaucrat.

If complementarity and diversity are really part of God's plan for the process of conflict, then we shouldn't always look for the troubleshooting roles either. Many of us find those roles most interesting. With our psychic training and self-image, we don't find it difficult to imagine ourselves as advocates with the virtuous underdogs. Yet the overdogs have a place in the process too, somehow, at least as enemies (and we're supposed to love our enemies), but usually more than that. They have a place as advocates of values that are also needed in the mix, and usually as the persons possessing the capacity to make things change.

Vulnerability and Suffering Love Are Keys for Receiving Truth

Now if we were to try to build a bridge from this subject matter to other things that theology traditionally has to talk about (human nature, the nature of community, the nature of wholeness, the nature of forgiveness), we would of course have to focus on many more things. I won't try to do that now, although some of these elements should come back in the ongoing conversation. I just want to point to one particular theological or perhaps spiritual focus that seems to me to be especially important. We touched on it in passing yesterday. In 2 Corinthians 4, the apostle Paul writes about his weaknesses. He uses the image of an "earthen vessel"—i.e., a very fragile, inexpensive, and unattractive container. Paul means that it is meaningful, and fitting, that the treasure that he carried, the Christian message, should be carried in unworthy, fragile vessels. His capacity to be a vehicle of the gospel is rooted in his being inapt and weak. Paul may be referring to a physical weakness. Or he may be referring to his difficulties with his colleagues; fellow workers always seemed to abandon him. More likely he is referring to the particular bind when both Jewish Christians and Gentile Christians felt he was "on the other side." In any case, Paul does not complain about his weakness, or resign himself to it in the stoic sense of saying, "I'll just hang on, and maybe it will blow over." He doesn't whistle in the dark and say, "This is not so bad." Instead, he says, "I glory in my weakness. Then it can be seen that the power that is working is God's power."

In a more modest key, something of that vulnerability is involved in the roles of intervention that we were talking about. I mean not simply that as a part of our personal emotional equipment, we need to possess the wherewithal to be vulnerable. Rather, vulnerability is a specific role, the strength of which is its weakness. The intervener has no standing except as it is given to him or her. He or she is the only person in the conflict like that. Everybody else has some kind of vested clout; each other player was sent there with some kind of defined power. The needed intervener is the one who has no standing at all except as it is freely given. That kind of vulnerability is a role, and not just a personal ploy. For that vulnerable role to keep on functioning, it will need to be subject to doubt and to periodic rejection from both sides. This function has no rights. The reason it is functional, the reason that this function has to be so weak, is that the only power it has is the truthfulness that shows through. There is nothing else to get in the way of truthfulness, of the factual communication and honest perception of the nature of the problem. That's the only power that's there. Therefore, it is a genuine kind of power.

When Mahatma Gandhi entitled his autobiography *The Story of My Experiments with Truth*, he gave us an understanding of his tactics. They were not specifically planned pressure tactics, although of course they were also that. They were not only true or insightful sociology, although sometimes they were that. Gandhi's own inner understanding of the meaning of the fasts, and sit-ins, and vigils, and the other practices that the movement enacted over the decade was that they were a way to open up channels for the truth. This truth people couldn't see otherwise, either because they didn't stop to hear or because nobody had helped to open their perceptions.

Paul's recognition of our fragility as vessels of the gospel in 2 Corinthians 4 offers a deep statement about the apostle himself, but it is also a statement about Christ. That is, the genuineness of the power of truth is related to its vulnerability, to its having no other props, no crutches, no sanctions, no clout, other than truthfulness itself. This profound and short word—*truth*—is maybe a better word for what is sometimes considered the notion of *neutrality*. Some of those usages seemed more affirmative than others. In one case study, *intervention* was talked about as neutrality. This wasn't quite the language that John Adams used when he told us the story firsthand. The American Arbitration Association, which recruits highly expert judges to help with commercial and legal conflicts, calls itself "neutral," but that is probably the wrong word. Yet, there is a desirable value that looks like what the ordinary person would call neutrality.

If I'm committed to a win-win solution, I'm on both sides. I'm not on either side, but neither am I on neither side. I'm committed to the interest of both sides. *Neutrality* is not a big enough word for that. If I'm an advocate of good process, and if my own self-interest is an investment in a good process and in a good resolution, then that is not neutrality, but neither is it partisanship. Having good contacts on both sides is not neutrality, but it certainly isn't partisanship. It demands effective concern for structuring the guarantees for both sides, finding techniques for keeping oneself color-blind. Neutrality isn't the word for this commitment to the overpowering and nonpartisan nature of truth, which is itself a constructive resource. It doesn't come automatically, and it doesn't come with every other kind of neutrality.

Next I'll identify a question that I suspect you will want to debate. Is this commitment to Christian vulnerability a virtue that can be asked of everyone? We have seen that some conflict intervention needs to buy into the mutual or reciprocal selfish interests of all parties; that is, the win-win solution has to be good for both of them. Some of us ask whether that's the best we can ask of everyone in every circumstance. Can't you sometimes ask people to do "the right thing" because of their idealism? Can't we at least suggest a higher definition for their self-interest? That's the surface level of the question I'm asking.

According to the biblical witness, Christians do expect to suffer. They expect to put other people's prospering ahead of their own and to suffer unmerited injustice. Is this a general virtue that should be preached to the whole society? Or to all Christians? One extreme form of the affirmative answer to this question is the preaching of submission to the underdogs, as was done to slaves in the American South,[18] as has long been done to women and children, and as is being done today by certain people in South Africa. They hold that such submissiveness is the same thing as New Testament nonresistance, and that it is to be preached to the people at the bottom of the pile. Certainly that won't work, because the people who preach it from the top of the pile don't apply it to themselves and thus have no right to commend it to others. But it's not what the New Testament meant either. In the New Testament, the apostles never imposed the acceptance of defeat on people who were defeated anyway.

Another answer, and one that looks easier at first glance, would be to say that turning the other cheek, or suffering love, is an upper-level heroic performance for high-quality Christians (like Mennonites), but that you can't ask that of ordinary humans. In this line of thinking, you have to let run-of-the-mill Christians seek self-interest as long as they do it decently, with dignity. In other words, I can abandon *my* rights, but I can't ask you (or a woman, or a child) to abandon *your* rights. Now that's credible. It's better than the other option. It would fit with the Catholic distinction between *precepts* and *counsels*. It does not extraneously project onto somebody else a denial of dignity that from his or her perspective can't be seen as whole or free.

Yet that dualistic ethic is, in the long run, not manageable either. It means ultimately denying that God's salvation is for the real world. We see this slant more often in some Mennonite thinking about politics, like the ideas of a Mennonite bishop with whom I spoke in 1962, just after the Cuban missile crisis. He disapproved of the Mennonite Central Committee Peace Section for having been critical of the Kennedy administration's threat of world war. The bishop said, "War is wrong for us, but it's right for them." That has been the standard way of boxing *nonresistance* into a privileged world and denying that it is good news for the rest of the world. That kind of dualism won't work here either, in the long run, to handle the questions of dignity and empowerment. We can't be happy with those who say: "Turning the other cheek, or suffering love, is not freedom. It's above and beyond the minimal demands of the law. It's something I can never recommend, never preach, and certainly never impose on somebody else." We can't ultimately admit that to love one's enemy is counter to human dignity, or that suffering love is ultimately the *alternative* to empowerment. That idea is only serviceable pedagogically, transitionally, in particular situations, where the persons whose dignity is coming to expression are in a different place in their growth and pilgrimage than the ones to whom Jesus is speaking.[19]

Social Change, Evangelism, and Faith

Now to play back a few more issues that surfaced in our conversations. Each of them would call for additional theologizing, although we cannot deal with them all here. It would certainly be out of place for me now to try to give, on each of them, what I think is the right answer. I'll just try to locate them. I'll state them negatively; that is, I have heard these negative criticisms addressed to the proposal of a model of structured, competent intervention.

Intervention, especially if it is motivated by fear of conflict, may lead to a premature resolution. A premature resolution of a conflict may hinder a necessary healthy process of heightened tension, leading to heightened awareness, heightened dignity, heightened responsibility, growing identity and empowerment of the complainant, a stronger challenge to the system, and a better final result. Thus a premature resolution may not serve the cause of justice in the long term. By satisfying the first complaint group with a first victory, it may remove the pressure. Advocating for the less powerful might be more important, in most cases, than serving as conciliating interveners. It is better to get the tension created in the first place. It's needed first that we be "on the right side," to get the thing in movement. *Then* intervention for reconciliation would be functional.

Scott Cheeseborough[20] unfortunately is no longer here. He stated a second criticism the most bluntly: namely, that *troubleshooting by well-intentioned peacemakers may merely make the basically bad system a little more livable.* Whether you make the point in Marxist terms, or in Anabaptist or Jehovah's Witness terms, doesn't really matter: the whole system of conflict intervention is wrong and oppressive. It may be like old leather patches on a new wineskin. We shouldn't be interested in helping the bad system work better. We should be so radically against the system that we would have very little interest in helping it work better. To resolve one of these conflicts does not make the system fundamentally better.

The next set of questions is broader. The presentations we have heard in the last day and a half didn't say much about *the relationship of this reconciling intervention in other people's conflicts to the rest of the life of the church.* Our speakers said only a little about the personal piety and self-understanding of the intervener as an arm of the church.

Nothing was said about the positive theology behind our commitment to social change, whether it be an old social gospel or a new social gospel. No one suggested that some other theology explained why it is important that we care about justice. We took it for granted that we care about justice; spelling out the reasons might have enriched our picture.

Nothing was said about the wider connection with less directly relevant matters like prayer, celebration, education, and all the other things that the church does and would be doing anyway. How do those things relate to justice in general and to intervention in particular? We just didn't talk about that.

We did not refer in this meeting to evangelism: that is, to our response to the fact that the relation to the Christian faith and to the person of Jesus is not the same for everybody in our society. Some people have decided, and some not, to follow Jesus. The invitation to people to make that decision is not the same thing as what we've been talking about. Yet the two invitations, one to peacemaking and social change and the other to becoming a follower of Jesus, must somehow relate. How? If we don't talk about them, then some people in Christian America will assume that everybody's in, or that the in-out variable is not significant for these purposes, because after all we are in a Christian culture. Others would say that the in/out or belief/unbelief variable is unimportant for the opposite reason: namely, that in the wider common culture faith is not supposed to be mentioned, but some equivalent of its substance is assumed always to be there. Other people will assume that the in-out variable with regard to Christian faith is *very* important. We haven't talked about how this relates to issues of conflict intervention.

We have not discussed what meaning a person we speak to sees in a new relationship to God in Jesus. Is that irrelevant? Is it relevant? We just didn't talk about it. The meaning of our silence in this kind of discussion is a very difficult thing to figure out. Some things we don't say because we take them for granted: we *do* agree about them, so we don't need to say them. Some things we don't say because we *don't* take them for granted: we *don't* agree about them, and we don't want to get stuck on debating them, because we only have two days together. The differences between those two kinds of silence are very hard to define. They certainly matter for our ability to interpret and relate to conflict. Sometimes, we are quiet because we don't want to get into a hassle on the bigger subject and we think that we can talk about the first-order agenda without that. Sometimes we don't need to mention it because it's clear to all of us. I suspect that in pacifist circles, commitment to the rejection of violence against persons is pretty clear to all of us. Therefore, we didn't talk about that because we didn't need to. But that lets a doubt persist on the edges.

We have to know about those things if we are to work at greater depths. To say this is by no means a criticism of conflict intervention know-how in itself. It's simply to acknowledge a limitation of our particular meeting, of the background we could bring to it, and of the way these broad themes could be handled.

Looking back at all of these observations about the limits of our process, I don't see that any one of them, looked at one by one, is itself a solid argument against having a place among the ministries of the church for explicit conflict resolution activities, as long as we have a place in the church for all the other things we should be doing. The other things we go on doing, including making our livings and raising our children and running our schools and our missions and our service programs—none of them challenges the whole system either. None of them is always on the side of the underdog. In all of them we are—in graduated ways, with more or less guilty conscience, and more or less clean hands, and more or less self-awareness—doing what we can of the many things that need to be done. The call to judge any particular intervention by asking whether it undercuts long-range injustice, or whether it is against the system, systematically enough, has to be taken seriously with regard to everything we do. I don't see that such a critique applies peculiarly with regard to this particular kind of troubleshooting, but it certainly identifies one of the things we want to talk further about.

The desire to make clear that we do not give our blessing to something that isn't categorically on the right track may be a new form of an old fearful Mennonite personality pattern. We want to be sure we are right; so when we look at something new to do, we have to ask, "Is it *really* on the right track?" Our case studies have concentrated on disadvantaged ethnic groups and their empowerment; this fact lets us be pretty clear that we are the right side. Therefore, it's easier for us to resurrect from our own cultural history the conviction that it is possible to find "the right side." Our Mennonite preference for simple issues, and for knowing who the virtuous underdog is, still follows us when, in more complex settings, we ask what forms our interventions might take.

Realistically Facing Tragedy, Unwinnable Struggle, and Irresolvable Ambiguity

There is another last set of issues to name. They relate to the solidity of the bases of our hope. The models of effective intervention we looked at yesterday may not be as representative as we hope they would be. They all fit within the North American context in which we picture the virtuous regularly winning out. This paradigm says that we can know what cause is right, and when that right cause properly comes to a head and is properly shepherded, the crisis can be worked through in such a way that the total system has moved forward rather than backward. That was true of all the cases we were told about. I don't doubt that the truth was told us in all those cases, but that's not the whole story in the rest of the real world. Not all battles are won. Not all victories turn out, with better knowledge, to have brought the world forward. In some parts of the American peace community, people are now rather disappointed in the victory of the campaign against the B-1 bomber. After stopping the bomber, we got instead the cruise missile, which may have more destabilizing effects on the attempt to halt the international arms race than the B-1. So not all battles won are necessarily moral victories.

Nor are all underdogs virtuous. It would have been good if we had looked at the recent Skokie religious liberties case, where the real underdogs were the Nazis, and where the powerful people in that culture were the Jews who now had the civil and economic power on their side (partly because they had been underdogs somewhere else).[21] What does hope mean there? Maybe the Civil Liberties Union was the underdog in this case, having lost half of its membership for taking a really liberal position, losing the income they had been getting from people who thought they were liberals when the cards were in their favor.

Not all conflictual issues go through a crisis process. Some come to a head in such ways that there cannot be the discernible interlocking of roles, models, and stages the theory needs. Initial empowerment is not the need in all issues. Someone mentioned to me yesterday that very often there is less room for intervention or hope when the parties are already somewhat empowered or organized and have their respective power structures. The black lawyers know how to do the black business, the labor lawyers know how to do the labor business: yet all these people who are now in on the game, and empowered, still keep losing their dignity. How does that fit? How do we bring resources to bear on that? Not all causes have part of the federal bureaucracy on their side. Since the civil rights movement, we're used to having part of the federal bureaucracy on the right side. There are not many parts of the world where you can count on that, and not even every part of America. Few social systems give to dissent the rights that it has in Anglo-Saxon polity. Whatever we all agree is wrong about the limits of the Anglo-Saxon world in terms of justice, at least it provides structures for the affirmation of minority dignity, which most of the world doesn't.

So, if we want to think more deeply about the success stories we talked about yesterday, asking to what extent they are typical of how and where most Christians deal with injustices, we come to a profound spiritual and theological question. What is the justification of working for justice when you won't win? Which side is God really on, if the wicked prosper? Which side will *we* be on, if we can't see clearly which side is right?

At least we have said that Christians are (or should be) willing to suffer when it's clear which side is right. Not many Christians even have to do that, at least most of the time in this part of the world. Sometimes we can't see clearly which side is right. Often we can't see that the suffering of Christians will be God's cause for growth. Not only is the triumph of iniquity something we haven't struggled with yet, but I don't know how we might struggle with the triumph of evil, in terms of simulations and experiences, analogous to what we have done here, where we have the leaders and the technical know-how to analyze things. We aren't yet engaged in the spiritual struggle with evil. We didn't come yesterday to the depths of Old Testament literature and its wrestling with the fact that the wicked prosper. We are still part of the generation that believes that the wicked won't really prosper, at least not for long, at least not if we do our job right. We believe that some of the people in power in Washington, DC, are on the side of the good; some of the oppressors' hearts can be touched, and some people will give in a little, if just to get us off their sidewalks. That the wicked *really prosper* is a piece of world history and a part of the Old Testament witness, and a part of the Jewish and black experience, that we have not learned to take with deep seriousness in North America.

If we aren't yet up to wrestling with the deepest crises of the Old Testament, then obviously we will need more help if we are to deal with the New Testament depths of the meaning of the cross. The cross drives us to a still deeper search for what is really new and victorious, by way of insight, love, and patience in the gospel, beyond what we have discussed. I hope we can continue talking about the themes of yesterday, about settings where we can contribute to the systems and scenarios in the privileged part of the world. But let's remember that it wasn't only in the privileged part of the world that God chose to be with his people, in the old covenant or the new, or in the Reformation. Some kind of awareness of solidarity with the places where the virtuous don't win is an ongoing part of our responsibility. Only then do we know what we're doing with the exceptional opportunities we have, in a society where at least there's room for dissent, and there are rights for minorities, and there is leeway (created partly by Christian witness over the past) for working on relative justice.

Seeing God Acting in the Midst of Struggles for Justice: Questions and Responses

Participant:[22] "We lived in Tanzania for three years from 1970–72. President Nyerere is one of the few people in the world of whom I would state that I believe he is a truly good person, and truly motivated by good and not self-interest. He is a Catholic and a practicing Christian. Yet one thing I could never resolve was that he very strongly supported FRELIMO, the guerrilla movement working in Mozambique to overthrow the Portuguese government. He not only let guerrilla forces stay in Tanzania and helped support the guerrilla fight in Mozambique. They drove the Portuguese government from Mozambique. Now the guerrilla bases still exist for the fight in Rhodesia. This has been a conflict that I've had myself: this really good Christian man, who I really believe is one of the truly good people, supports a violence that I have trouble dealing with."

Other participant: "You talked, John, about resources of the Spirit being present in the church. As yet, our justice system has decided mainly on the side of maintaining social systems. To what degree is this theological concern, about the other side's dignity being present through the Spirit, one of the energizing factors that may make a change, beyond human rationalizing, for good?"

Yoder: I am immediately aware of two problems in that connection. You were pointing mostly to the second. Yet it is something to be embarrassed about, that we do not want either to say a clear "no" to the question: "Are there Christian resources in the social process in America?" Most people in office claim to be Christians. People in high office make much of their being Christians and of bringing their values into their function in public office. It won't do to be completely cynical about that, but neither should we be completely gullible about it. That's not just a judgment on those people, but also on the structures in which they work. Since we're in a post-Christian culture, we haven't even finished disentangling to what extent anything Christian should properly or improperly come into the nonchurch discourse.

That's the question we have here that we wouldn't have in the USSR or China. We need to avoid both the gullibility that honors every religious claim, and the blanket rejection of every religious appeal today, on the grounds that our society is "secular" or because we have to debunk some people's gullible trust in their "Christian world."

Your other question was the deeper one. Is there hope for new, specific input derived from a faith commitment? Is there potential for change that isn't in the system? If so, where would it come from? It would come from outside the system as it is, but how would you recognize it? How would you comment on it? Should you comment on it? Should you pray when negotiations are beginning, or when they collapse? Jimmy Carter did pray at Camp David. What difference did that make? Would prayer be just a psychological gimmick, or might it open up something that wouldn't have happened otherwise?

The difficulty is that, whenever something happens, then the social scientist Jim Laue can put it on his map of all the factors. Then it will be one more natural phenomenon subject to social science analysis. If it doesn't happen, then of course we can't tell that it belongs on the map. We can't prove transcendence, ever, on the grounds of something that happened, because once it happens it isn't transcendent. You can argue that some breakthrough was unexpected, or unlikely, or atypical, or creative, but you can't prove that something that happened in a social process just simply couldn't have happened, so that therefore it must have been a miracle.[23]

Some of our Pentecostal friends can do this with healing, because we do have notions about organic continuity. Most of us believe that cancer doesn't just go away. Some Pentecostal believers have before-and-after x-rays to show, so that they can argue at least that something organic happened that could not have happened except by some transcendent intervention. But our physiology of social cancer is not clear enough that we can know that something couldn't have happened, so that once it *does* happen, as it should not have, we can give God the credit.

Nevertheless, I think there should be room for socially active believers to operate on a faith assumption as a whole. That is, there should be room for the expectation (*hope* may be too strong a word in modern English) that something saving may happen, something that did not previously seem possible. Christians and Jews don't accept a closed-system analysis as a valid reason for giving up on doing the right thing. (That is, once something good has happened, we know it could happen after all; therefore, you can't prove philosophically that God alone did it.) Nevertheless: people who believe in the resurrection are responsible, on the grounds of that faith context, to go through life believing that problems can be solved for which the solution is not yet evident. Such people are more likely to find new answers than people who believe there are none. The solution will be more likely to come if you don't shortcut for a violent solution. If you allow yourself to resort to violence, then you won't wait for the resurrection. If you don't authorize violence, you might not get a resurrection, but at least there's also room for an unforeseen saving outcome.

Notes

Introduction Jesus Is No Sectarian: John H. Yoder's Christological Peacemaking Ethic

1. John H. Yoder, *The Politics of Jesus* (Grand Rapids: Eerdmans, 1972 and 1994), chap. 12, "The War of the Lamb."

2. See "The Political Meaning of *Hope*," chap. 3 below.

3. Ibid.

4. Ibid.

5. "The Political Meaning of *Hope*." Also mentioned in "Gospel Renewal and the Roots of Nonviolence," chap. 2 below.

6. Reinhold Niebuhr, "Why I Leave the F. O. R.," *The Christian Century*, January 3, 1934, and in Niebuhr, *Love and Justice*, ed. D. B. Robertson (Louisville: Westminster John Knox, 1957), 254–55.

7. Reinhold Niebuhr, "Why the Christian Church Is Not Pacifist," in *Christianity and Power Politics* (New York: Scribner, 1952), 8; cf. 10.

8. Reinhold Niebuhr, "Pacifism Against the Wall," *The American Scholar* (Spring 1936), in *Love and Justice*, 261.

9. Niebuhr, "Why the Christian Church Is Not Pacifist," 4–5.

10. Niebuhr, "Pacifism Against the Wall," 257.

11. For Yoder's more extensive, parallel response to Niebuhr, see his *Christian Attitudes to War, Peace, and Revolution,* ed. Theodore J. Koontz and Andy Alexis-Baker (Grand Rapids: Brazos, 2009), chaps. 18–20.

12. Mark Thiessen Nation, *John Howard Yoder: Mennonite Patience, Evangelical Witness, Catholic Convictions* (Grand Rapids: Eerdmans, 2006).

13. Glen Stassen, *Living the Sermon on the Mount: Practical Hope for Grace and Deliverance* (San Francisco: Jossey-Bass, 2006); Stassen, "The Fourteen Triads of the Sermon on the Mount: Matthew 5:21–7:12," *Journal of Biblical Literature* 122, no. 2 (Summer 2003): 267–308; Stassen, "Concrete Christological Norms for Transformation" in Glen H. Stassen, John H. Yoder, and D. M. Yeager, *Authentic Transformation: A New Vision for Christ and Culture* (Nashville: Abingdon, 1996), 172–73. Our shared interest in making this correction, as on many other themes, is a major reason for our close friendship.

14. Yoder, *Nevertheless: A Meditation on the Varieties and Shortcomings of Religious Pacifism* (Scottdale, PA: Herald Press, 1971), 95–96, 123–27.

15. Yoder, *Christian Attitudes to War, Peace, and Revolution,* 317.

16. Yoder, *Christian Witness to the State* (Scottdale, PA and Waterloo, ON: Herald Press, 1964 and 2002), 7.

17. Ibid., 180–81.

18. Yoder, *For the Nations: Essays Public and Evangelical* (Grand Rapids: Eerdmans, 1997), 3–8.

19. Yoder, *Christian Attitudes to War, Peace, and Revolution.*

20. Yoder, *The Priestly Kingdom: Social Ethics as Gospel* (South Bend, IN: University of Notre Dame: 1984), 180–81.

21. "The Changing Shape of the Conversation Between the Peace Churches and Mainstream Christianity," chap. 7 below.

22. See his explanation in Stassen, Yoder, and Yeager, *Authentic Transformation*, 82.

23. Michael Walzer, *Thick and Thin: Moral Argument at Home and Abroad* (Notre Dame, IN: University of Notre Dame Press, 1994); and Walzer, *Interpretation and Social Criticism* (Cambridge, MA: Harvard University Press, 1987).

24. Stassen, Yoder, and Yeager, *Authentic Transformation*, 67–71.

25. Yoder, *Anabaptism and Reformation in Switzerland: An Historical and Theological Analysis of the Dialogues Between Anabaptists and Reformers*, trans. David Carl Stassen and C. Arnold Snyder (Kitchener, ON: Pandora Press, 2004).

26. Mark Thiessen Nation, "The Politics of Yoder Regarding *The Politics of Jesus*: Recovering the Implicit in Yoder's Holistic Theology for Pacifism," (unpublished lecture, Indianapolis, Indiana, March, 2009, and Tokyo Biblical Seminary, June, 2009); forthcoming in John Nugent, ed., *Radical Ecumenicity: Pursuing Unity and Continuity after John Howard Yoder* (Abilene, TX: Abilene Christian University Press).

27. Yoder, *Nevertheless*, 135.

28. Ibid., 136.

29. Yoder, "The Kingdom as Social Ethic," in *The Priestly Kingdom: Social Ethics as Gospel* (Notre Dame, IN: University of Notre Dame Press, 1984), 92.

30. Yoder, *Nevertheless*, 135.

31. Ibid., 136.

32. Yoder, *The Christian Witness to the State*, 73.

33. Yoder, *For the Nations*, 2–3.

34. Ibid., 121.

35. Stassen, Yoder, and Yeager, *Authentic Transformation*, 67–71.

36. Yoder, *Body Politics: Five Practices of the Christian Community Before the Watching World* (Scottdale, PA: Herald Press, 1992 and 2001).

37. Yoder, *Priestly Kingdom*, 61–62.

38. Yoder, *For the Nations*, 49.

39. Ibid., 42.

40. Ibid., 115.

41. Ibid., 7.

42. The following quotations are all drawn from Yoder, *Nevertheless*, chap. 18, "The Pacifism of the Messianic Community," 124–28. In the revised edition (Scottdale and Waterloo: Herald, 1992), see pp.133-7.

43. See Yoder, *Authentic Transformation*, 61–65, 84–87, 141–42.

44. Yoder, *Preface to Theology: Christology and Theological Method*, ed. Alex Sider and Stanley Hauerwas (Grand Rapids: Brazos, 2002), 202. He argues similarly in *Authentic Transformation*, 61–65; see also 138–42 for a qualification of how this applies to H. R. Niebuhr.

45. For example, Paul Martens, "Discipleship Ain't Just about Jesus: or On the Importance of the Holy Spirit for Pacifists," *The Conrad Grebel Review* 21, no. 2 (Spring 2003): 32–40.

46. Yoder, *For the Nations*, 217.

47. Ibid., 228.

48. The following quotations are taken from "Gospel Renewal and the Roots of Nonviolence," chap. 2 below.

49. Ibid.

50. "The Changing Shape," chap. 7 below. Yoder developed these themes more fully in his *For the Nations*, and his *The Jewish-Christian Schism Revisited*, ed. Michael Cartwright and Peter Ochs (Grand Rapids: Eerdmans, 2003).

51. Ibid., 32–33.

52. Yoder, *Priestly Kingdom*, 50–54; *Authentic Transformation*, 82–89.

53. "Gospel Renewal and the Roots of Nonviolence," chap. 2 below.

54. Yoder, "A Think Piece on How Just War Thinking and Pacifism Coinhere," unpublished essay.

55. Ibid.

56. Ibid.

57. Yoder, "The Church and Change: Violence and its Alternatives," chap. 13 below.

58. The following notes come from these unpublished memos.

59. Yoder, *The Original Revolution: Essays on Christian Pacifism* (Scottdale, PA and Waterloo, ON: Herald Press, 1971, 1977, and 2003), 38.

60. Yoder, *The Royal Priesthood* (Scottdale, PA: Herald Press, 1994), 143–167.

61. "Just War and Nonviolence,"chap. 6 below.

62. "Gospel Renewal and the Roots of Nonviolence," chap. 2 below.

63. Yoder, *For the Nations*, 2, 6, 7, et passim.

Chapter 1 A Theological Critique of Violence

1. This chapter was written for two lectures presented at Elmhurst College on July 29 and 30, 1991, and published as "A Theological Critique of Violence," *New Conversations* 16, no. 3 (1995): 2–15.

2. 1 John 3:11–12, 15–18: "For this is the message which you have heard from the beginning, that we should love one another, and not be like Cain who was of the evil one and murdered his brother. And why did he murder him? Because his own deeds were evil and his brother's righteous. . . . Anyone who hates his brother is a murderer, and you know that no murderer has eternal life abiding in him. By this we know love, that he laid down his life for us; and we ought to lay down our lives for the brethren. But if anyone has the world's goods and sees his brother in need, yet closes his heart against him, how does God's love abide in him? Little children, let us not love in word or speech but in deed and in truth."

3. Gen. 4:14.

4. The term "mimetic" is borrowed from the very creative but very tentative synthesis of René Girard, whose numerous works have created a school in which primeval violent mimesis explains most of the origins of culture.

5. Gen. 4:15. Nothing is said as to who will inflict that retaliation. In the somewhat parallel judgment of Gen. 9:5–6, the agent of retribution is human. It would then seem that the same people who kill Cain will kill his killer, and that what Yahweh predicts or promulgates is an escalation of the same mimetic retaliation that Cain needs to be protected against.

6. I offered a very brief capsule of René Girard's thesis in a review of his *The Scapegoat* (Baltimore: Johns Hopkins University Press, 1986) in *Religion and Literature* 19, no. 3 (Autumn 1987): 89ff. Cf. his *Violence and the Sacred* (Baltimore: Johns Hopkins University Press, 1972).

7. Mark I. Wallace, "Postmodern Biblicism: the Challenge of René Girard for Contemporary Theology," *Modern Theology* 5, no. 4 (July 1989): 309–24, identifies ways in which Girard's approach is less able to deliver a "general field theory" of violence, society, and religion than some had thought.

8. The First Gulf War was a fresh memory at the time of the conference.

9. We also call it the family, the clan, the corporation (all usually patriarchal). I name the civil realm first because most moral theology begins at the top; the logic of affirming the legitimacy of domination is parallel.

10. C. S. Lewis, "The Humanitarian Theory of Punishment," reprinted in *God in the Dock: Essays on Theology and Ethics* (Grand Rapids: Eerdmans, 1972), 287–301. Lewis's actual case is against social workers who would make criminal sentencing arbitrarily flexible out of a manipulative intent to "rehabilitate" offenders rather than honoring them with a retribution worthy of their offense. Lewis did not apply this argument to the death penalty, but readers have.

11. Editors' Note: Yoder mentions a specific news story, but the account is timeless.

12. Cf. review of these passages in H. Wayne House and John Howard Yoder, *The Death Penalty Debate* (Dallas: Word, 1991), 133–137.

13. 2 Cor. 10:4.

14. Others in the Elmhurst symposium reported a similar consequentialism, by which morality pertains never to means but only to ends, and which can be calculated on a simply utilitarian basis.

15. Properly interpreted, the just war discipline is thus an instrument of restraint, forbidding war when it does not meet the criteria. Not all who use the terms respect this intent. Cf. my *When War is Unjust* (Minneapolis: Fortress, 1984), 42–71.

16. "Violence therefore can be understood as any breach of the community of humankind as we are led to understand it in the light of Christ." Violence can also be defined "as the cause of the difference between the potential and the actual in human self-realisation": Consultation on "Violence, Nonviolence, and the Struggle for Social Justice" report, Cardiff, Sept. 3–7, 1972, and report from World Council of Churches, Geneva, Nov. 1972, par. 4 and 9.

17. Is the picture made truer by calling all evils by the same name? Many cultural forces (shame, fear, respectability, concepts of divine order) aggravate injustice without coming close to being "violence." Many social arrangements, without evil intentions, victimize or violate persons by virtue of their sex, race, or status. As a white male with a steady job and status, I participate in such injustice, sometimes culpably. Yet to boil down all evil monodimensionally to "violence" is a disservice to the necessary moral argument.

18. Editors' Note: Yoder is here giving his own summary of the message of Frantz Fanon in *The Wretched of the Earth* (New York: Grove Press, 1963 and 1968), not a quotation from the book. Yoder comments by way of footnote: In less brutal forms similar prices are exacted wherever social change moves by pendulum swings. Compensatory measures to provide marginalized persons a level playing field may be paid for by others who had no share in the history of discrimination.

19. Too few deal with the power of the "recreational" media in forming and reinforcing social values.

20. See Walter Wink, *Engaging the Powers* (Minneapolis: Augsburg Fortress, 1992), 45ff.

21. Out of respect for those who use this language and a mode of reckoning, I here go, ecumenically, a second mile, though I consider it both fundamentally inadequate at best and corrupt in ordinary usage.

22. Killing is not clearly the worst thing a human being can do to another. Physical or psychological torture, gang rape, or slavery might *in some ways* be worse. But no one advocates doing those things as a purposive political program. What we are evaluating here is the case for willingly and wittingly choosing violence as a less-evil political strategy.

23. A footnote to par. 9 of the Cardiff document cited above suggests that the broadest definition ("cause of the difference between the potential and the actual") has been "enlarged to the point of uselessness." I would say that such abstract extension of meaning has some use, but not in the contested calculation of lesser evils.

24. References to the "just revolution" argument, as made or alluded to in the Elmhust symposium, regularly posited such conditions as: "when it is possible in a brief time with rela-

tively little cost to establish a better regime." Yet there was no consideration of the difficulties of knowing when in a "revolutionary situation" such a sanguine prospect actually obtains.

25. When this was said it was most obviously true of the Warsaw Pact governments, the former Yugoslavia, and the southern tier of former Soviet republics.

26. Thinkers who transpose just war thought to the setting of revolution are right about the existence of substantial parallels; they are, however, seldom overtly and ecumenically self-critical about this one crucial difference.

27. That the values are incommensurable identifies the point of the present discussion. A more profound theological critique would point out that national "liberty," "sovereignty," "honor," "justice," and the other quasi-transcendent values for which modern militancy is ready to kill and to die, tend (as operationally defined) to be ill-defined, provincial, self-serving, and idolatrous.

28. Measured by the criterion of total purity, every sin, by being sin at all, is of course quantitatively the same (Rom. 14:23, James 2:10ff). The argument here, however, is about social utility, not purity.

29. Some descriptions of the argument against violence presented in the Elmhurst symposium suggested that the believer need do nothing, on the grounds of her or his trust in providence. This is an exaggeration. The believer in the lordship of the Crucified is called to do many aggressive, costly, and risky things; the believer is not called, however, to choose to do evil that good may come.

30. Editor's note: This is not an exact quote of the Nicene or Apostles' Creed, but is an accurate summary of the creeds as we have them; that, I think, is Yoder's intent. It is closer to the wording of the Apostles' creed.

31. "The good news of the gospel is not the law that we ought to love one another. The good news . . . is that there is a resource of divine mercy which is able to overcome a contradiction within our own souls. . . . In this doctrine of forgiveness . . . Christianity measures the full seriousness of sin. . . ." Reinhold Niebuhr, "Why the Christian Church Is Not Pacifist," 2.

32. My book by that title (Grand Rapids: Eerdmans, 1972) reviewed the social-ethical import of the gospel on the basis of the scholarship of the times. In the past twenty years others have made the same point, not because they got it from me but because in the face of the agenda of our age, many scholars could not but notice the same message.

33. Perhaps the fundamental distortion behind all of the abuses just named is the notion that preaching the cross is compatible with patriarchy. This particular issue became especially visible in the Elmhurst conversations. This kind of patriarchy differs from the Rambo and Schwarzkopf patterns, in that its conscious intention is benevolent. I have personally experienced that such good intentions can nevertheless lead to abusive relationships.

34. The most important omission in this paper, as in the overall programming of the Elmhurst symposium event, was a study of the relationship between the ethos of the people of God and the ethos of the wider society. Biblically the two must be distinguished though not separated. Since Eusebius they have tended to be confused, at great cost. Cf. my "The Constantinian Sources of Western Social Ethics" in *Priestly Kingdom*, 135–47. How the believing community is called to be paradigm or pilot project for the world's renewal is portrayed in John Howard Yoder, Doug Gwyn, George Hunsinger, and Eugene Roop, *A Declaration on Peace: In God's People the World's Renewal Has Begun* (Scottdale, PA: Herald Press, 1991). Cf. also my *Original Revolution*, 153–76.

Chapter 2 Gospel Renewal and the Roots of Nonviolence

1. The context for which this paper was written was a conference, May 2-4, 1984, on the religious roots of nonviolence. The event was convened by a study center of the State University of New York at Stony Brook, whose primary area of disciplinary concern is Asian religions, so that the frame of reference is broader than Christian. It was revised and published in *Faith*

and Freedom (Australia) vol. 4/4 (December,1995) 5-10, and edited February 1997 for inclusion in this volume.

2. The label "radical reformation" was given currency by George Huntston Williams, *The Radical Reformation* (Philadelphia: Westminster, 1962; 3rd edition, Kirksville, MO: Sixteenth Century Journal Publishers, 1992). The history of its most representative movements is presented in Donald F. Durnbaugh, *The Believers' Church: The History and Character of Radical Protestantism* (New York: Macmillan, 1968; Scottdale, PA: Herald Press, 1985).

3. For a general summary of the radical reformation stance in ethics, see my *Priestly Kingdom*, 105–34. For an exposition of the notion that a series of reformation events across the centuries follow a certain pattern, see my "The Free Church Syndrome" in *Within the Perfection of Christ: Essays on Peace and the Nature of the Church*, ed. Terry L. Brensinger and E. Morris Sider (Nappanee, IN: Evangel Press, 1990), 169–76. There exists no adequate general narrative history of the entire movement, but the earliest days of the Swiss movement were recounted in a lively way by Fritz Blanke, *Brothers in Christ: The History of the Oldest Anabaptist Congregation* (Scottdale, PA: Herald Press, 1961). *The Sources of Swiss Anabaptism,* ed. Leland Harder (Scottdale, PA: Herald Press, 1985) is the definitive documentary survey. The fullest recent overview is C. Arnold Snyder, *Anabaptist History and Theology* (Kitchener, ON: Pandora Press, 1995). Editors' Note: Also now see a translation of Yoder's early research in John Howard Yoder, *Anabaptism and Reformation in Switzerland.*

4. This part of the picture is by no means as self-evident as it might seem. Gerhard Ladner, *The Idea of Reform: Its Impact on Christian Thought and Action in the Age of the Fathers* (Cambridge, MA: Harvard University Press, 1959) demonstrates how broadly the Neoplatonic roots of medieval thought led critics of Christendom to give priority to nonformal diagnoses, and therefore to cures that did not cure. The positions that historians call "spiritualizing" regularly claimed that to care about fixing forms was by definition not radical since it did not give priority to the inward. Cf. my *The Royal Priesthood* (Scottdale, PA: Herald Press, 1994), 69–72, and my *Priestly Kingdom*, 68ff.

5. Franklin H. Littell, one of the last generation's foremost interpreters of the radical reformation vision, capsuled this point in the distinction between the ideal type notions of "reformation" and "restoration."

6. Cf. "Radical Reformation Ethics in Ecumenical Perspective" in my *Priestly Kingdom*, 105–22.

7. Cf. "The Authority of Tradition" in *Priestly Kingdom,* 63–79, esp. 69ff.

8. The term *magisterial* was given currency by George Huntston Williams, to combine the notions of magistrate (what we call *state*) and normative teaching (*magisterium*).

9. The ambivalence of the reformers' reception of the just war heritage is spelled out at length in my "The Reception of the Just War Tradition" in *History of European Ideas* 9 (1988): 1–23, and more briefly in *When War Is Unjust,* 19–24.

10. A debate continues among historians of ethics concerning whether the early Christians were "pacifist." I have written on that question in "War as a Moral Problem in the Early Church," in *The Pacifist Impulse in Historical Perspective*, ed. Harvey L. Dyck (Toronto: University of Toronto Press, 1996), 90–110. It is partly a semantic quibble. Here I have intentionally written that Christians rejected Caesar's wars, a fact that no historians deny. The debate is about just why they did so. Editors' Note: Also see Yoder's lecture on the early church, chapter 3 in his *Christian Attitudes to War, Peace, and Revolution.*

11. Cf. "The Constantinian Sources of Western Social Ethics" in *Priestly Kingdom,* 135–47.

12. This fleshing out of the claim to fulfill the law is of course most simply put in Matt. 5:21–48. Cf. "The Political Axioms of the Sermon on the Mount" in my *Original Revolution,* 34–51; also "Jesus' Life-Style Sermon and Prayer" in *Social Themes of the Christian Year: A Commentary on the Lectionary,* ed. Dieter T. Hessel (Philadelphia: Geneva Press, 1983), 87–96.

Editors' Note: The latter has since been reprinted as "The Moral Axioms of the Kingdom Coming," in *To Hear the Word* (Eugene, OR: Wipf & Stock, 2001), 28–38.

13. The appeal to God as model is simplest in Matt. 5:45 and Luke 6:35; its wider connections are the theme of chap. 7, 112–38, in my *Politics of Jesus*, 2nd ed. (Grand Rapids: Eerdmans, 1994).

14. See *The Politics of Jesus* on the ways in which Jesus was a political figure (21–59), and the many ways in which Christians are called to imitate him (112–33).

15. This point was relatively novel when originally presented in the Stony Brook meeting. Since then I have spelled it out more fully in "War as a Moral Problem in the Early Church" (in Dyck, *The Pacifist Impulse in Historical Perspective*) and in "On Not Being in Charge," in *War and Its Discontents: Pacifism and Quietism in the Abrahamic Traditions*, ed. J. Patout Burns (Washington, DC: Georgetown University Press, 1996), 74–90. Cf. also "The Jewishness of Early Christian Pacifism," Kroc Institute and website. This insight has yet to be taken account of by academic historians of ethics. Without it, the unique interfaith stance of the radical reformation is misunderstood. Editors' Note: For these latter two essays, now see chap. 9 and chap. 2 in John Howard Yoder, *The Jewish-Christian Schism Revisited*.

16. Cf. my essay, "On Not Being in Charge," in *War and Its Discontents*.

17. Not every item of the law was held by the later rabbis to be worthy of sacrificing one's life to obey it. The rejection of bloodshed, the rejection of incest, and the rejection of blasphemy are the three points where such costly faithfulness is called for. On other matters, a Jew might accept an evil that someone asks him to do, for the sake of saving his life or that of someone else (*Babylonian Talmud*, Sanhedrin 74a). This does not mean, however, that the martyr's death "sanctifies the Name" *only* when it is inflicted for the sake of one of those three kinds of refusal to conform.

18. *Babylonian Talmud*, Sanhedrin 74a.

19. *Babylonian Talmud*, Berakhot 10a.

20. *Babylonian Talmud*, Sanhedrin 74a.

21. I have gathered numerous of these rabbinic testimonies in "Jewish Nonviolence from Jeremiah to Hertzl," chap. 3 in my paper, "Chapters in the History of Religiously Rooted Nonviolence," the Joan B. Kroc Institute for International Peace Studies, 1996; and website. Editors' Note: http://theology.nd.edu/people/research/yoder-john/documents/thenonviolence ofjudaismfromjeremiahtohertzl.pdf; and see chap. 10 of Yoder, *Christian Attitudes to War, Peace, and Revolution*.

22. The global impact of "Constantine" as an event, not merely as a person, is summarily described in my *Priestly Kingdom*, 135–47.

23. Geoffrey Nuttall, *Christian Pacifism in History* (Oxford: Basil Blackwell, 1958), shows how the antiwar testimonies of the several radical reformations were both alike and different.

24. As acknowledged above, Geoffrey Nuttall, in the chapter "The Law of Christ" in his *Christian Pacifism in History*, very well characterizes this understanding.

25. Murray L. Wagner, *Petr Chelčický: A Radical Separatist in Hussite Bohemia* (Scottdale, PA: Herald Press, 1983).

26. As noted in endnote 3 above, the sources are gathered in the volume edited by Harder and an early narration was provided by Fritz Blanke. There is no agreement on how to interpret these beginnings. Editors' Note: However, for the most up-to-date narration, see C. Arnold Snyder, "The Birth and Evolution of Swiss Anabaptism (1520–1530)," *The Mennonite Quarterly Review* 80 (October 2006): 501–645. Yoder had high respect for Snyder's scholarship, and we share that high respect.

27. See "suffering" in *Anabaptism and Reformation in Switzerland*.

28. Numerous of these kinds of progress were especially visible in the work of William Penn, but he was not alone. He was preceded by Roger Williams and aided by the German pacifist immigrant communities.

29. These social contributions are "second-order" in another way as well. They reflect patterns of loving community in the wider society, which are first meaningful within the faith community. Cf. my "Sacrament as Social Ethics" in *Royal Priesthood* and my *Body Politics*.

30. Cf. my essay, "The Free Church Syndrome," in *Within the Perfection of Christ*, 169–76.

31. See the description of the interreligious nature of the context for this paper in endnote 1 above.

32. This does not mean that they all followed through with the realization of a totally renewed pattern of ministry after the Pauline model. As I said in "The One or the Many: The Pauline Vision and the Rest of the Reformation" in *Servants of the Word*, ed. David B. Eller (Elgin, IL: Brethren Press, 1990), 51–64: not all of the elements of the New Testament vision of the church were implemented by later reformations.

33. The Salvation Army does without the visible sacraments, because in their view they are a service agency rather than a church. On the other end of the spectrum of nineteenth-century renewal, the Disciples made much of restoring believers baptism and the weekly Lord's Supper.

34. Littell citing Troeltsch in Franklin H. Littell, *The Origins of Sectarian Protestantism* (New York: Macmillan, 1964), 154.

35. I have argued the inadequacy of that traditional kind of "method" debate in my essay, "Walk and Word: The Alternatives to Methodologism," in *Theology Without Foundations*, ed. Stanley Hauerwas, Nancey Murphy, and Mark Nation (Nashville: Abingdon, 1994), 77–90, 312–17.

36. Editor's note: By "established-church versions" of Christianity, Yoder means something like Ernst Troeltsch's "church type"—receiving official authority from a government, and intending to include all citizens in the state ruled by that government. Its definition of membership must be metaphysical and invisible, rather than visible indications of belief and regeneration, since it intends to include everyone in a realm, regardless of their visible discipleship. Established-church versions have a Constantinian understanding of the relation of church and state. But so do free-church versions that have taken on nationalism or a dominant ideology.

37. Only polemically preoccupied misinterpretation would substitute an "either/or" formulation for the above "not so much . . . as. . . ." The radicals made much of contemplation and of clarifying insights; but they did not seek the primary leverage for renewal there.

Chapter 3 The Political Meaning of *Hope*

1. This chapter is part of the second lecture of the Heck Lectures delivered at United Theological Seminary, Dayton, Ohio, in May 1983.

2. Leo Tolstoy, *The Confession* (New York: W. W. Norton & Co., 1984); Tolstoy, *What I Believe* (Whitefish, MT: Kessinger Publishing, 2004); and Tolstoy, *The Kingdom of God Is Within You* (Lincoln: University of Nebraska Press, 1985).

3. Gen. 4:24.

4. The chronicler of this nonresistant/conscientious objector tradition is Peter Brock. He wrote many volumes on this history. They are summarized in: Peter Brock, *Varieties of Pacifism: A Survey from Antiquity to the Onset of the Twentieth Century* (Syracuse: Syracuse University Press, 1999). Some documentation of the tradition within the U.S. is provided in Staughton and Alice Lynd, eds., *Nonviolence in America: A Documentary History*, rev. ed. (Maryknoll, NY: Orbis Books, 1995).

5. Walter Wink, *Engaging the Powers* (Minneapolis: Augsburg Fortress, 1992), 184–86. Editors' Note: See also Clarence Jordan, *Substance of Faith* (New York: Association Press, 1972), 69; John Ferguson, *Politics of Love* (Nyack, NY: FOR, 1979), 4–5; Willard Swartley, "War and Peace in the New Testament," *Aufstieg und niedergang der römischen Welt* (Berlin: Walther de Gruyter, 1996), 3:2338; Glen H. Stassen, "The Fourteen Triads of the Sermon on the Mount: Matthew 5:21–7:12," *Journal of Biblical Literature* 122/2 (Summer, 2003), 267–308.

6. Tolstoy did have enough unresolved personal problems to make him vulnerable to the kind of description represented by H. Richard Niebuhr's caricature of radicality in his *Christ and Culture* (New York: Harper & Row, 1951); that does not, however, make the *ad hominem* critique fair. The characterization is motivated by Niebuhr's own agenda, like that of his brother Reinhold: namely, the intent to prove a polarity between the Jesus of the Gospel accounts and the realm of morally autonomous "culture." It is Reinhold Niebuhr who told three generations of American ethicists that Jesus taught a limp and historyless nonresistance, thus driving a wedge between Tolstoy and Gandhi as well as between Jesus and the real world.

7. M. K. Gandhi, *Gandhi's Autobiography: The Story of My Experiments with Truth,* trans. Mahadev Desai (Washington, DC: Public Affairs Press, 1960), 172, 198.

8. On Moses, see my "Exodus and Exile: Two Faces of Liberation," in *CrossCurrents* (Fall 1973): 279–309. This is also true of Abraham; see "If Abraham Is Our Father," in *Original Revolution*. Scriptural narrative is often more sociologically realistic than our reading of it.

9. See James Wm. McClendon Jr., *Ethics* (Nashville: Abingdon, 1986), 27–34, for the characterization of "baptist" identity.

10. Editors' Note: Yoder had intended that this essay would follow his essay on the meaning of hope and of the full incarnational humanity of Jesus for faithfulness and effectiveness, especially in the thought of Martin Luther King Jr. That essay, however, has already been published as "The Power Equation, Jesus, and the Politics of King," chap. 6 of *For the Nations*. We recommend reading that essay along with this one.

11. Gandhi, "We Can Wait." Editors' Note: We searched the books on Gandhi's writings, and Linda Gerber-Stellingwerf of the Fourth Freedom Forum conducted several keyword searches on the CD-Rom of Gandhi's writings, but we have not found a writing specifically on that topic. However, the phrase appears several times in Gandhi's speeches and writings, and in ways that confirm Yoder's interpretation.

12. Editors' Note: "The Church and Change: Violence Versus Nonviolent Direct Action," chap. 13 below.

13. Cf. Richard B. Gregg, *The Power of Nonviolence* (New York: Schocken, 1966); Krishnalal Shridharani, *War Without Violence: A Study of Gandhi's Method and Its Accomplishments* (New York: Harcourt Brace Jovanovich, 1939); and Gene Sharp, *The Politics of Nonviolent Action,* 3 vols., (Boston: Porter Sargent, 1973).

14. *A Testament of Hope: The Essential Writings of Martin Luther King, Jr.,* ed. James M. Washington (San Francisco: HarperCollins, 1991), 11.

15. Ibid., 14.

16. Editors' Note: Here Yoder's footnote refers us simply to "Richardson." In *For the Nations* (125), Yoder writes: "Herbert W. Richardson wrote in *Commonweal* that King had been "the most important theologian of our time, . . . because of his creative proposals for dealing with a structure of evil generated by modern relativism. . . . I may not follow Richardson on relativism as the essence of the modern challenge. I do however support Richardson in the claim that there is profound learning yet to be gained by the Christians of North America in the unfinished appropriation of the meaning of the black struggle and of its unfinished state." In his lectures in Warsaw, Yoder commented on Richardson's *Commonweal* article: "In order to overcome this kind of evil, faith does not attack the men who do evil but the structure of evil which makes man act violently. Hence there must be an *asymmetry* between the form in which evil manifests itself and the form of our opposition to evil. We should meet violence with nonviolence. . . . To meet hate with retaliatory hate would do nothing but intensify the distance of evil in the universe. Hate begets hate; violence begets violence; toughness begets a greater toughness. We must meet the forces of hate with the power of love; we must meet physical force with soul force. Our aim must never be to defeat or humiliate the white man, but to win his friendship and understanding." Yoder concluded: "There is not a disjunction between, on the one hand, taking the way of the cross as a matter of blind faith, come what may, and on the other hand,

taking rational responsibility for historical process which always needs to include violence. . . . For those who confess the Lamb that was slain as risen Lord worthy to receive power, there can be no ultimate need to choose between suffering love and social effectiveness."

17. Editor's note: Yoder also quoted this Lowell poem in his *For the Nations*, 133, where he pointed out that Martin Luther King Jr. "used the quotation six times in the talks collected by James Washington," *The Essential Writings and Speeches of Martin Luther King, Jr.* (New York: HarperSanFrancisco, 1991).

18. E.g. Paul Hanson, *The Dawn of Apocalyptic: The Historical and Sociological Roots of Jewish Apocalypse Eschatology*, rev. ed. (Philadelphia: Fortress Press, 1979), on the setting.

19. See Hendrik Berkhof, *Christ and the Powers* (Scottdale, PA: Herald Press, 1962), and Walter Wink, *Naming the Powers* (Minneapolis: Augsburg Fortress, 1986), and Wink, *Engaging the Powers* (Minneapolis: Augsburg Fortress, 1992).

20. Editors' Note: See Leonhard Ragaz, *Signs of the Kingdom: A Ragaz Reader*, ed. and trans. Paul Bock (Grand Rapids: Eerdmans, 1984). Yoder has said that Ragaz and Christoph Blumhardt were influential in the early theology of his teacher, Karl Barth, because they combined an approach to apocalyptic thinking with political involvement in rather unique ways that Barth found intriguing.

21. Eberhard Arnold, *God's Revolution: The Witness of Eberhard Arnold*, ed. and trans. John Howard Yoder and the Hutterian Society of Brothers (New York: Paulist Press, 1984), with introduction by Yoder, 5–22.

22. Thomas C. Oden, *Radical Obedience: The Ethics of Rudolf Bultmann* (Philadelphia: Westminster Press, 1964).

23. Dietrich Bonhoeffer, *Ethics* (Minneapolis: Augsburg Fortress, 2005), 48, quoted in Larry Rasmussen, *Dietrich Bonhoeffer: His Significance for North Americans* (Minneapolis: Fortress, 1990), 158.

24. The so-called Apostles' version of the creed adds here a few more otherworldly words; this probably earlier, less otherworldly wording is attested by Marcellus (d. 308).

Chapter 4 From the Wars of Joshua to Jewish Pacifism

1. Part of a lecture series on "Nonviolence in Cultural, Historical, and Theological Perspectives" prepared for presentation in Warsaw, Poland, May 10–20, 1983, at the invitation of the *Polska Rada Ekumeniczna* and its President W. Benedyktowicz. This was lecture 6.

2. This widespread modern confidence that the New Testament has nothing more to tell us was the primary challenge to which my *Politics of Jesus* initially responded.

3. As a guest in the Slavic world, which was so long victimized by Christian imperialisms (whether Germanic, Roman, or Russian), I considered it significant when visiting Warsaw that this particular oversimplified critical angle on the abuse of power was at home in the Slavic world.

4. Tolstoy characterized the thrust of Matt. 5:38, "but I say to you, do not resist the evil one," as "the key to the gospel."

5. Von Rad's 1959 pamphlet did not appear in English until 1991: *Holy War in Ancient Israel*, trans. and intro. Marva J. Dawn, Ben C. Ollenburger, and Judith E. Sanderson (Grand Rapids: Eerdmans, 1991).

6. Judg. 9, 1 Sam. 8.

7. E.g. Deut. 17:14–20.

8. 2 Chron. 20:17. I have spelled out this point more fully in chap. 4 of *The Politics of Jesus*, 2nd ed. (Grand Rapids: Eerdmans, 1994), 76ff.

9. The modern reader's notion that we can distinguish what an author "was trying to say" from what the text says is one of the most current easy ways of insulating ourselves against the gospel having a message for us.

10. A few elite Jews, the Maccabees, were violent two centuries before Jesus, and a few were violent 66–70 and 132–135 CE. But most Jews had been nonviolent since the end of the Davidic kingdom in the age of Jeremiah, as we shall go on to see.

11. The "state" is of course our modern concept. What Judea lost in 586 was the complex of kingship, army, and royal city.

12. Cf. my paper "See How They Go With Their Faces to the Sun " in *For the Nations*.

13. I referred above to one trait in the Ezra story; namely, that he renounced a military escort because of the concept of trusting Yahweh. The stories of Ezra and Nehemiah document the abandonment of statehood and army, since both men were functionaries of the eastern empire. Yet neither man's notion of how to get Palestinian Judaism going again revoked the mission to Diaspora or sought to restore kingship.

14. Cf. my research résumé "Jewish Nonviolence from Jeremiah to Hertzl" on my website. Editors' Note: John Howard Yoder's website is http://theology.nd.edu/people/research/yoder-john/. For this research resume, see http://theology.nd.edu/people/research/yoder-john/documents/thenonviolenceofjudaismfromjeremiahtohertzl.pdf.

15. That is, of course, the message of Job, Lamentation, and Habakkuk.

16. The best current descriptions of Jewish nonviolence are *The Challenge of Shalom,* ed. Murray Polner and Naomi Goodman (Philadelphia: New Society, 1994), and Evelyn Wilcock, *Pacifism and the Jews* (Gloucestershire, UK: Hawthorn Press, 1994).

Chapter 5 Jesus: A Model of Radical Political Action

1. Previously published in *Faith and Freedom: A Journal of Christian Ethics*, and then in *Faith and Freedom: Christian Ethics in a Pluralist Culture*, ed. David Neville and Philip Matthews (Adelaide, Australia: ATF Press, Australia, 2003). Reprinted by permission.

2. See Matt. 5:1–16.

3. See Matt. 5:21–48.

4. Matt. 5:43–48; Luke 6:32–36.

5. My brief interpretation of Jesus's ministry in this light in chap. 1 of *The Politics of Jesus* continues to be reinforced by the work of scholars, some of which has been provoked by S. G. F. Brandon's overstated thesis that Jesus was in fact a violent Zealot.

6. The immense variety of modes of participation/discipleship is surveyed in chapter 7 of *The Politics of Jesus.*

7. Editors' Note: By "distraction and reform," Yoder must be referring to the previous paragraph, which contrasts compromise and reform, or apostasy and reform. He means compromises that distract us from discipleship that faithfully follows the call of Jesus.

Chapter 6 *Just War* and *Nonviolence*: Disjunction, Dialogue, or Complementarity?

1. This chapter was originally a lecture presented at the World Conference on Violence and Coexistence, Montreal, August 1992. Published in *Proceedings: International Association for Scientific Exchange on Violence and Human Coexistence*, Second World Congress, Montreal, July 13–17, 1992, 171–78.

2. The nonviolent activist has no choice but to assume the existence of a social system in which other parties will continue to be violent, without her approval. Usages differ widely as to whether unjust social situations where there is no military activity should be called "violent." Moralists in the just war mode often redefine careful nuances of the concept of the "morally unacceptable," such as "sinful but necessary" or "imperfectly just" or "materially but not morally evil."

3. In *War or Peace? The Search for New Answers*, ed. Thomas A. Shannon (Maryknoll, NY: Orbis, 1980), 40–58; also in Childress' book of essays, *Moral Responsibility in Conflicts* (Baton Rouge: Lousiana State University Press, 1982); and his "Just-War Theories: The Bases,

Interrelations, Priorities, and Functions of their Criteria," *Theological Studies* (September 1978): 427–45.

4. The most careful list of the traditional criteria is the compilation on 147–61 of my *When War Is Unjust*. Childress does not in fact itemize all of the criteria. Nor does he demonstrate in detail how each of them serves in the way he says they do. He says that his list is not exhaustive. I count eleven items in his list, but as he describes them they shade into one another. His concern is first to show that they can all be boiled down to the single logic of *prima facie* duties or rights, and then to explore whether one can ask that all the criteria be met. He is less concerned with formulating each of them so that it could be implemented accountably.

5. The individualism and the consequentialism underlying this version of the language of rights and duties can be challenged. Paul Ramsey rejects the reduction of political obligations to "non-harming" in *Speak Up for Just War or Pacifism: A Critique of the United Methodist Bishops' Pastoral Letter "In Defense of Creation"* (University Park, PA: Penn State University Press, 1988), 83–84, 108–9.

6. The just war theory, properly so-called, must be distinguished from some of its variants, which would more properly be called "holy" or "realistic," even though they are often claimed as "just" by their advocates. Cf. my survey, "How Many Ways Are There to Think Morally About War?" *Journal of Law and Religion* 11, no. 1 (1994): 83–107.

7. Some recent moralists would call it "pre-moral" or "material" evil, to distinguish the fact that war inflicts harm from the question of its moral justification.

8. Ralph B. Potter, *War and Moral Discourse* (Atlanta: John Knox, 1969), and Potter, "Moral Logic of War," *McCormick Quarterly* 23, no. 4 (May 1970), 203–33. J. Bryan Hehir, "The Catholic Church and the Arms Race," *Worldview* (July-August 1978), 13–18, and elsewhere.

9. Editors' Note: In Yoder's tentative outline of *The War of the Lamb*, he considered including an essay arguing that "Paul is out of step. Paul Ramsey is being left behind by the Charles River clique." The "Charles River clique" refers to Harvard University scholars Potter, Childress, and Hehir. We do not have this essay. The debate is summarized by David P. Gushee, "Just War Divide," *The Christian Century*, August 14–27, 2002, 26–28.

10. Editors' Note: Yoder is referring to the U.S. Catholic bishops' document, *The Challenge of Peace*, drafted primarily by J. Bryan Hehir, as explained below.

11. Richard B. Miller, "Christian Pacifism and Just-War Tenets: How Do They Diverge?" *Theological Studies*, 47 no. 3 (Summer 1986): 448–72. Marking the coherence of the two views is already a program within the complementarity thesis, which he then argues is taken with inadequate refinement by the various authors he criticizes. That thesis adds more appearance of cohesion to the debate than really fits.

12. For obvious reasons I must limit my description here to the "popular" expressions. A fuller treatment would gain from reviewing Richard B. Miller's *Interpretations of Conflict: Ethics, Pacifism, and the Just War Tradition* (Chicago: University of Chicago Press, 1991). Miller takes off from Childress's assumption to analyze the way he sees pacifism and just war "converging" in five different systems.

13. U.S. National Conference of Catholic Bishops, *The Challenge of Peace: God's Promise and Our Response* (Washington, DC: United States Catholic Conference, 1983).

14. *Gaudium et Spes,* par. 79, "Curbing the Savagery of War." The U.S. bishops had recognized "selective" refusal to participate in unjust wars for the first time in the Viet Nam period. Cf. my review "The Moral Responsibility to Refuse to Serve in an Unjust War: The Movement of 1968–75 and Its Prehistory," Joan B. Kroc Institute for International Peace Studies, University of Notre Dame, Document (3:WP; 9–95) 1992. But also see note 3 above, Childress, *Moral Responsibility in Conflicts*. In the second draft of the bishops' document, this recognition of the moral claims of pacifism had been pressed on the bishops by their review of the vision of peace in the New Testament and the early church. Then in order to restore the just war theory

to its customary preeminence, the third draft moved the discussion of the early church from just after the New Testament to par. 111ff.

15. *The Challenge of Peace*, par. 120–21. That the two views are complementary does not mean that they are symmetrical. Only just war is applicable to governments, as bearers of the moral obligation of self-defense. Only for conscientious individuals is nonviolence legitimate. The non-Catholic will discern here a vestige of the classical distinction between "precepts" and "evangelical counsels" as founding two different moral systems for different kinds of actors.

16. Par. 221–30. The interlocking of just war and nonviolence rationales is again explicit in par. 224 and par. 226.

17. Here the bishops refer to the work of Gene Sharp, to which I shall return below.

18. *In Defense of Creation* (Nashville: Graded Press, 1986). There are several interlocking texts, the fullest of which is called "Foundation Document."

19. The Roman Catholic text rejects nuclear deterrence in principle, but then condones keeping it after all, as long as the justification for keeping it is to negotiate it away. The United Methodist text uses stronger words, yet renounces unilateral disarmament after all, in favor of "reciprocity," i.e., not taking risks if the enemy does not. Thus neither document called on the nation to take real risks.

20. A similar line of argument was carried further by a statement produced within the United Church of Christ, and adopted by their General Synod 15 of 1985. Cf. *A Just Peace Church*, ed. Susan Thistlethwaite (New York: United Church Press, 1986). Paul Ramsey castigated this kind of effort to avoid making the hard choice between just war and "pacifism" as trying to have it both ways.

21. Paul Ramsey's very careful critique in his *Speak Up for Just War or Pacifism* shows, I believe correctly, that whereas the Roman Catholic text subsumes pacifism within the just war, the United Methodist rendering of the reciprocity tilts the other way. It says in principle that it is pacifist (i.e., recognizing no really valid grounds for war) but is then unwilling on political/ pastoral grounds to follow through with the implications of that basic commitment. This is thoroughly analyzed and criticized by Stephen Long. Editors' Note: Long's book on the topic is *Living the Discipline: United Methodist Theological Reflections on War, Civilization, and Holiness* (Grand Rapids: Eerdmans, 1992).

22. Cf. above my reference to the other types. Also my paper "A Historic Peace Church Perspective" in *Peace in a Nuclear Age: The Bishops' Pastoral Letter in Perspective,* ed. Charles J. Reid Jr. (Washington, DC: Catholic University of America, 1986), 273–90.

23. Michael Walzer has identified the use of the term "realism" as an ideal type over against his advocacy of just war theory in his *Just and Unjust Wars* (New York: Basic Books, 1977). In different ways Clausewitz, Hans Morgenthau, and Machiavelli represented this posture. Hugo Grotius ascribed the same position to "cynics" among the ancient philosophers. It posits, paradoxically but thereby honestly, the claim that it is morally accountable to state that moral considerations do not apply in interstate conflict. Cf. my description in my "How Many Ways Are There to Think Morally About War?"

24. James Turner Johnson, in *Ideology, Reason, and the Limitation of War* (Princeton: Princeton University), 9ff., 134ff., overdoes his partly valid critique of the notion that "holy war" constitutes a different type, as Roland Bainton had interpreted that contrast. Johnson agrees (15ff.) with my present point: namely, that in early modern times the just war theory lost its capacity to impose effective restraint. "How Many Ways Are There to Think Morally About War?" discusses further how Johnson does and does not clarify types.

25. Editors' Note: In the final paragraphs of this section, we are inserting some material from a parallel unpublished essay of Yoder's, "How Just War Thinking and Pacifism Do and Do Not Coinhere," which he called a "think piece." He began with this three-paragraph note to himself, in which we have inserted references in [brackets]:

"My purpose here is not to make debating points, but to clarify the substance of a perennial debate by looking at the diverse ways in which language is used to attempt to make sense of the debate but at the same time also (often unintentionally) to obfuscate.

"This review has been triggered by an argument in the same mode by James Sterba, but is not offered as a response on the same level, since my intent is to challenge not so much Sterba's argument as his assumptions.

"Take note of other parallel efforts by Duane Friesen in Whitmore book [Friesen, "Peacemaking as an Ethical Category: The Convergence of Pacifism and Just War," in *Ethics in the Nuclear Age*, ed. Todd Whitmore (Dallas: Southern Methodist University, 1989)], and by Richard Miller [in *Interpretations of Conflict: Ethics, Pacifism, and the Just War Tradition*]; possible paper on the theme of bridging over. Bounce it off Paul Ramsey on 'come clean' [Paul Ramsey, *Speak Up for Just War or Pacifism*]. The main point is that the just war people who invest all their energy in discussing their relationship to the few pacifists on their left are in political reality tacit allies to the unjust warriors on their right."

26. John Courtney Murray denounced the U.S. law according to which it is illegal for any agents of the U.S. government to do any contingency planning about the possibility of surrender. This law is still on the books, although some of our military educators disobey it.

27. Jesuits John Ford in the 1940s and John Courtney Murray in the 1950s get a lot of deserved credit for saying this; I do not want to detract from that. But my point is that Catholicism was not saying that. Most bishops, most parish priests, most moral theologians, and most military chaplains were not saying it. Ford and Murray were almost alone. One of the odd things about Roman Catholicism is the way the next generation takes credit for the right positions that were not listened to at the time.

28. As I have sought to describe it in chap. 1 of my *Nevertheless*, 15, the way that popes from Benedict XV to the present have condemned war, as in John XXIII's *Peace on Earth* and in Paul VI's visit to the United Nations, has its own special "pastoral" shape. When set up against the fourfold or fivefold typology I have described, it is "none of the above" and has been compatible with all of them.

29. This imperative is described in detail in *The Challenge of Peace*. See also Gene Sharp, *The Politics of Nonviolent Action*.

30. One of the first persons to make this claim was Commander Sir Stephen King-Hall of the British Royal Navy, in his *Defense in the Nuclear Age* (1957). As a nonpacifist and a lecturer in military science, King-Hall was clear on utterly pragmatic grounds that democracy cannot be defended by nuclear destruction. Therefore, means for defending democracy must be found which are compatible with the end. His term, "psychological warfare," was inadequate; but his point was the same as the one Sharp was to make a generation later. The alternative to a military establishment planning for new ways to use killing or the threat of killing is not doing nothing but doing something else, something which demands no less planning, no less courage, no less risk.

31. Martin Luther King Jr.'s argument of this type is that it is legitimate, for purposes of public order, that a parade should need a permit; yet if the issuance of a permit is denied on racial grounds, then the intrinsically acceptable law has become illegitimate and it can be imperative to parade without a permit.

32. A Roman Catholic canon lawyer argues with a straight face that it is possible successfully to wage war without lying: Joseph Macksey, SJ, "War," in *The Catholic Encyclopedia* vol. XV (New York: 1911), 550. The argument that lying to someone is worse than killing him continued to be advocated with some seriousness by George Orwell and by my Notre Dame colleague Robert Rodes.

33. Gandhi's autobiography bore the title *The Story of My Experiments with Truth*. Vaçlav Havel places a similar accent on truth telling as the hinge of political legitimacy.

34. One phrase used by early Friends to bespeak the unity of spirituality and ethics was "the terror and power of the Light." That is, the same divine power that brings the sinner to conversion forbids coercing or killing the neighbor. If God could win me over to righteousness by the pure power of the truth, I must count on that same power to operate between my neighbor and me. Cf. the chapter "The Terror and Power" in Hugh Barbour's *Quakers in Puritan England* (New Haven: Yale University, 1964).

35. *Why We Can't Wait* (New York: Mentor, 1963), 54–58. In order not to predispose the results of a runoff election in Birmingham, the details of tactical planning for the civil rights campaign in that city were initially kept secret. King recognized that from a Gandhian perspective this was a questionable decision, needing to be explained.

Chapter 7 The Changing Conversation between the Peace Churches and Mainstream Christianity

1. This chapter was a lecture presented September 29, 1995, as a guest of Swarthmore College, a historically Quaker (Society of Friends) college well-connected with peace concerns.

2. I gathered a review of both the institutional shape and the common content of this shared witness in Douglas Gwyn et al., *A Declaration on Peace*, Appendix C, 93–105.

3. These three groups are only the core of the much wider story of Christian pacifist conviction. Their common American experience made them visible and capable of collaboration, yet many other renewal movements have also been pacifist: Franciscans, Waldenses, Czech Brethren, Churches of Christ, some Wesleyans, Pentecostals, and the Salvation Army.

4. An example of the few efforts to converse on the theme is the "Consultation on the Christian Witness to Peace" convened at the World Council's study center at Bossey after the planning for Uppsala in the coming summer was done: see *On Earth Peace*, ed. Donald Durnbaugh (Elgin, IL: Brethren Press, 1978), 306ff. The entire Durnbaugh volume testifies to the persistence of the historic peace churches in sticking by their witness despite minimal response.

5. ". . . every war in which churches on each side condone or support the national effort becomes a civil war within the church. Is not this state of affairs where Christian kills Christian an even greater breach of ecumenical fellowship than the deplorable confessional differences that have rent our unity? Indeed, can we Christians expect the Lord to restore our unity in worship as long as we put one another to death on the field of battle . . . ?" *Peace Is the Will of God* (1954), reproduced in *A Declaration on Peace* (1991), 70.

6. *The Church's Peace Witness*, ed. Marlin E. Miller and Barbara Nelson Gingerich (Grand Rapids: Eerdmans, 1994).

7. Sincere and superficial interpreters may believe that only just war and pacifism are serious options. In "How Many Ways are There to Think Morally About War?" I demonstrated that there are other morally serious stances. Historically, just war discipline has rarely been taught by clergy or implemented by statesmen. See also Yoder, *When War Is Unjust*, rev. ed.

8. Editors' Note: We have imported section III from Yoder's Heck Lectures given at United Theological Seminary, Dayton, Ohio, January 1980.

9. National Conference of Catholic Bishops, *The Challenge of Peace*, 28–31.

10. Robert W. Tucker, *The Just War: A Study in Contemporary American Doctrine* (Baltimore: Johns Hopkins University Press, 1960), 11, 21, 25, 61–66, 74–79, 86; Robert W. Tucker and David C. Hendrickson, *The Imperial Temptation, the New World Order, and America's Purpose* (New York: Council on Foreign Relations, 1990), 133–34.

11. *The Challenge of Peace*, 35–37.

12. Ibid.

13. Richard B. Miller, "The Morality of Nuclear Deterrence: Obstacles on the Road to Coherence," in *Ethics in the Nuclear Age*, 35–58; Yoder, "Bluff or Revenge: The Watershed in Democratic Deterrence Awareness" in *Ethics in the Nuclear Age*, 79–92.

14. *The Challenge of Peace*, 92–99.

15. Ibid., 51–56.

16. By no means was Pennsylvania alone in this. Penn was also a founder of the colonies of Jersey and Delaware. Other Friends were leaders in the pre-Revolutionary governments of Rhode Island and North Carolina, and in the Indies.

17. Häring, *The Healing Power of Peace and Nonviolence* (New York: Paulist, 1986).

18. Sider, *Nonviolence: The Invincible Weapon?* (Dallas: Word, 1989).

19. My essay "The Free Church Syndrome" in *Within the Perfection of Christ*, 169–76, reviews the diversity of starting agenda points of the many believers-church beginnings.

Chapter 8 Gordon Zahn Is Right: Going the Second Mile with Just War

1. Editors' Note: In his memo of September 4, 1997, Yoder indicated he had just edited this essay for inclusion in *The War of the Lamb*: "Gordon Zahn, senior Catholic pacifist, disapproves of my selling out on just war. He is right about the limits of the moral validity of the just war system. Edited except bibliography as of September 1."

2. Paul Ramsey, *Speak Up for Just War or Pacifism: A Critique of the United Methodist Bishops' Pastoral Letter "In Defense of Creation"* (University Park, PA: Penn State University Press, 1988), 83–84, 108–9.

3. Joseph L. Allen, *War: A Primer for Christians* (Nashville: Abingdon, 1991).

4. My argument to that effect was first published in *The Christian Witness to the State*, 48f.: "That there can be a just war in the Christian sense of the word *just* or *righteous* is, of course, excluded by definition; we can make the point only negatively. When the conditions traditionally posed for a just war are *not* fulfilled, then a war is unjust to the point that even a state, resolved to use violence, is out of order in its prosecution."

Since then I have written several papers on the theme, summarized in my "How Many Ways are there to Think Morally about War?" in *The Journal of War and Ethics* 11, no. 1 (1994): 83–107, and *When War Is Unjust*. No other pacifist of my acquaintance has taken that tradition as seriously.

5. They do not always thus refuse. Several times nonpacifist institutions have invited me to make this argument. Charles Lutz, who as denominational administrator had led Lutheran agencies in applying just war notions critically to the Vietnam War, invited me to write *When War Is Unjust*, 1st ed. (1984) for Augsburg Press, and commended it to nonpacifist readers. The University of Notre Dame for decades largely left it to me to offer their curriculum in this area.

6. One of my earliest publications was a work of ecumenical advocacy, *The Ecumenical Movement and the Faithful Church* (Scottdale, PA: Herald Press, 1958). My commitment to ecumenical involvement, committed in principle to going the second mile to address interlocutors in their own terms, has recently been summarized in *Royal Priesthood*.

7. Cf. my paper "On Not Being in Charge," on the cultural style common to Jews since Jeremiah and Christians in the early generations, in *War and Its Discontents*, ed. J. Patout Burns, 74–90.

8. That I was paying nonpacifists this compliment was already recognized by Charles Lutz, one of those who courageously led Lutherans in the Vietnam era to retrieve the critical edge of their long-forgotten just war tradition, in his preface to the first edition of my *When War Is Unjust*. The preface has been retained in the second edition (Maryknoll, NY: Orbis, 1996).

9. My cultural roots in the Amish Mennonite ethnic culture make it especially easy for others to discount what I say on the grounds of my being an odd outsider; but similar distancing techniques are used as well to decrease the claims of Jesus; some of the more common ones are listed in my *Politics of Jesus*, 2nd ed., 1–8 and 15–19.

10. One statement of this argument "from inside" is the outline, "The State of the Question" in *When War Is Unjust*, 119–29. Academically oriented arguments of the same kind were "The Credibility of Ecclesiastical Teaching on the Morality of War" in *Celebrating Peace*, ed. Leroy S. Rouner (Notre Dame, IN: University of Notre Dame Press, 1990), 31–51, and "The

Credibility and Political Uses of the Just War Tradition" in *Morals and Might,* ed. George A. Lopez and Drew Christiansen, SJ (Boulder, CO: Westview, 1997), 11–24. My phrase "who *say* they hold to it" is meant seriously. Most of those who affirm loyalty to the tradition do not in fact honor it in hard decisions, and many of them, when challenged, will make an argument for not honoring it firmly.

11. Conscientious objector: *Another Part of the War: The Camp Simon Story* (Amherst: University of Massachusetts Press, 1979). Sociologist: See a descriptive study of the social backgrounds of conscientious objectors in *Civilian Public Services during World War II* (Washington, DC: Catholic University of America), 1953; also *The Military Chaplaincy: A Study of Role Tension in the Royal Air Force* (Toronto: University of Toronto, 1969). Historian: *In Solitary Witness* (Springfield, IL: Templegate, 1986); *Franz Jägerstäter, Martyr for Conscience* (Erie, PA: Pax Christi, 1984). We owe it largely to Zahn that the martyrdom of Franz Jägerstätter has become widely known and that the Vatican is seriously considering his beatification; *German Catholics and Hitler's Wars* (New York: Sheed and Ward, 1962). Editor: Thomas Merton, *The Nonviolent Alternative* (New York: Farrar, Strauss & Giroux, 1980), previously *Thomas Merton on Peace*. Author: *War, Conscience, and Dissent* (1967); *Vocation of Peace* (Baltimore: Fortkamp, 1992).

12. Gordon Zahn to Orbis Press, cited by permission.

13. My honoring their modesty more than they do might be called a kind of backhanded pedagogy. If their system is corrupt, as I think it is, then one good way to demonstrate that should be to let it do its thing and see that in fact it does not work, that it may even make things worse.

14. At that time I was a doctoral student in the [Reformed] Theological Faculty of the University of Basel. The ecumenically committed historian Ernst Staehelin, later my dissertation director, invested more effort in being ecumenically fair to that new doctrine than any of my Catholic neighbors at Notre Dame have invested in commending it to me.

15. The World Council of Churches was constituted legally by its first Assembly in 1948 in Amsterdam; yet the principle of its formation had been decided upon at the Assemblies of its primary parent agencies at Oxford and Edinburgh in 1937. The ecumenical conversations on the war question, in which I was privileged to participate later, began then. Some of the story of that attempted conversation is chronicled in Doug Gwyn et al., *A Declaration on Peace*, Appendix C, 93ff.

16. Cf. my arguments to that effect in *Royal Priesthood*, 221–41 and 300ff. In the World Council setting it was always difficult to get a serious hearing for dissent about war (*On Earth Peace*, 388–89), but at least the overruled dissent can be noticed. For a nonconciliar ecclesiology in an atmosphere of overwhelming "convergence" it is still hard to be noticed. One very promising exception is the modest effort of the North American Faith and Order conversations reported in *The Church's Peace Witness*, ed. Marlin E. Miller and Barbara Nelson Gingerich. Editors' Note: An additional volume from these promising Faith and Order dialogues was subsequently published: *The Fragmentation of the Church and Its Unity in Peacemaking*, ed. John Rempel and Jeff Gros (Grand Rapids: Eerdmans, 2001).

17. Most thinkers who participate in depth in interfaith dialogue, whether among Christian traditions or with other faiths, would argue that any conversation between people of differing convictions is only serious if each interlocutor is susceptible to some degree of being convinced by the other's authenticity. Cf. the several writings of Kenneth Cragg on Islam. Note the theme of "passing-over" which appears frequently in the topic indexes of the writings of John Dunne, CSC, *The Way of All the Earth* (Notre Dame, IN: University of Notre Dame Press: 1982), 239, and *The Church of the Poor Devil* (Notre Dame, IN: University of Notre Dame Press, 1982), 178.

18. The chapter "Pacifism and the Just War" that Gordon Zahn contributed to *Catholics and Nuclear War*, ed. Philip J. Murnion (New York: Crossroad, 1983), 119ff., named numerous of the more-than-ethical dimensions of the reality of war that should matter in Catholic piety.

19. This claim is often made without using the *adjective* "Catholic," since in the American experience that term has come (paradoxically?) to have sectarian overtones. Mainstream Protes-

tantism, as represented by the major denominations that collaborate ecumenically in the conciliar movement, and by their divinity schools, tends to take this same patronizing stance.

20. I stand in puzzled awe of the capacity of some of my friends to feel at home and go forward "in the Roman obedience" despite its inhospitability on the episcopal level to their concerns. For their sake I shall not name them.

21. Their writings have been reviewed by a host of historians, most fully in the several excellent publications of James Turner Johnson, and have been built upon in popular literature like the 1983 episcopal pastoral letter *The Challenge of Peace*. That letter gives the false impression that the tradition that it summarizes was in fact applied effectively in most Western Christian history. That impression is categorically false, though the bishops who gave it may not have been conscious of that. Cf. my paper "A Historic Peace Church Perspective" in *Peace in a Nuclear Age*, 273–90.

22. Frederick H. Russell, *The Just War in the Middle Ages* (Cambridge and New York: Cambridge University, 1975) is not about the decision of rulers to go to war, but about Catholic thinkers seeking to discipline illicit killing. The most concrete thinking was in the rules developed by confessors for application in the practice of the sacrament of forgiveness. The cultural question was not "when is war a good thing?" but "how can it be forgiven?" James T. Johnson reminds us of this in criticizing Lisa Sowle Cahill's overvaluing of Aquinas.

23. Francisco de Vitoria is the best example; he was first to lay out the just war tradition in the scale of a book (i.e., the record of an entire lecture series). He was perhaps the first to identify the specific form of challenge to just war integrity represented by the Iberian adventures in the New World, thereby thinking about the moral status of non-Christian peoples, and perhaps the first formally to criticize his own rulers' imperial policy.

24. I have argued before that the just war tradition has never been declared authoritative by the means that Catholicism recognizes as making any doctrine authoritative. No council or pope has ever promulgated the doctrine as binding. Refusal to kill has never been addressed by a formal *damnamus*. No pacifist theologian has been condemned canonically of heresy. A Roman Catholic pacifist is outvoted, but cannot technically be called a heretic, for what she or he rejects was never a dogma. Only a few specific rulings of medieval councils on prohibited weapons, on "the peace of God" or "the truce of God," are in the record. They were seldom enforced, and they are only a small sliver of the just war system. Here, however, my point is not that the doctrine is not dogma, but that church leaders have not established a credible record of particular accountable acts of implementation judging particular wars.

25. Cf. my display of most of the logically available repertory of types of thought in my "How Many Ways Are There to Think Morally about War?" One category missing from that list, which was in fact present, even decisive, in the militant expansion of Europe around the globe, is the conviction that the "natives" or "savages" do not have the same rights we fully human people do.

26. "Theology and Modern War," *Theological Studies* 20 (1959), 40–61, and often anthologized: "The tendency to query the uses of the Catholic doctrine of war initially rises from the fact that it has for so long not been used, even by Catholics. That is, it has not been made the basis for a sound critique of public policies, and as a means for the formation of a right public opinion. . . . I think it is true to say that the traditional doctrine was irrelevant during World War II."

27. War of 1812: See the section on "The unsystematic nature of just war theory" in chap. 4 of Yoder, *Christian Attitudes to War, Peace, and Revolution*. War against Mexico: The best-known critics were Lincoln and Thoreau. It is noteworthy that those who used just war arguments did not appeal to ecclesiastical tradition; their doubts about "last resort" or "just cause" were matters of commonsense logic.

28. See my informally published working paper, "David Urquhart and the Challenge of 'Just War' at Vatican I." Had the Council not had to spend its first months on infallibility and then

dissolve unfinished because of the outbreak of war, the proposal had some serious chance of passage.

29. Zahn confirms this function of serving "the individual's moral obligation to make a personal exploration of conscience before supporting or participating in modern warfare."

30. I can testify to its being taken seriously by colleagues responsible for reserve officer training at Notre Dame.

31. Howard Zinn, *Declarations of Independence* (New York: HarperCollins 1990), 98.

32. David Irving, *The Destruction of Dresden* (Ballantine: 1965), quoted in Zinn, 98.

33. Ronald Clark, *Einstein; The Life and Times* (New York: World, 1971), 370. This spurious moral rigor did not keep Einstein from supporting the preparation of the atom bomb, on the ground that the Germans might do it first. Author Clark himself deplored Einstein's lack of realism. Zinn (*Declarations of Independence,* 34ff.) has gathered other similar statements from Sigmund Freud and E. O. Wilson. One branch of anthropology maximizes the contribution of our genetics to human aggressiveness; see Thomas Merton "Is Man a Gorilla with a Gun?" in his *Faith and Violence* (Notre Dame, IN: University of Notre Dame Press: 1968), 96ff.

34. Drew Christiansen's contribution to *When War Is Unjust*, rev. ed. (1996), 102ff., identified numerous points at which some Roman Catholic thinkers and bishops have come to be more careful about this or that implication of the just war discipline. Yet I do not observe that non-pacifist moral theologians wrestle adequately with this "trigger" phenomenon as it has worked itself out in all our major wars. There is one analogy to it in the notion of a "nuclear firebreak." People who have not thought seriously about escalation in conventional war sometimes get the point when they think nuclear. Yet they are often ready to remain uncritical up to the nuclear threshold. Nor do I see them (including Christiansen) ever wrestling with Gordon Zahn's claim that a system which *claims* to be an instrument of effective discrimination is refuted in its status as normative doctrine if it is in fact not thus implemented in most of history.

35. Editors' Note: Yoder surely intended Robert Tucker, not Osgood, as in the previous chapter: Robert W. Tucker, *The Just War: A Study in Contemporary American Doctrine* (Baltimore, MD: Johns Hopkins University Press, 1960), 11, 21, 25, 61–66. 74–79, 86; Robert W. Tucker and David C. Hendrickson, *The Imperial Temptation, the New World Order, and America's Purpose* (New York: Council on Foreign Relations, 1990), 133–34.

36. Childress: in *War or Peace? The Search for New Answers*, ed. Thomas A. Shannon (Maryknoll, NY: Orbis, 1980), 40–58; also in Childress's book of essays, *Moral Responsibility in Conflicts* (Baton Rouge: Lousiana State University Press, 1982); and his "Just-War Theories: The Bases, Interrelations, Priorities, and Functions of Their Criteria," *Theological Studies* (September 1978): 427–45. Potter: *War and Moral Discourse*. Hollenbach: David Hollenbach, *Nuclear Ethics* (New York: Paulist Press, 1983). To see the general shape of moral discernment as constituted by presumptions modified by exceptions is what Philip Wogaman projected in his *A Christian Method of Moral Judgment* (Philadelphia: Westminster, 1976).

37. Paul Ramsey, *Speak Up for Just War or Pacifism*. For Ramsey, justifiable war is not an exception to a general rule against harming; it serves an independent imperative of love to defend the innocent, even though it does that by harming another.

38. Paul VI was the authority who had most recently rejected conscientious objection. Now the American bishops recognize the vocational morality of integral pacifism and call for legal recognition of "selective conscientious objection," in addition to defining the just war as a subset of pacifism.

39. Gordon Zahn's mentor Dorothy Day is cited in a note in *The Challenge of Peace*. Her witness to the bishops in the course of the second Vatican Council had been widely noted. David O'Brien called her the nation's most important Catholic.

40. Patricia McNeal, *Harder than War* (Piscataway, NJ: Rutgers University Press, 1992) chronicles the life of the pacifist undercurrent in Catholicism from 1927 to 1983, but without seeking to provide any measurement of its numerical importance. Despite their very small

numbers, Catholic pacifists had so changed the atmosphere that in 1980 the bishops could not write them out of the story.

41. None of the other traditional criteria (from four to over a dozen, depending on how carefully they are stated; see *When War is Unjust* [1996], 147–60) were tested seriously in *The Challenge*. Seven of the criteria *ad bellum* are explained with no discussion of their application; of *in bello* criteria, only innocent immunity is taken seriously, while the others are simply ignored. In "The Challenge of Peace: A Historic Peace Church Perspective" in *Peace in a Nuclear Age,* 273–90, I noted some of the ways in which the historical account in *The Challenge* was (I trust innocently) misleading; but I did not pursue the tacit implication that on only one of the many criteria were the bishops willing to contemplate the possibility that U.S. policies might be found wanting. Nor did I underline the fact that this position cost no one any sacrifice, since the policy of unrestrained accumulation of arms beyond "sufficiency," which they condemned, was not politically or strategically rational and was advocated by no one.

42. Dorothy Day is named, together with Gandhi and King, in the text of *The Challenge of Peace*, par. 117.

43. Actually there are no "teeth" in *The Challenge of Peace*. The bishops encourage everyone to be good, but there is no specification of the point at which, for example, a munitions worker or a missile technician ought to refuse to work.

44. At the time of the death of Princess Diana, who had made land mines a public issue, the United States agreed to join the negotiations around a possible banning of land mines (it appeared in early September), but only in order to weaken the treaty. In all the flurry of diplomacy there was no attention to the fact that discussions were limited to the level of a treaty. No one had the integrity to say that in recent generations the use of land mines was a blatant case of the intentional targeting of noncombatants.

45. We remember Murray saying that the Ten Commandments are not made irrelevant by the fact that they are not obeyed. Yet the credibility of those who teach them is not independent of whether they see to their implementation.

46. It may well be argued that the criteria were met by some of the Central American resistance efforts against U.S.-supported oligarchies, but one cannot vouch for "legitimate authority" in the absence of electoral process. Cf. John Lewis, *The Case against Pacifism*, for a nonpacifist's best candidates.

47. In his response to *When War Is Unjust*, Drew Christiansen, SJ, reports several ways in which some of the criteria of the just war tradition are defined more clearly in recent writings than they were before. Yet he grants repeatedly that the Roman Catholic communion as a whole is not set up to make the discipline stick. He writes of "the growing lack of social conditions for authentic and effective use of the just-war analysis" (103), as if there had ever been such conditions before their "lack" grew.

48. Cf. again "The State of the Question" in *When War Is Unjust*, rev. ed., 119–29.

Chapter 9 Lisa Sowle Cahill Is Generous: Pacifism Is About Conversion and Community, Not Rules and Exceptions

1. Lisa Sowle Cahill, *Love Your Enemies: Discipleship, Pacifism, and Just War Theory* (Minneapolis: Augsburg Fortress, 1994).

2. Editors' Note: Yoder wrote the following note in his plan for *The War of the Lamb*: "Lisa Cahill's carefulness and good manners in her glancing attention to me in *Love Your Enemies* do not in fact advance the conversation since she wants to find some minimum to agree on. To be written on the bases of two earlier texts. Helpful beside the Gordon Zahn piece as another specimen of entering dialogically into the others' view." We have one of Yoder's "earlier texts," and we present it here; but we do not have the other. Yoder said to me [Glen Stassen] that he especially appreciated the carefulness and appreciative assessment with which Lisa Cahill treated his position. He mentioned this when we were finishing writing *Authentic Transformation*, and

suggested we ask Lisa to be one of the book's endorsers for the book jacket. We did ask her, and she agreed; she wrote a thoughtfully appreciative endorsement, for which we were grateful.

3. Editors' Note: We added this paragraph to summarize Cahill's presentation relative to Yoder's point. The quotation comes from Lisa Sowle Cahill, *Love Your Enemies*, 213.

4. Editors' note: The title of Cahill's book is *Love Your Enemies*. Yoder probably means that her including the Crusades in her book does not imply that she sees the Crusades as forms of loving your enemies.

5. Editors' Note: We added this sentence of explanation for clarity.

Chapter 10 The Science of Conflict

1. This was chap. 6 in the unpublished text developed from the Heck Lectures, presented at the United Theological Seminary, Dayton, Ohio, in January 1980; it is substantially parallel to lecture 6 in the Warsaw series.

2. The widely used German proverb that I quoted in the Polish setting was *Auf der Gewalt ruht kein Segen,* ("no blessing rests on violence").

3. I think especially of the work of economist Kenneth Boulding, sociologist Elise Boulding, and educator Adam Curle, major contributors to the origins of conflict resolution studies as a social science.

4. This is especially the case for the work of Gene Sharp.

5. Cf. Paul Wehr, *Conflict Regulation* (Boulder, CO: Westview, 1979). Saying "management" or "regulation" is intended to ward off utopian misunderstandings about possible "resolution." More recently some have chosen "conflict transformation" as a more optimistic vision.

6. Other practitioners of conflict could have been added. I note here those who make most of their tactical hardheadedness.

7. Gene Sharp, *Exploring Nonviolent Alternatives* (Boston: Porter Sargent, 1970).

8. In the Warsaw series, previous lectures had narrated the learnings of Gandhi and King. It was from cases like theirs that Gene Sharp drew most of his anecdotes. Yet it is striking that those who *first* did those creative things were *not* guided by such science.

9. This is what I have argued in chap. 6 of *For the Nations*.

Chapter 11 Creation, Covenant, and Conflict Resolution

1. From the Heck lectures at United Theological Seminary, Dayton, Ohio, January 1980.

2. Editors' Note: Here Yoder is summarizing his argument in "The Changing Shape of the Conversation between the Peace Churches and Mainstream Christianity," chap. 8 above.

3. Editors' Note: "The Political Meaning of Hope," chap. 3 above. Yoder was also referring to his lecture on the meaning of hope and the full incarnational humanity of Jesus for faithfulness and effectiveness that is now published as "The Power Equation, Jesus, and the Politics of King," chap. 6 of *For the Nations*.

4. The "reaching back" to the older roots occurred especially when Niebuhr moved from occasional writings of social criticism to his Gifford lectures on human nature and human destiny.

5. That distributive or modalist understanding of Trinity is sketched in Stassen, Yoder, and Yeager, *Authentic Transformation*, 61ff.

6. To say "God wills" may be inappropriately anthropomorphic. Many thinkers on the "reason" side of this debate suggest that "personal" language is not to be taken seriously.

7. Catholics often call this given moral order *nature*, while Lutherans and Calvinists call it *creation*. The moral prescriptions are basically the same.

8. Jeremiah's redefinition of the meaning of the dispersion is the real beginning of Jewish identity. Whether the "Jeremiah of history" or the specific message of Jeremiah 29 was in fact the historical cause of the vision of a mission to "seek the peace of that city," accepting Babylon as the new locus of Jewish survival became the hinge to the new chapter of Hebrew history.

Cf. my "Exodus and Exile," 297–309, and "See How They Go With Their Faces to the Sun" in *For the Nations*.

9. Editors' Note: Sentence added to provide transition to Pretoria panel presentation.

10. The following is an assigned panel contribution at the South African Christian Leadership Assembly, Pretoria, July 6, 1979. A paper read at a different section of the same assembly is "The Spirit of God and the Politics of Men" in my *For The Nations*, chap. 11.

11. Cf. "Binding and Loosing" in my *Royal Priesthood*, 323ff.

12. Editors' Note: Yoder wrote: "Which of these aspects of the work of Jesus, as of ours, calls forth conflict?" But the context indicates that he intended to suggest that each aspect *does* call forth conflict, yet nevertheless the end and the means are reconciliation. He has been arguing throughout that "conflict is a sign of life and growth"; "conflict is provoked by God's righteousness"; conflict is not necessarily evil but can be healing. So here God's action does bring conflict, and also brings reconciliation. Although this edit may have changed Yoder's meaning, we are seeking faithfulness to his intent.

Chapter 12 Conflict from the Perspective of Anabaptist History and Theology

1. Presented at Mennonite Graduate Fellowship's annual session at Ithaca, NY, December 28, 1969, drafted after the meeting from notes used at Ithaca, circulated only privately. The Mennonite Graduate Fellowship was a self-governing, self-perpetuating group that functioned from 1958 to 1972, with some support from the denominational student services committees. The term "Anabaptist" indicated the mentality of the time, considering the denominational identity of modern Mennonites as derived from, and therefore subject to guidance (or judgment) from, ideal sixteenth-century origins.

2. Editors' Note: We added "and I call a practice" to connect Yoder's citation of Burkholder here with what he later called practices in *Body Politics*, in the concluding chapter of *Royal Priesthood*, and elsewhere. See Michael Cartwright's insightful summary of the development of practices in Yoder's writings in his introduction to *Royal Priesthood*.

3. Editors' note: Yoder is probably referring to Michael Sattler here. See *The Legacy of Michael Sattler*, Classics of the Radical Reformation, Vol. 1 (Scottdale, Pa: Herald, 1973).

4. Editors have added verses 45–46 in the context in Matthew that Yoder's interpretation is referring to, for clarity. These verses come immediately before Jesus says in verse 48, "Be perfect (complete, all-inclusive) like your heavenly Father."

5. Editors' Note: We do not recognize the exact source for Yoder's quotation here, but the sentiment fits well with 2 Cor. 4:16–18 as well as with Anabaptist martyrs.

Chapter 13 The Church and Change: Violence Versus Nonviolent Direct Action

1. Lecture presented to the annual conference of the South Africa Council of Churches (SACC), Hammanskraal, July 24, 1979. The General Secretary of the SACC at the time was Desmond Tutu, who had assigned me the topic, and who made a first response. Major guest speakers on the program were Jesse Jackson of Operation Breadbasket, Chicago, and Andrew Kirk, author of *Liberation Theology: An Evangelical View from the Third World* (London: Marshall, Morgan and Scott, 1979). The conference theme was "The Church and the Alternative Society," a theme borrowed from the missiological thought of the late professor David Bosch. Rewritten by request after the event but then never published. That I publish this text after all this time is a grateful tribute to Archbishop Tutu in recognition for all that he has done since then to realize the potential of Christian reconciliation. Editors' Note: We have included only the second half of the lecture, since the first half repeated what is already included in previous chapters of *The War of the Lamb*.

2. Editors' note: "Masada" refers to a last-ditch stand of Jews unwilling to surrender to Roman conquest, so they resisted to their death. "Laager mentality" is a South-African term that means "resistance to the end" by circling the wagons and resisting change.

3. Bishop Manas Buthelezi was a participant in the SACC meeting in Hammanskraal, July 24, 1979, where John Howard Yoder presented this address.

4. A two-year study of "Violence and Nonviolence in the Struggle for Justice," under the auspices of the Division of Studies of the World Council of Churches, led to a report to the Central Committee in August 1973; cf. *Ecumenical Review* (October 25, 1973): 434–46, partially reproduced in *On Earth Peace,* 373–85.

5. Vatican II praised "those who renounce the use of violence in the vindication of their rights and who resort to methods of defense which are available to weaker parties"(*Gaudium et Spes*, 78). It is true that people without guns can claim power through noncooperation, obstruction, and surprise. Yet that is not the priority moral claim against killing. The main case for renouncing violence is *not* that it is something that underdogs can do.

6. In March 1960, over seventy unarmed demonstrators were massacred in the street by the police. For most patriots this event is counted as the point where the nonviolent commitment of the African National Congress finally ended, because nonviolent struggle "does not work." Yet since then, many times that many have laid down their lives (and taken lives) without anyone's deciding that armed struggle does not work.

7. In 1979 the South African government was promoting an informal consultation process which some hoped would begin movement toward greater justice. Others feared that it would be just one more way to co-opt black and colored leadership and divert their energies away from adequately profound demands for change. Koornhof was the Minister for Interracial Affairs, who had just addressed the South African Christian Leadership Assembly.

8. This point has since been argued strongly, with special concern for South Africa, by Walter Wink, in his *Violence and Nonviolence in South Africa: Jesus' Third Way,* (Philadelphia: New Society, 1987).

9. Cf. the fifth note in this chapter on the linkage between nonviolence and weakness.

10. This is part of what Gandhi meant when he said, "They are not in control; we are."

11. This program was a new undertaking of the World Council of Churches, which had been developed after its 1968 Assembly, whereby moral and financial support was given to ethnic independence movements, especially in Africa. Critics, especially in the British and German churches, objected to what they thought constituted support for revolutionary violence. Editors' Note: Dr. Gqubule is likely Dr. Simon Gqubule, then of the University of Pretoria.

Chapter 14 Politics: Liberating Images of Christ

1. John Howard Yoder, "Politics: Liberating Images of Christ," in *Imaging Christ: Politics, Art, Spirituality*, ed. F. A. Eogo (Villanova, PA: Villanova University, 1991), 149–69. Reprinted here by permission.

2. Editors' Note: we have edited these two sentences for clarity. The original says "It is not enough, with the first commandment, to say that other gods should not be *worshiped*. The second commandment recognizes that, since other gods are unreal, making their images is a human activity, and commands that it should not be done."

3. Numerous very respectable people, from Karl Barth, *Church Dogmatics* III/4 (Edinburgh: T&T Clark, 1961), 117–18, to Douglas John Hall, *Imaging God: Dominion as Stewardship* (Grand Rapids and New York: Eerdmans and Friendship Press, 1986), have used the "divine image" passages for quite different purposes. Barth finds in it a normative vision of human sexuality, Hall of ecology. I like what both say on both subjects, but I am moved to doubt by their canonically questionable assumption that one can read Genesis independently of the Decalogue.

4. "Divine state" (*morphe*) or "equality" (*einai isa*) in Phil. 2:6; "appointed to inherit" (*etheken kleronomon*), "radiant light" (*apaugasma*), "perfect copy" (*charakter*) in Heb. 1:2f.

5. Yoder, *The Politics of Jesus*.

6. Ibid.

7. Cf. my survey, "The Wider Setting of 'Liberation Theology,'" *Review of Politics* (Spring 1990): 285–96.

8. José Miguez Bonino, *Christians and Marxists: The Mutual Challenge to Revolution* (London: Hodder & Stoughton, 1976).

9. Helder Camara, "What Would Saint Thomas Aquinas, the Aristotle Commentator, Do If Faced with Karl Marx?" *The Journal of Religion,* Supplement to vol. 58 (1978): 174–82.

10. What collapsed in Eastern Europe in the late 1980s was not socialism in any way but rhetorically; it was Byzantine bureaucracy.

11. Cf. my "Withdrawal and Diaspora: The Two Faces of Liberation," in *Freedom and Discipleship*, ed. Daniel Schipani (Maryknoll, NY: Orbis, 1989); an earlier treatment of the same theme was "Exodus and Exile," 297–309.

12. Judaism is very aware of the wrongness of applying the liberation metaphor self-righteously or gleefully. God restrained the angels from praising at the occasion of the Reed Sea victory: "How can you sing hymns while my creatures are drowning in the sea?" (Megillah 10b). This tradition is widely known because of reminders tied to the use of the *Hallel* in the daily prayers and in the Passover ritual. This simple summary was facilitated by the aid of Dr. Roger Brooks.

13. Cf. my *Priestly Kingdom*, 49–54.

14. I spell out in *Priestly Kingdom* (53) the ways in which all five passages defend specifically the human historicity of Jesus. As to this vision of the place of the development of trinitarian thought, see Catherine Mowry LaCugna, "The Trinitarian Mystery of God," in *Catholic Systematic Theology*, ed. F. Fiorenza and J. Galvin (Philadelphia: Fortress, 1990), and "Re-Conceiving the Trinity as the Mystery of Salvation," *Scottish Journal of Theology* 38 (1985): 1–23.

15. What changed with "Constantine" (not the man, but the symbol of historic reversal) was far more than just a reading on the ethics of the state; cf. my *Priestly Kingdom*, 135–71. Eusebius may be more responsible for this worldview shift than was Constantine himself.

16. George Huntston Williams, "Christology and Church State Relations in the Fourth Century," *Church History* 20 (1951): 3/3–33 and 4/3–26.

17. The very term *idealism* in this standard account signals the *a priori* Neoplatonic assumptions of the critic.

18. The most common reproach—impracticality—ignores the real experience of the Quaker William Penn and the Baptist Roger Williams in founding viable societies.

19. They used the term "nonresistance" because of their understanding of the translation of the wording of Matt. 5:39. Neither Tolstoy nor Garrison took that term to mean what their critics, from their contemporaries to Reinhold Niebuhr, read into it; namely, that one should let evil happen without opposing it. Both Garrison and Tolstoy were politically active, even to the point of challenging the laws. Nor was literal "nonresistance" what Jesus meant; cf. Walter Wink, *Violence and Nonviolence in South Africa,* 12ff.; Ronald J. Sider, *Christ and Violence* (Scottsdale, PA: Herald Press, 1979), 46ff.

20. Krishnalal Shridarani, *War Without Violence* (New York: Harcourt, Brace, 1939); Gregg, *Power of Nonviolence*.

21. Cf. my capsule summary of Girard's thought in the context of a review of *The Scapegoat*, in *Religion and Literature* 19 (Autumn 1987): 89–92.

22. Tolstoy used the title, "Key to the Gospel Teachings," in the first chapter of his *What I Believe (1884)* [English Translation, *Oxford World* Classics 229 (Oxford: 1921)], but "Resist not the evil one" permeates the entire pamphlet as dominant hermeneutic clue. By "key" he does not mean moral rigorism or a superficial view of the power of evil. He means it as a hermeneutic password; he writes as *littérateur*. In terms of rhetorical structure, it is for him the

passage that makes the Sermon on the Mount, or the entire Gospel of Matthew, hang together as discourse.

23. Mubarak Awad, "Nonviolent Resistance: A Strategy for the Occupied Territories," in *Nonviolent Struggle in the Middle East* (Philadelphia: New Society, no date, ca. 1985); Marjorie Hope and James Young, "Christians and Nonviolent Resistance in the Occupied Territories," *The Christian Century*, April 27, 1988, 430–32; Beth and Jonathan Kuttab, "Nonviolence in the Palestinian Struggle," *Fellowship*, October/November 1988, 7–8. The main meaning of the *intifada* is not the confrontations in the streets, but the community building in the back rooms, the development of cells of local self-government, of elementary education to replace the schools the Israelis have closed, of local gardens and workshops to replace the economy the Israelis have closed. As I wrote in late May 1990, the still growing Israeli repressiveness is close to pushing the Palestinians beyond the discipline that they have maintained for more than two years; that does not change my point. If the Palestinians, in their despair, reach for their guns after all, they cannot "win" in any meaningful sense. Editors' Note: Yoder is referring to the first, or popular, *intifada*. His prophetic prediction turned out to be right: the second *intifada* was characterized by the violence of suicide bombing of civilian targets, and has pushed Israeli politics to the reactionary right and lost what gains had been temporarily achieved. See Mohammed Abu-Nimer, *Nonviolence and Peacebuilding in Islam* (Gainesville: University of Florida Press, 2003).

24. If the ANC and the *intifada* are effective without military superiority, why do they not avow a nonviolent commitment? To answer this would call for a deep analysis of the power of macho ideology, dominating the minds even of those whose experience contradicts it.

25. Gene Sharp, *Exploring Nonviolent Alternatives* and *The Politics of Nonviolent Action*.

26. In his *Christianity and Power Politics*, Niebuhr was not careful in reporting that the non-pacifist Christian churches (that is to say, the mainline nonpacifist theologians) had traditionally held to the just war tradition, which sets firm limits on war. Niebuhr did not spell out or affirm either such limits or the just war notion as such. Thus Niebuhr's claim to speak for the classical tradition was not precisely true.

27. William Miller, *Nonviolence: A Christian Interpretation* (New York: Schocken Books, 1966).

28. Leslie Griffin replicates this misunderstanding by ascribing to me a preoccupation with purity, in "The Problem of Dirty Hands," *The Journal of Religious Ethics* 17 (Spring 1989): 31–61, especially 36–37. Griffin forsakes Kant and Niebuhr and follows Sartre (and tacitly, the cultural anthropologists) in using the metaphor of dirt instead of the categorical command, but the misunderstanding is the same. Whether the metaphor be purity or absolute command, to be concerned primordially with the integrity of the agent belongs to the disciplines of catechesis or pastoral care. In ethics, the question that matters is the source and status of the moral imperative. Is the ultimate moral value the preservation of American social values or the word and work of Christ? Niebuhr's ethic is no less deontological, shows no less moral passion, than the ethics of discipleship. What differs is not whether moral standards are binding, but which standards are binding. Choosing to serve Yahweh instead of idols demands the metaphor not of dirt, but of choice. I do not refuse to kill my neighbor because I do not want blood on my hands, but because I want my neighbor alive. I honor the sovereignty of Yahweh in the dignity that the divine image confers on my neighbor, even if it be an enemy neighbor.

Chapter 15 A Theologically Critical Perspective for Our Approach to Conflict, Intervention, and Conciliation

1. The following text was rewritten from a transcript taken from the tape recording of extemporaneous remarks made at the Mennonite Central Committee Peace Theology consultation in Park City, a Kansas City suburb, April 6–8, 1978. The Peace Section of the MCC often used "Peace Theology Colloquia." This particular study event was part of a longer, focused process

that lasted several years, under the leadership of Dr. William Keeney, which ultimately culminated in the creation of the "conciliation service" as a new kind of ministry active in numerous places, and to the development of "conflict transformation" as an academic specialization. The conference planners assigned the title to me. These remarks followed workshops that had been led by Dr. James Laue, one of the founders of conflict resolution as an academic discipline and as a social action profession. The transcript was made by a secretary who had not been at the meeting, from a tape of evidently bad quality. Thus the reconstruction does not claim literal adequacy. It seems fitting to retain in the text the references to its concrete setting, as testimony to the historic importance of the study process, and of this particular event, for the peace church communities, and because any effort to make the presentation less concrete would not make it any more clear. No attempt has been made in 1997 to fix what *should* have been said back then. Editors' Note: We think this chapter's more interactive format provides a lift, a personal touch, and a "sending forth" that climaxes *The War of the Lamb* nicely. Because of the format, we edited this chapter a bit more actively than other chapters for clarity and readability, but sought always to stay precisely faithful to Yoder's meaning.

2. Several times, I heard a senior staff person of the World Council of Churches describe the working method of WCC study conferences. The theologians were put in one room to write the preface, and the experts were then free to draft the main substance of the report. Theology or spirituality can illuminate motivation but cannot determine moral substance. Experts provide the substance; technical expertise is the ministry of the laity. This assumes of course that ethics is reduced to the expert management of consequences, while theology is a matter for preambles.

3. Professor James Laue, the primary outside resource person at the conference, is one of the fathers of the field of conflict resolution as a social science and as a social service skill. He taught at the University of Missouri, and then George Mason University. A lynchpin of his method is the analysis of the variety of roles needing to be played in a conflict situation. Someone needs to be an advocate for the absent, someone a "neutral" observer, someone a communicator, someone a liaison to the wider public. Adam Curle's *Making Peace* (London: Tavistock, 1971) is an early classic of this kind of analysis. To teach this kind of method awareness was part of the laboratory process at the Kansas City conference.

4. Dr. William Keeney, professor of Bible and then dean at Bluffton College and then at Bethel College, was a pioneer in peace studies at Bethel College, with the support of President Harold Schultz. Later Keeney became the executive of the Consortium on Peace Research, Education, and Development, a networking entity based first at Bethel College and then at Kent State. For years, Keeney had been the chair of the MCC Peace Section. He bore special responsibility for the study process in which this event was a major link, and the ultimate result of which was several pioneer initiatives of Mennonite agencies in the field. It is respect for those developments, and for the many persons who have followed them up, which has led me to the concreteness in this paper.

5. Deut. 17:14–20 thus portrays an understanding of the royal role analogous to the narrative of 1 Sam. 8.

6. Deut. 16:18 (KJV).

7. Matt. 16:19, Matt. 18:18.

8. Matt. 18:20.

9. A study guide on this theme from the New Testament is offered in my *Royal Priesthood*, 323–58.

10. 1 Cor. 6:7.

11. 1 Cor. 6:5.

12. This function still exists in those synagogues with a strong sense of their history and culture. It is called *beth din* ("house of judgment"). The synagogue discharges a conflict resolution function that the Gentile world will not and need not provide for Jews. See James Yatte, *So Sue Me! The Story of a Community Court* (New York: Saturday Review Press, 1972).

13. See Heinold Fast, "The Anabaptists as Trouble Makers" *Mennonite Life*, April 1976, 10–13.

14. At the time of the conference, these were young brash radical evangelical journals, expressing more respect and support for pacifism and nonviolence than Mennonites had previously encountered among evangelicals. Both are still going strong in 1997. Editors' Note: *The Other Side* has since ceased publication.

15. Of course, if that wide gamut of different roles is required in every situation, then sometimes a particular person may need to fill one role because it's needed, even though it isn't the role he or she feels most called to fill. I have said this more fully, but without special focus on conflict resolution, in my booklet *The Fullness of Christ* (Elgin, IL: Brethren Press, 1987). It is a frequent mistake to paraphrase this, as some do, as "the priesthood of all believers."

16. The other outside resource person in the conference, besides James Laue, was John Adams, a minister made available by the Methodist church for ministries in places of conflict, such as political conventions. His personal narrative of the Wounded Knee conflict, *At the Heart of the Whirlwind* (New York: Harper & Row, 1976), gave his witness special depth and moral authority.

17. In my study of the dynamics of punishment, *You Have It Coming* (Shalom Desktop packet, 1996), I have discussed the functional value of having an authority figure to shoot down.

18. Editors' Note: On this and other points, everyone should read Howard Thurman's classic *Jesus and the Disinherited* (Boston: Beacon, 1996), 30–31, *et passim*.

19. In this concluding sentence, Yoder is saying something similar to William Spohn's advocacy of "analogical imagination": On the one hand, Jesus's way gives us a word that is God's will for the world; we are not to fence it in and marginalize it as only for true Christians. But at the same time, we are not to interpret it legalistically as applying to all persons and situations without creative adaptation. We need to study carefully what Jesus's teaching means in Jesus's original context, and then study carefully what would be the analogous meaning for persons in another personal and social context. See Spohn, *Go and Do Likewise: Jesus and Ethics* (New York: Continuum, 1999). In personal conversation, Yoder explained that we should not first reduce Jesus's teaching to a principle, then carry that principle over to a current context, and apply the principle to the new context. Too much distortion enters into the process of reducing and then applying, and a principle is too thin to give concrete guidance. We should exegete Jesus's meaning thickly in its original context, and bring the whole teaching with its rich meaning to our context, exegeting how it would function analogously in our context. [GHS]

20. A sociologist who taught at Mennonite colleges and at Chicago's Urban Training Center, Scott had left the meeting early, after making the very helpful contribution to which I refer here.

21. The staff of the Chicago offices of the American Civil Liberties Union courageously jeopardized much of their financial support by defending the rights of the American Nazis to hold a parade in Chicago, as guaranteed to all persons and groups by the First Amendment to the Constitution, guaranteeing "the freedom of speech," and "the right of the people peaceably to assemble." Donald B. Downs, *Nazis and Skokie* (Notre Dame, IN: University of Notre Dame Press, 1977; James L. Gibson, *Civil Liberties and Nazis: The Skokie Free-Speech Controversy* (Santa Barbara, CA: Praeger, 1985); David Hamlin, *The Nazi Skokie Conflict* (Boston: Beacon, 1980).

22. Here the transcript begins to pick up the question/answer format with which the hour ended. It is impossible to identify the voices.

23. I know a social scientist who argued against taking the political changes in Eastern Europe in 1989 seriously, because they were atypical and therefore not "ontological."

Index

227